AFRICA FROM
EAST TO WEST

AFRICA FROM EAST TO WEST

A JOURNEY FROM THE RED SEA TO THE ATLANTIC

DAVID HAPPOLD

The Book Guild Ltd

First published in Great Britain in 2018 by
The Book Guild Ltd
9 Priory Business Park
Wistow Road, Kibworth
Leicestershire, LE8 0RX
Freephone: 0800 999 2982
www.bookguild.co.uk
Email: info@bookguild.co.uk
Twitter: @bookguild

Typeset in Aldine401 BT

Printed and bound in Great Britain by CPI Group (UK) Ltd, Croydon, CR0 4YY

ISBN 978 1912575 343

British Library Cataloguing in Publication Data.
A catalogue record for this book is available from the British Library.

MIX
Paper from
responsible sources
FSC
www.fsc.org   FSC® C013604

CONTENTS

ACKNOWLEDGEMENTS

Old friends are the great blessing of one's later years… They have a memory of the same events and have the same mode of thinking.

(Horace Walpole)

I wish to thank the many people – bus drivers, children, government officials and many others – who I met on this journey and who offered assistance, advice and hospitality. Their help added so much to the enjoyment of this long journey. Also, I want to acknowledge friends who lived in Khartoum and/or Ibadan at the same time as I did, as well as others who shared my earlier African adventures. All of them (here listed alphabetically as I knew them in the late 1950s and the 1960s) have remained loyal and valued friends for 50-60 years, and for this I am truly grateful: Mark Coode, Rosemary and Andrew Forson, Charles Hilary Fry, Liz and Dan Goddard, Jill and Edward Hackford, Elaine and Rob Oldham, Tony and Sally Pettet, Roger Polhill, Mary and John Twidell, and Valerie and Colin Wood-Robinson.

Sketch map of Africa showing the author's route.
The complete country boundaries are shown only for the countries
through which the author travelled.
The country names are as they were in 1965–1967.

Legend:

Southern Guinea Savanna

Rainforest

Somalia-Masai semi-desert bushland

Sahel Savanna

Sudan Savanna

Northern Guinea Savanna

⬭ Ethiopian Plateau

········· Travel route

Scale (Kilometres): 0 160 320 480 640 800 960 1120 1280

Compass: N E S W

Latitude lines: 20°N, 15°N, 10°N

RED SEA

ERITREA

Asmara
Massawa

ETHIOPIA

Lake Tana

Axum

Blue Nile

EGYPT

SUDAN

Atbara

Nile

Jebel Qeili

Khartoum

White Nile

Jebel Marra

Geneina

Nyala

Abeche

CHAD

Lake Chad

Ati

Mongo

Fort Lamy

Chari

CENTRAL AFRICAN REPUBLIC

NIGER

Maiduguri

Kano

CAMEROUN

Benue

NIGERIA

Zaria

Ibadan

Lagos

Dahomey Gap

DAHOMEY

TOGO

GHANA

Accra

Half Assini

Abidjan

CÔTE D'IVOIRE

MALI

MAURITANIA

SAHARA DESERT

Bamako

Niger

Senegal

SENEGAL

Dakar

ATLANTIC OCEAN

ix

1

PROLOGUE

I am not really sure when I became interested in Africa. I remember I had some books on African animals when I was a boy, and I became fascinated by elephants, giraffes, zebras and antelopes. I also remember being taken to Whipsnade Zoo, the wonderful open-air zoo on the Chiltern Hills north of London, when I was about five years of age. Pictures in books are wonderful, but seeing these majestic animals 'in the wild' was magical. However, at this time of my life, I never thought that I would ever go to Africa; I was young, it was the middle of World War II, Africa was far away, and my whole world was confined to within a few miles of home. There were just two African connections that brought Africa a little closer. The first was a very dear friend of my mother's who had an apple orchard in South Africa, and she kindly sent me a book called *Our South African National Parks* by Colonel Stevenson-Hamilton published by a cigarette company in South Africa.[1] It was a large book with much more information than I needed at this stage of my life. There were very few pictures in the book, but lots of 'frames' where pictures could be pasted. The idea was that 'cigarette cards', each with a photograph of a South African animal and supplied within every packet of cigarettes, could be collected and pasted into the 'frames' of the book. I did not understand about advertising or why people bought cigarettes, but I waited with great anticipation for any letters from South Africa that might contain these 'cigarette cards'. Over the years, my book filled with pictures, and I increased my knowledge of African animals. The second connection was my godfather who was a District Officer (and later District Commissioner) in the Gold Coast (now Ghana) during WWII. It seemed a wonderful job to me and I wondered whether I could ever get a job like this when I was older. Both of these 'connections' gave me the idea that one day I might be able to go to Africa even though the possibility seemed very remote.

There were two other themes in my early life that eventually enabled me to obtain an appointment in the Sudan where this story begins: animals and travel. Firstly, I have always been fond of animals and they have been a source of wonder and enjoyment ever since I was small. My mother told me that when I was about three years of age, I spent hours at a time crawling around our garden on the chalk downs of Wiltshire following snails and any other bugs that I could find. My parents encouraged me to have many sorts of animals as pets, and I was very lucky that we had a large garden for all of them. At various times, I had Dalmatian dogs, bantams, guinea pigs, rabbits, tadpoles and frogs, newts, and fish caught in the local streams. Sometimes, I found injured birds; I brought them home and kept them until each one was fit enough to fend for itself again. Special favourites were a chaffinch, a jackdaw and several blackbirds. Looking for birds' nests was a wonderful pastime in the spring. I learned a lot about our local species by quiet observation, and I was told that I must never do anything that might disturb the adult birds or prejudice the survival of the fledglings. I made a collection of butterflies and moths; these were the days when there were clouds of butterflies everywhere on the downs and in the gardens, and there was no need to feel guilty about catching two or three individuals for a collection. It was possible, in those days, to purchase the eggs of various butterfly and moth species from the 'Butterfly Farm'. The eggs arrived by post in little pillboxes, and I then placed the eggs in special cages with the correct plant food. During the following weeks, I was able to watch the hatching of the eggs, the growth of the caterpillars, the formation of the pupae, and finally the emergence of the adults. It was utterly fascinating and wonderful! Other activities that gave me lots of happiness were 'tiddling' for minnows and sticklebacks that I then placed in my aquaria, falconry with an expert falconer who lived nearby, and expeditions with the local Boy Scout group. This upbringing was perfect for a boy who wanted to be a zoologist.

Secondly, all my early travels were by train, bus, and bicycle. My family – like most families – did not have a car. A train journey from my home in Salisbury to Devon, London or Bournemouth was a great adventure, particularly because the steam engines were huge, noisy, and spewed great plumes of smoke and steam. I realised that I enjoyed travelling and seeing new places. I think I must have inherited this characteristic from my maternal grandmother (whom I never met). In the early years of the twentieth century, before WWI, she travelled with her photographer husband through the Balkans and the Middle East. This was an amazing feat for a 'Victorian' lady; more so because she wrote four books about her adventures,[2] which were wonderfully illustrated by her husband's photographs. My grandmother was also, like me, concerned with animal welfare; she recorded in one of her books that she had founded a hospice for maltreated donkeys in Palestine in 1910. My mother, too, loved travel especially in Europe and she introduced me to the wonders of Switzerland and Austria in the 1950s. All our travels in those years were by land or sea – this was decades before air travel and mass tourism.

These threads in my ancestry and formative years resulted in my determination to become a zoologist and to specialise in African zoology. I was fortunate enough during my obligatory National Service to be seconded to an African regiment in Kenya. It was a wonderful opportunity to experience Africa and African mammals at first hand. When not involved in my military duties, I collected butterflies, visited a few game reserves, and had the opportunity to visit some farms near Nanyuki where I was stationed. Here I was able to experience the sights and smells of the African bush, and watch birds, squirrels, smaller antelopes and warthogs at close range. I knew, after these experiences, that when my formal training was completed, I would look for employment in Africa.

So, some six years later, I started my African career at the Zoology Department of the University of Khartoum in the Sudan. I began to study small mammals in the desert – a challenging project which involved catching and observing small mammals, fieldwork at night, and longer expeditions to interesting places. But not only this – I enjoyed seeing the many environments of northern Sudan, the different peoples, the seasonal changes in climate, and learning about the immensely rich history of the Sudan. In time, and wanting to see more, I began to think about other places and countries bordering Sudan. Gradually the idea of seeing the whole of

Africa, from east to west, at roughly the latitude of Khartoum, was born. The idea began with a journey from Khartoum to Nigeria. Other travels in the Butana (Chapter 4) and northern Ethiopia (Chapter 3) seemed to extend the scope of the adventure, and finally my move to Nigeria enabled me to contemplate continuing the journey to the far west of the continent.

This tale describes my journeys across the width of Africa from east to west roughly along the 15°N parallel of latitude (hereon referred to simply as the '15th parallel'). The journey began at Massawa (15° 36' N) in Eritrea and ended at Cape Verde (14° 44' N) in Senegal, a distance of about 3,800 miles (6,100km) in a straight line. This line of latitude runs roughly parallel to and slightly south of the Sahara desert, in the rather arid environments between true desert to the north and the moister savannas to the south. However, my journey was not in a straight line because, in the middle section, it dipped southwards through the savannas to the rainforests of coastal Nigeria and westwards along the coast to Côte d'Ivoire (5°N to 6°N)[3] before going northwards to the 15°N parallel again in Mali; as a result my journey was c. 5,500 miles (8,850km). The journey was made in four separate expeditions at different times between November 1964 and July 1967 but here they are described as if they were one continuous journey.[4] I travelled on trains, lorries, buses, cars and a boat, and on foot – in fact anything that was going in the direction that I wanted to go. As a zoologist and ecologist, I was fascinated by animals, plants, landscapes and biological systems, and hence my diaries and notes tended to focus on these topics, but I was also interested in how people live and survive in the environment, and the way in which history has determined the present states of affairs in the countries through which I travelled. An engineer, linguist, anthropologist or politician, for example, would have had a completely different focus to mine. Hence, this book is very much a personal narrative of what was interesting to me. For two places where I lived for a number of years, Khartoum and Ibadan (chapters 5 and 12), I record just a series of vignettes that collectively form an impression rather than a continuous narrative.

2

A BRIEF INTRODUCTION TO THE 15ᵀᴴ NORTH PARALLEL

When Emmanuel Bowen published his map of Africa in 1748, very little was known about the interior of Africa. In previous centuries, mariners had sailed around the continent and as a result the outline of the continent was reasonably well known. Many rivers were given names but where these rivers originated was not known; each is shown simply as a wiggly line originating somewhere further inland. The interior of Africa was completely unknown and many of the geographical features on the map were just speculation.

A good example is the Senegal River. Bowen placed the mouth of the river in the correct place (just to the north of Cape Verde and the present city of Dakar); however, he did not know that the river is formed from several smaller rivers that rise in the mountains of Guinea and on the plateau country of western Mali. Rather, his map showed that the source of the Senegal River was far to the east in what is now the Central African Republic. From here, according to Bowen, it flowed due west into 'Lake Bourn', then into 'Lake Guardia' (roughly where Lake Chad is situated), and on to 'Tombut' (probably modern Timbuktu) and finally to the coast north of Cape Verde. With hindsight, we now know that Bowen confused the Niger and Benue river systems with part of the Senegal river system. Bowen correctly showed the bulge of the Niger delta in the Bight of Benin, but without any river flowing into it. It was not until the epic journeys of Mungo Park in the 1790s and 1800s, and the journeys of Hugh Clapperton,

Richard Lander and John Lander in the 1820s and 1830s,[1] that the Niger and Benue rivers were shown to flow into the sea through the Niger delta, that the Senegal and Niger river systems were completely separate, and that 'Tombut' was located on the Niger River and not on the Senegal River.

On the eastern side of the continent, Bowen's map showed, correctly, the Nile River flowing northwards through Nubia and Egypt to the Mediterranean Sea. The map also showed the origin of the (Blue) Nile in the Ethiopian highlands; but the (White) Nile, which we now know originates in the lakes area of central Africa, was not shown at all. Interestingly, another early map (that of Bonne, a cartographer in Paris, published in 1771) showed the Nile (his 'Riviere Blanche') originating in the highlands of southern Ethiopia just to the south of the origin of the Blue Nile. The search for the source of the White Nile is one of the great sagas of African exploration and was only solved by the numerous travels of Richard Burton, John Hanning Speke and James Grant in 1856 to 1863,[2] nearly 100 years after Bowen published his map.

Bowen's map was, of course, not very different from other maps published in the previous two or three centuries. New information about Africa was rare at this time, and hence maps changed very little. The course of the Senegal River and the absence of the Niger River in Bowen's map was exactly the same as in the 1574 map of Abraham Ortelius. The course of the (Blue) Nile River was also rather similar in both maps, except that Ortelius did not show a lake in the Ethiopian highlands – just a multitude of small rivers flowing north-eastwards from the highlands to the Nile – but he did show a (White) Nile originating from two lakes in the regions of modern Mozambique and Angola. Cartography at this time in history was an interesting blend of slender facts, vivid imagination and speculation! Some of these early maps included small drawings of African animals, particularly elephants, lions, leopards and giraffes. The pictures added interest and an air of mystery, especially to people at the time of publication who probably had never seen such animals in the flesh. However, the position of the animals did not bare much relationship to where these animals actually lived!

It is fascinating to look at these old maps and to wonder how cartographers decided what to put in their maps. Was it better to leave a large area blank – which is rather dull – or to add some geographical feature even if there was no real evidence that such a feature existed? How much did cartographers rely on travellers' anecdotal stories? During the 200 years since Bowen published his map, almost all the 'blanks' have been filled in and now there are hardly any totally unmapped regions on the continent; however, detailed accurate maps are still not available for some modern African nations. For my travels, I had to rely mostly on two general maps: Michelin 153 Afrique (Nord et Ouest) and Michelin 154 Afrique (Nord -Est). They were good enough for my purpose even though the scale was only 1:4,000,000 (1cm = 40km).

The country through which I travelled is less known and less studied than either the Sahara desert to the north or the savannas and rainforest to the south. Yet it is of great interest with a rich history, dramatic seasonal changes in climate, wonderful and varied sceneries, and great diversity in plants and animals. Compared with other parts of Africa to the south, there are relatively few humans because of the hot climate, low rainfall and low productivity of the land. In spite of these drawbacks, there are many ethnic groups and languages across this great swathe of Africa.

In general terms, all the countryside within one or two degrees of the 15°N parallel is semi-arid. Climatologists and biologists refer to this country as the Sahel Savanna; to the north is the Sahara Desert (even more arid) and to the south is the Sudan Savanna (generally less arid). The average annual rainfall is low: for example, at Khartoum it is 160 mm/annum but it increases further westwards (e.g. 510 mm/annum at Fort Lamy, 696 mm/annum at Kano, and 1100 mm/annum at Bamako). The majority of the annual rainfall falls during a short "wet season" in July and August although in some years there may be rain in May and in September. [3] Importantly there are 6-8 months of "dry season" when there is very little or no rain. In April in Khartoum, the average rainfall is 0.4 mm (1/64th inch) and this when the average maximum temperature is 40°C (104°F). Under these conditions, evaporation is high and there is a negative water balance. Such conditions are very challenging for animal and plant life. The climate is considerably more arid in the east than in the west.

The climate of these semi-desert regions, indeed of all of Africa between the Tropic of Cancer (23°N) and the Tropic of Capricorn (23°S), is governed to a great extent by the movements of the "Inter-tropical Convergence Zone" (ITCZ). [4] The "convergence" is an area of low atmospheric pressure that forms where the air mass of hot moist air from the Atlantic Ocean and Gulf of Guinea meets the air mass of hot dry air of the Sahara. Where the two masses meet, the air pressure is reduced, and the moist air is forced upwards so that the water vapour condenses into liquid water that then falls as rain. In July, in West Africa, the ITCZ is at its northernmost limit (i.e. around 20°N). Between July and the end of December, it moves southwards across the Equator into the Bight of Benin (and even further south in southern Africa), and from January to the end of June it moves northwards again. The ITCZ is a band several hundred miles wide and it forms a wavy line from east to west in relation to topography. To illustrate how the movements of the ICTZ affect the climate (and every aspect of life), here are two examples. In Khartoum (and indeed at the same latitude all the way to the west coast of the continent), the ITCZ is overhead only during June, July and August, providing a short wet season. The climate is warm and humid and the amount of rain that falls is rather small, and occurs during only a few rainstorms. By September, the ITCZ has moved southwards and the 'dry season' has begun – so there is no more rain, and the temperature declines as cooler air flows southwards from the north. The winds bringing cooler air also bring fine particles of desert dust, colloquially called the 'harmattan' in West Africa. The months of January and February are cool (at least by Sudan standards); in these months, the ITCZ is far to the south, and there is no rainfall. In February, March and April, the temperature gradually increases as the ITCZ progresses northwards. Eventually, by June, the ITCZ arrives over Khartoum again and rain falls. This welcome rain is the first since the previous September, eight or nine months previously. The second example is at Ibadan near the West African coast at about 6°N. The pattern of the movements of the ITCZ is the same as the previous example, except that the ITCZ stays over this region for much longer each year and passes over twice each year – once going south and once going north. The result is a longer wet season from February to October/November, and a dry season from only November to February. In Ibadan (and all of southern Nigeria), the wet season has two peaks with a little 'dry season' in August (when the ITCZ is at its furthest north) but this is not in fact a real "dry season" but only a slight drop in the monthly rainfall. The Sudan is the most arid of the countries at 15°N because of its proximity to the deserts of Egypt and the Arabian Peninsula. Further westwards in West Africa, the climate is ameliorated by the monsoons from the Atlantic Ocean and is less harsh.

The Sudan and Sahel Savannas along the 15th parallel have a semi-arid environment. Rainfall is low and highly unpredictable, rivers are no more than dry river beds (*wadis*) for most of the year (or for many successive years), and the soils are sandy or sandy-loam with low fertility. Plant life is mostly sparse and low-growing, and trees are restricted to the edges of wadis and the bases of rocky hills. However, when there is rain, the country bursts into life. Within a week or so, the seeds of grasses and herbs have germinated, and the growth, flowering and production of new seeds are accomplished in just a few weeks. Trees produce new foliage and flowers. All this activity is short-lived, and by two months after the end of the rains, the countryside is dry and parched and has lost its greenness. The dryness of the landscape means that productivity of the vegetation is low, and most of the country is unsuitable for agriculture (unless crops are irrigated). Likewise, animal productivity is low and there are few animals.

Living in the Sahel and Sudan savannas is not easy because of the lack of water, high radiation from the sun, high temperatures during the daytime, and the limited resources. Animals have evolved a number of strategies to survive in this harsh environment: these include nocturnal activity, physiological adaptations to prevent overheating and water-loss, and changes in life-history (especially reproduction), all of which help to ensure the maximal utilisation of resources when conditions are good (such as after rains), and to survive when conditions are poor (such as during droughts).[5] Humans have also developed strategies for survival: they wear long flowing wide robes and turbans to keep cool and reduce evaporation, and to minimise the effects of solar radiation. They build houses (of brick or mud) with thick walls, and verandas to provide a cool environment. They reduce activity at the hottest time of the day. They construct wells and locate villages near water sources (such as a river, oasis or well), and they store food to provide nourishment during the "dry season". Humans have had to be as resourceful as the animals with whom they share this environment.

Humans have, to some extent, overcome the shortage (or absence) of water by digging wells. Some of the wells are fairly shallow, but others are deep and the water has to be hauled up in buckets to the surface. These wells extend down into the artesian aquifers where water has accumulated during previous centuries and millennia. There are many such wells across the Sahara-Sahel-Sudan region; the location of the wells has been important in determining the caravan routes across these arid and semi-arid regions.

Other wells are located where there are seasonal grasses and where nomads herd their domestic animals. In contrast, there are two places in these arid lands where water is abundant: the Nile and Niger rivers. This seemingly paradoxical situation is because the waters of these rivers originate in hills and mountains far removed from the arid regions. Where they originate, the level of each of these rivers rises during the wet season. The consequent increase in the volume of water takes several weeks or months to travel downstream; but eventually it arrives in the arid lands, and the water level of the rivers rises and floods over the river banks.

The countryside is comparatively flat with few obvious topographical features. Views are extensive extending for miles across the sandy plains to the horizon. Here and there a solitary tree, or a line of trees beside a wadi, interrupts the flat horizon. Any inclines up or down are very gradual, and frequently imperceptible. The most notable features of the countryside are the rocky hills, called 'jebels' in Sudan and 'inselbergs' in West Africa. These may be big or small; some are single huge domes of rock, others are 'mountains' of huge boulders, and the largest are massifs of uplifted rock with cliffs, crags, hidden valleys, and rock pools. One really notable jebel, Jebel Marra, is an extinct volcano (see chapter 7).

Travelling from east to west along the 15°N parallel, most altitudinal changes are slight and occur over long distances. Beginning in the east at Massawa (10m a.s.l.) on the coast of the Red Sea, the land rises very steeply to the northern part of the Eritrean-Ethiopian Plateau (Asmara 2,325m a.s.l.); this is the northernmost part of the Afro-Alpine Biotic Zone, and has a temperate climate and a flora and fauna quite different from that of the Sahel and Sudan. To the west of Asmara, the land declines steeply to Kassala (550m a.s.l.) and finally to the Nile Valley (Khartoum 380m a.s.l.). From here, it rises slowly to the western Sudan (El Geneina, 805m a.s.l.) – this over a distance of about 1,100km (690 miles). Continuing westwards, the altitude declines again towards Fort Lamy (now N'Djamena, 300m a.s.l.) and then rises again towards Kano (480m a.s.l.). The next section of this east-west traverse, if I had followed it, passes along the upper Niger River through Niamey (202m a.s.l.), Timbuktu (263m a.s.l.) and Bamako (324m a.s.l.). Finally, the land rises slightly again before descending to the coast at Dakar (4m a.s.l.). Although these changes in altitude may seem small (except in Ethiopia), especially considering the large distances involved, they are extremely important because they determine the flow of water and the catchment areas of the major rivers in this part of sub-Saharan Africa. These landforms result in five adjacent river systems; three have very large catchments, and two have smaller catchments. The first – on the east – is the Nile River catchment which occupies most of the Sudan, the northern half of Ethiopia and the highlands of eastern East Africa; the second (further west) is the Lake Chad catchment which occupies all of Chad, eastern Niger and the northern parts of Cameroun and Nigeria; the third is the Niger-Benue River catchment of Nigeria, western Niger, southern Mali and the Guinea Highlands; the fourth is the Volta River catchment of Ghana and parts of Burkina Faso (previously called Upper Volta); and the fifth is the Senegal River catchment of Senegal, Guinea, Liberia and parts of western Mali and Mauritania. These catchments were more extensive and of greater significance in the past, when this part of Africa was wetter than it is now.

In the past, the climate in this region of Africa was not as dry and harsh as it is today. There is considerable evidence from archaeology and paleoclimatic research to indicate that 15,000 – 5,000 years ago, the current Sahara Desert was a savanna with extensive cover of savanna trees and grasses, lakes, and running waterways. The rainfall was much higher than at present. This period has been given a number of names: 'African Humid Period', 'Green Sahara', Neolithic Subpluvial', and 'Holocene Wet Phase'. Likewise, the areas just south of the Sahara, such as those at 15°N, were savannas probably similar to the savannas of present-day East Africa. During this humid period, the Sahara, and the Sahel and Sudan Savannas, supported elephants, giraffes, hippopotamus, lions, crocodiles, fishes, and no doubt many other forms of wildlife. Many of these species have been depicted in the rock art (both paintings and engravings) of the region. Communities of humans were able to survive permanently in this rich environment; there was water in the lakes and rivers, and they were able to obtain adequate food by hunting and fishing. Now the "African Humid Period" has ended, the landscape is desert and semi-arid, most of the water sources have dried up, the larger animals are locally extinct, and the number of humans has declined (at least until very recently). This pattern of alternating wet periods and dry periods is thought to have occurred many times in the last million years. It was an interesting and rather sobering thought, that if I had travelled 7,000 years earlier, I would have witnessed lush savannas, many large trees, abundant rivers and lakes, and lots of large wild animals.

Religion has always played a part in the lives of the peoples of the Sahel and Sudan savannas, and has had a strong influence on the rise and fall of kingdoms. Traditional religions were widely practiced until about 300 AD when Christianity spread through Egypt, upper Sudan and Ethiopia. Whether Christianity spread to West Africa at this time is uncertain; if it did, it may have reached West Africa via the trans-Sahara trade routes from Roman North Africa. Christianity has survived in the highland regions of Ethiopia since 300 AD[6] and the only places in Ethiopia that converted to Islam are the coastal regions near the Red Sea. The Ethiopian Orthodox Church (which is closely related to the Coptic Church in Egypt) has remained the universal religion of Ethiopia for over 1,800 years. In contrast, from about 700 AD, the traditional religions of most of the Sudan and Sahel savannas have been replaced by Islam.[7] Islam did not extend further south into the rainforest and wet savannas of West Africa where the indigenous African people continued to practice traditional religions. Christianity was introduced into these southerly regions only very recently during the European missionary and colonial periods, and has now become the main non-traditional religion in most of Africa south of about 5° North.

Over the centuries, there have been many kingdoms and political entities along the southern fringes of the present-day Sahara, each with its own culture, language, arts and religion. Many of these kingdoms were formidable in their day, but none of them exist now. In northern Sudan, around the Nile River (an area often referred to as Nubia), there has been a succession of kingdoms: the Kingdom of Kush flourished from about 1000 BC to 350 AD. In about 400 AD, the Kingdom of Axum (from the Ethiopian highlands) overthrew Kush and established the Kingdom of Nubia. This Christian Kingdom survived until about 1500 AD when Islam became the main religion, and Nubia gradually became integrated into the Arab world. Further west, was the Kingdom of Darfur (1200-1400 AD), centred around Jebel Marra, but this was just one of a series of kingdoms that, over time, occupied what is now Darfur Province of Sudan. The Kanem-Bornu Empire (700 – 1900 AD) was one of the great empires of this region which originated in the Lake Chad area but subsequently extended its influence to both east and west. Also in this region was the Kingdom of Baguirmi, which at times was part of the Kanem-Bornu Empire, and the Kingdom of Ouddai or Wadai (1635–1909), an offshoot of the Kingdom of Darfur.[8]

In 'West Africa' as we now know it, several great Empires were formed, rose to power, and then declined. The most important of these, with the greatest geographical spread, were Songai (1464–1591 AD), Ghana (not to be confused with the modern state of Ghana, 300–1200 AD), Mali (again not to be confused with the modern state of this name, 1235–1600 AD) and Great Fulo (1490–1776 AD). Each of these empires had a similar type of history: each originated in a small area, and then by conquest became larger and more powerful. Finally each was defeated and their lands were either absorbed into a new large empire or fragmented into smaller states. The early empires followed some sort of traditional religion but as Christianity spread across northern Africa, many became Christian states. Then between c. 800 AD to 1500 AD, the traditional religions and Christianity were replaced by Islam. The colonial era of the late nineteenth and early twentieth centuries resulted in the end of these great empires (and also the many conflicts between them) and established the modern Nation States of the present time. The history of these great African empires is as complex as the history of the contemporary states of Europe, but is much less well known to the outside world and there are fewer historical records than in Europe. Most of the information about these empires, kingdoms and sultanates was recorded by North African Arabic scholars of previous centuries, and is based on the records of pilgrims travelling to Mecca and the stories of travellers who ventured across the Sahara desert. There is also a very rich source of information in Arabic texts, songs and oral history that is much less well known – and then only to scholars of African history.[9] More recently, modern historical and archaeological evidence has provided a better understanding of these great empires.

The humans of these arid lands have always been great travellers. In prehistoric times (for which we have only a little information), nomadic herdsmen must have moved from place to place following the new grasses that sprout after rain. In later times, probably from when the Romans occupied north Africa, trade routes were established along the North African coast and southwards across the region we now call the Sahara (which at that time was a savanna), as well as within the Sahel and Sudan savanna zones. Gold and salt were the most valuable commodities of trade, but many other everyday items were also traded. After the arrival of Islam, believers made the pilgrimage to Mecca; those from west and central regions of the Sahel savanna either travelled to the North African coast and then continued eastwards, or travelled south of the Sahara towards Khartoum and then across the Red Sea.[10]

There are many languages and dialects across the parallel – far too many to describe here; most of these are local and spoken in only small geographical areas. However, there are three widespread languages, and a traveller like myself was able to get by with English (in ex-British colonies), French (in ex-French colonies) and Arabic (widespread in countries of the Sahel). With these three languages, I never had any difficulties during my travels, and I was always able to make myself understood.

3

ERITREA AND ETHIOPIA

My journey began in Massawa, the port town of Eritrea on the shores of the Red Sea.[1] It was December, the so-called winter season, but even so the temperature and humidity were high. One does not feel like being energetic, and the best 'activity' is to sit in the shade and have a long cold drink. Massawa is steeped in history. Long ago it was just a sleepy fishing village within the Christian Kingdom of Axum. But after about 800 AD, Massawa was ruled by a series of Sultanates and was also, at one time, part of the Ottoman Empire when it was developed into a major port. One of the darkest episodes of its history was when it was a port for the Arab Slave Trade, transporting Africans for slaves in Arabia.[2] In the late nineteenth century and during the early twntieth century, it was the main seaport of Italian Eritrea. After the end of World War II it was briefly a British Protectorate before becoming a Province of Ethiopia in 1952. At the time of my visit, Eritrea was part of Ethiopia and the long struggle for Eritrean independence had not yet begun.

I arrived at the railway station in Massawa after the rail journey from Asmara. The railway (and the road which follows a similar route through the hills) was built by the Italians between 1897 and 1911. My only apprehension was that I was told to look out for *shifta* (or bandits) who were regularly robbing people travelling between Asmara and Massawa. (Thankfully I did not meet any of them!) In my diary, I recorded my impressions:

The diesel train left Asmara for Massawa at 7.15 in the morning. It was cold and the early morning mists were rising through the eucalyptus forests. There were lots of local people in the train – just a single carriage – and it was rather a crush. The single line track (built by the Italians) twists across the hillsides through cuttings and forest. The air was sweetly scented and bracing. The journey takes just under four hours, and the railway drops down 6,000 ft (1830 m) to Massawa. It is one of the most fascinating train journeys in the world. At first, the track descends through steep rocky hills, thick with Prickly Pear (Opuntia), but later the country becomes green with a variety of shrubs which I could not identify. Some parts of the hills are terraced and used for growing crops. The track twists down and down over innumerable bridges and escarpments, and through tunnels. In places, I could see the track looping downwards five or six times and several hundred feet below me. We stopped at Nefasit and at the halfway station of Ghindu to buy nectarines and egg sandwiches. All the way, range after range of hills with steep slopes and small valleys rolled away into the far distance; the view was ever-changing as the train twisted and turned along its narrow single track. Many of the women in the carriage wore gold earrings, bangles, necklaces and brooches. The young girl sitting opposite me had a necklace of gold with a George V gold coin. The women fed me with roasted wheat – a favourite food here. As time progressed and the train descended, the air became warmer and warmer, the hills were left behind, and the coastal plain came into view.

On arrival at Massawa railway station, I asked a small boy to take me to the Albergo Primavera hotel where I had booked a room for the night. He evidently did not know where to go, and he led me through a number of sleepy sleazy streets to what he said was the Albergo Primavera. In fact he took me to a brothel and, as I discovered later, Massawa was seething with prostitutes! After finding the Albergo, and having a snack and meeting an American Peace Corp volunteer, we hired a rowing boat to go to Green Island, a small uninhabited island in the bay about one mile from Massawa; there were no facilities, no landing stage, and it seemed miles from anywhere. The island is entirely sandy with a broken cover of low xerophytic shrubs, and its shores were thick with hermit crabs scuttling over the dazzling white sand; the sea was clear and still without any waves. We swam and lounged in the tepid water trying to keep cool. To the west, we could see the beach-front and harbour of Massawa; all the buildings were white. Especially majestic was the Imperial Palace with its white high-domed central roof, curved white arches and surrounding green garden and tall palm trees. A Palace has stood here since the days of the Ottoman Empire, but the present palace was constructed in 1874. In the end, the heat and the glare of the island sent us scuttling back to the mainland for a drink and a sleep. In the cool of the evening, I met some more Peace Corps volunteers; we had soup, fish steaks and fruit at an Italian restaurant and then explored the beach-front and some of the neighbouring streets, often being accosted by the ever-present prostitutes. Massawa has a very Italian feel because of the many Italian-style buildings. Some of the older buildings around the harbour were destroyed by an earthquake in 1921 and were rebuilt by the Italians over the following years. Later on in the evening, we sat in front of the Savoy Hotel, drinking coffee, until 11p.m. There were several ships in the harbour, and there were many more Europeans wandering around than we expected; most, we assumed, had disembarked from the ships that stop regularly at Massawa on their way between Italy and the Indian Ocean. It was pleasantly cool when bedtime arrived.

Massawa was the most easterly point of my journey; from now on, I travelled westwards (for nearly 4,000 miles). Asmara, the capital town of Eritrea, is situated on the top of the Eritrean-Ethiopian plateau. In December, the countryside is green and verdant, and there are many flowers, shrubs and trees in bloom. Everywhere is very Italian, more so than in Massawa. After settling into the 'Centrale Pension', I walked around the streets of central Asmara. The main street, Haile Selassie Avenue, was a wide tarmac-surfaced thoroughfare lined with three or four storey buildings and palm trees. The ground floor of these buildings was mostly shops with big awnings that provide shade on the pavements. There were many cyclists, a few two-wheeled carts pulled by donkeys, and lots of cars imported from overseas – lovely elegant old-fashioned cars with chrome hubplates and chrome bumper bars. Asmara was clean and the air was clean and refreshing. There were many drink and coffee bars, and shops full of cakes and pastries. In the evening, I found Reno Restaurant, and had a glorious meal of escalope of veal, followed by a plate of assorted cheeses, and a glass of beer.

All the Ethiopians that I met were delightful and helpful. Ethiopians have brownish skin, black wavy hair, and their facial features are aquiline; all of which indicate their origin – part North African, part Near East, and, in some, a bit of African. Men wore European trousers and jackets, or the traditional dress of white trousers and a huge white shawl wrapped around the shoulders and chest. The women wore a *shama* (or *shamma*), a white dress with a full skirt to the knees, bordered by decorative patterns, that is rather reminiscent of the national dress in the European Alps; and they do not normally wear any covering on the head. Other people seemed to have come from elsewhere; a few of the women I saw wore a *tobe*, a long length of cloth which is wrapped around the body and head; I suspected that these people came from the border with Sudan. Cowrie shells were often used as ornaments. I saw several leather bags ornamented with shells, especially bags used by women for carrying their babies.

On one morning, I walked along some of the smaller side streets where the houses are single storey, made of brick and concrete, usually painted white, and with corrugated iron sloped roofs, wooden doors and window shutters. The streets were relatively broad, not little alleyways, as found in the Sudan and Sahel arid zones to the west. I found the local market, bustling with activity; like all African markets there was a vast variety of food and household wares for sale, but there were also stalls selling pictures, crucifixes, and all manner of odds-and-ends. Much of the produce arrived in huge hessian sacks or in large baskets woven from palm fronds. Most African markets have a characteristic aroma – a mixture of earth, vegetables, fish, meats, human sweat, animals, leather... and often decay. But the aroma here was quite pleasant, due partly I suspect to the cool dry climate. Notices in the markets were written in Italian and Amharic.

Later on, after a lunch of ravioli, prunes and coffee at the Italian restaurant, I found a bus to take me to the local bus station where I purchased a ticket to take me to Axum on the following day. While I was there, it poured with rain – being in a rainstorm was so wonderful, especially having lived in an arid environment in the Sudan for several years. When the rain stopped, I walked onto the hills surrounding Asmara. The rocky hillsides had a sparse covering of green grass mixed with flowering scabious, wild roses, thistles and *daphne* (?), all plants of the temperate Palearctic. Nearby were plantations of eucalyptus trees from Australia, imported to provide wood for fuel and building. In one place, I found aloes and miniature wild irises sheltering in the lee of the rocks. I was surprised to find these un-African species of plants, relicts of the time long ago when the ice ages had forced the Eurasian flora and fauna much further south than they are now. As I walked back to the town, I met an old man driving three donkeys laden with goods; he looked poor but around his neck he wore a brilliant Ethiopian crucifix that shone brightly on his large white shawl. A beautiful traditional sight! As I returned to Asmara, it rained again – lovely! – and I found another restaurant for coffee and cakes.

On the following day, I caught the bus to Axum (Aksum) because I wanted to see the famous stelae, probably the most important remains of ancient Ethiopia. I travelled with John (a Peace Corps volunteer whom I met in Massawa). The bus was already full when we arrived at the bus station, so we decided to try to hitchhike (as many people like us did in those days). The driver kindly offered to take our luggage, and we willingly accepted (in retrospect, this was perhaps not a sensible thing to do, but it was common courtesy and we were much more trusting in those days). In the end, we caught another bus, which went the wrong way, then a horse-drawn cart, and finally a VW minibus. On our way, we passed *our* bus, with our luggage on the top! We stopped for the night at Adi Ugri, and I spent the night with some more Peace Corps volunteers. The house was rather crowded but I slept well enough on the floor. The countryside here is rather bare and open; there were lots of rocks and only a few trees. The next day, I continued on towards Axum in a brightly coloured red bus:

I got a seat near the front of the bus. The open country, with many small hills, is dotted with small bushes and eucalyptus plantations. Much of this region of Ethiopia has parkland-like scenery, without substantial forests. The road twists down an escarpment to a more arid region of familiar trees – Acacia, Balanites and Ziziphus – all of them now in leaf. Half way across the valley below the escarpment is the Magreb (Mereb, Mareb) River where the Province of Eritrea and the tarmac road end. On the other side of the valley I could see the high peaks of Adua (Adowa). On the way, we passed a similar bus to ours that had fallen over the cliff two days previously; it got stuck in a tree and luckily no-one was injured. Adua is famous for its church, and for a major battle when the invading Italians were defeated in 1896. When I arrived, I had tea with two of my fellow Ethiopian passengers, and then I found my way to the church – the first round Ethiopian Orthodox church that I had seen. A circular wall made of local stones surrounded the inner churchyard, and entry was through a tall square stone porch; inside the wall were many huge trees which cast a deep shade. It was peaceful and tranquil, and small parakeets were twittering in the foliage. The church itself was painted white, with many windows each protected with wooden lattice shutters. Sadly the bus driver was not able to wait for too long, and I had to leave sooner than I had hoped.

It was only eighteen miles from Adua to Axum. In Axum, I found a hotel in the centre of town for just one Ethiopian dollar per night (= about UK 2/9d). It was not luxurious, but the owners were kind; they brought a fly-spray, a new multi-coloured blanket and a bowl of water. Not so welcome were the few bedbugs that shared my bed during my two nights stay there! In the afternoon – what was left of it – I walked around parts of the historical part of the town and found the Touring Hotel where I had a drink of beer and some supper.

Axum is the oldest town in Ethiopia. It was the capital city of the Kingdom of Axum that flourished from 100 to 940 AD. During these years, it was a major trading centre and it expanded its influence far and wide, including into the Kingdom of Kush in Nubia. I spent a whole day – 7th December 1965 – immersed in the history and environment of Axum:

Apart from finding a bedbug in my bed when I woke up, it was a good day. The cool air is a pleasant change after the heat of Khartoum, so I had the energy to keep going and explore all day. After fried eggs and bread at the hotel, I started up the hill to the Tomb of Kaleb, the "King of Eritrea", who died in 542 AD. I was joined by three small children, one of whom, Futsum Gabremaria ('Servant of Christ'), spoke good English and was very helpful. The hillside is bare except for grasses and bushes. Some of the land had been cleared for growing tef, the local wheat looking rather like grass, which is used for making Ethiopian bread or injera. The Tomb of Kaleb, and his son Maskel, is on the top of a ridge. The entrance to the tomb is guarded by two huge rectangular blocks of stone, with a lintel stone on top; steps lead down into the ground (similar in form to those in the Valley of the Kings in Egypt). The tomb is lined with stone, and there are a few broken sarcophagi on the floor. It was a very simple tomb for a famous king, and the ravages of the centuries have removed all the evidence of royalty. From the ridge, a pageant of hills stretched away to the peaks of Adua. The sky was blue and dotted with clouds, and much of the land was broken into little patchworks of differently coloured fields and bushes. Above the ridge is another hill covered with bushes, trees and euphorbias, and on the summit is the Church of Likanos which commemorates Abba Likanos (Liqanos), one of the "Nine Saints" who are credited for bringing Christianity to Ethiopia in the late fifth century. (It is uncertain where these saints came from – Alexandria, Constantinople, Anatolia? – but they were welcomed by the Axumite king of the time.) We – the children and I – pushed our way through the bushes to the top, and to my surprise, there were several people sitting near the top. Even more surprising was the church built of stone just below the summit. Here in the courtyard were several hundred people listening to the priests, and from the open doors of the church drifted the singing of a litany. It was most impressive, especially on a Tuesday morning. On the path down from the church, an old lady was selling gum which is burnt (as incense) in the church. I bought ten cents worth which Futsum took to the church as an offering.

We walked down the hill and across some rough ground to another hill. On the top is the Church (or monastery) of Pentalewon which commemorates Abba Pentalewon, another of the 'Nine Saints'. A ring of bushes and stone walls surround the hill; inside this are the houses of the priests, and then there are steep steps up to the church perched on the top. There is only just room for the church, and on one side there is a steep vertical cliff. Before we left, the children stopped, said a few prayers and kissed a special stone. Like all the children I have seen here, these three wore crucifixes around their necks.

In the afternoon, I continued my explorations, visiting the stelae, the Church of St Mary of Zion, the Church of Mary Magdalene and the Bath of the Queen of Sheba. For most of the afternoon, I was escorted by a small Muslim boy named Awal. Later, I learned that about half of the population of Eritrea is Muslim – a fact that greatly surprised me. There are many stelae, clustered in a small area on one side of the town. A stela is a memorial to a deceased person; it is a huge carved piece of rock, rectangular in shape, very elongated, usually made of granite and placed in an upright position. The surfaces of a stela are carved – there are two 'false' doors, and decorations which resemble windows all the way up to the top. They vary in size, probably according to the social status of the deceased person. The largest stela in Axum (The Great Stela of Axum) is said have been constructed in *c*. 400 BC (so now about 1,700 years old) and is 24 m tall.

(Sadly this stela was not in Axum during my visit. It has had an interesting history: having fallen to the ground many centuries ago, it was taken by the Italians to Rome in 1937. It remained in Rome until 2005 when it was repatriated to Axum and re-erected.) There are also many other smaller stelae, many of which have fallen to the ground and have fractured into several pieces. It is presumed that each stela marked the site of a burial chamber in the ground below. The last stela was built in about 400 AD when the Kingdom converted to Christianity. Although the Great Stela was still in Rome, there was another very impressive large stela that Awal (incorrectly) called the Great Stela. I was intrigued how these steela were transported from the quarries, and how they were placed in an upright position; the stonemasons must have faced similar problems to those of the builders of Stonehenge on the chalk downs of Wiltshire.

I found my way to the church of St Mary of Zion; this small square church has special significance in Ethiopia because it is where the Emperors of Ethiopia were crowned and, according to local tradition, it houses the Ark of the Covenant. The original church was built in 300 AD, but has been rebuilt several times. Unfortunately, the church was closed so I was unable to see the lovely coloured paintings inside – ecclesiastical paintings of the Ethiopian Orthodox church are well known for their strong lines, bright colours, luminance and beauty. Nearby is a modern church with a large domed roof built by Emperor Haile Selassie in the 1950s. It is elegant in a modern sort of way but, to me, it does not have the majesty or presence of the 'Old Axum'. My final wanderings took me to The Baths of Sheba where the Queen of Sheba was reputed to bathe. The story of the Queen of Sheba is of great importance in the history of Ethiopia. According to legend (and there are many interpretations of this legend), Sheba visited King Solomon in Jerusalem so that she could sample the 'great wisdom of Solomon'. Many Ethiopians believe that a relationship between Sheba and Solomon resulted in a son, Menelik, who founded the Solomonic Dynasty in Axum in the tenth century BC. At that time, the dynasty embraced Judaism. When he was a young man, Menelik visited Jerusalem to see his father, and before he left Jerusalem he stole the Arc of the Covenant and took it to Axum. Later Menelik became the first King of Ethiopia – Menelik I – and his descendants (through different lineages) have ruled Ethiopia ever since, until 1974 when the revolution ended the Ethiopian monarchy. The Christian Ethiopian Orthodox Church replaced Judaism when the 'Nine

Saints' arrived in about 300 AD. There are so many stories about these early days and the foundation of Christianity that it is difficult to separate fact from legend. Nevertheless, Ethiopia has a rich and fascinating history, partly because of all its legends. Especially fascinating to me is that Ethiopia has remained a Christian nation, with it own special brand of Christianity, for the last 1,700 years while surrounding countries have embraced Islam.

The Queen of Sheba Baths were disappointing; a flight of rough-hewn steps up a rock face lead to the bath, but it was completely empty of water. One can only imagine what it may have been like. My wanderings were made particularly enjoyable because of the children who accompanied me. They were very keen to show me their schoolbooks, many of them just simple 'picture books'. They were eager to learn, and their attitudes were so different to those of the children I met in the Sudan. They were friendly too – shouting "Bambino" and "Hello" as I passed them in the street.

Looking back, I now realise how different the peoples and culture of this eastern part of the 15th parallel are compared with anywhere else further west. These differences are due almost entirely to the historical and geographical isolation of the Ethiopian highlands, the strong influence of Christianity, and the absence of conquest and settlement by foreigners (except for the Italians in the nineteenth and twentieth centuries – a relatively short time in the long history from the Solomonic Dynasty to the present time). From here, my journey took me to the low-lying semi-deserts of the Sudan where the climate, environment, peoples and religion are very different to Ethiopia.

4

THE BUTANA PLAINS

In eastern Sudan, there is an extensive flat plain – the Butana Plain – bounded by three rivers: the Nile on the west, the Blue Nile on the south and the Atbara river on the north, and by the highlands of Ethiopia on the east. In theory, I could have travelled to the Butana Plain along the Gash River from Ethiopia; I had passed over this river when travelling from Asmara to Axum (Chapter 3). However, it would have been a long and difficult journey because of the river snakes through the highlands and steep-sided gorges to the town of Kassala in eastern Sudan on the eastern edge of the Butana Plains. The river flows only during and immediately after the Ethiopian wet season and in some years it causes extensive flooding in and around Kassala; however, for most of the year it is a dry river bed with just a few pools of water. After leaving the highlands, where the country is flatter, the river is lined by a narrow fringe of trees and bushes, and to the south of Kassala there are small seasonally irrigated fields. To the north of Kassala, the river peters out because all of its water has drained into the desert sands. There is another larger river on the Butana Plains – the Atbara River – to the west of the Gash; this river rises in the Ethiopian highlands to the north-east of Lake Tana and it is also highly seasonal. The Atbara river provides water for a large irrigation scheme at New Halfa (just west of Kassala) and for some small irrigated fields near the town of Atbara. It flows into the Nile at Atbara, north of Khartoum. The Atbara River is the only river to enter the Nile north of

Khartoum before it reaches the Mediterranean. Amazingly it was shown correctly in Bowen's map of 1748.

The Butana Plain is within the Sahel Savanna Biotic Zone, and is characterised by having a low rainfall, many months of no rain, sparse vegetation, and very high temperatures throughout most of the year. However, grasses and herbs germinate and grow immediately after the short 'wet season' providing fresh forage for animals and (later) poor-quality 'hay'. Trees are uncommon except where sub-surface water is available. The soils of the Butana Plain are composed mainly of clay, with a surface of sand, but close to the Nile valley the soil is almost pure sand. In a few places, rocky jebels stand above the plain, and are visible for miles around. Although the plain is essentially flat, dry wadis cross the plain, some of them so silted that they are recognisable only as slight depressions in the ground.

I travelled on the Butana Plain in November 1965.[1] The short 'wet season' was over; the grasses had turned pale golden yellow in colour, and had dried to form 'hay'. Many grasses had already been broken by the wind or trampled and grazed by cattle and goats. I was on my way to Jebel Qeili, a large jebel in the middle of the Butana Plain. My diary recorded that…

After crossing the Blue Nile bridge from Khartoum to Khartoum North, we headed westwards on the road to Kassala. There were three of us on this expedition: Hassan Sati (the departmental driver), Awad my cook, and myself. We travelled in the big Ford Mercury truck – an excellent vehicle with a very high clearance essential for desert driving. The truck was heavily laden with collecting equipment, tables, chairs, canvas camp beds, water, food, and all the paraphernalia needed for camping in arid country. We attached zanzameers to the front of the truck (to provide cool water). There were innumerable tracks in the sand leading eastwards and it was often difficult to know which was the 'main road'. There was no tarmac and there were no signposts. There were several times when we thought we were not on the road, so we turned either north or south until we reached a better 'road'. Sometimes the road was discernable only by deep ruts in the sand – then at least it was easy to see where we had to go. This sort of driving would seem very unpredictable and haphazard to anyone used only to driving in western and non-desert countries. The country was bare and overgrazed near Khartoum, but further east, the Acacia trees and grasses grew more thickly.

Eventually, in some places, the country looked a bit like the open plains of East Africa. We passed two villages of simple mud houses with flat roofs, each with an elaborate tomb close by. Each tomb was built of brick with proper doors and freshly painted windows and topped by a silver-painted dome. What a contrast between the habitations of the living and the dead; of course, it would only be a very important wealthy sheik who could have a tomb like this. Herds of cattle wandered among the bushes, all of them in excellent condition. Two varieties of cows lived on the Butana Plain: the dark russet-coloured 'Butana' and the whitish 'Kenana'; both are good dairy cows and provided milk for Khartoum. Eventually we reached Abu Zukkeig where we stopped for tea – a favourite drink here served in small glass tumblers.

From here on, the ground rose gently to the Butana Plain; the soil was more like the black cotton soils of East Africa, and trees became scarcer. There were a few large wadis, only a foot or two deep, which crossed the Plain and it was only here that bushes were growing. Eventually the landscape was just golden grass swaying in the breeze. It was gloriously attractive country reminiscent of the prairies of Alberta and Saskatchewan in Canada. The openness of the Butana Plain gave me a wonderful feeling of freedom and I felt that I could go unhindered in any direction I wanted. Soon, the huge rock mass of Jebel Qeili (Jabal Qayli) appeared on the horizon, obscure because of the distance; as we got closer, the jebel appeared to become smaller. This odd effect is because of the mirage – what you see at first is the real jebel sitting above the mirage jebel. We continued at a good speed across the grassy plain, bumped across several more dry wadis, and reached the jebel. We found a huge boulder at the base of the jebel on the south side which gave some protection from the wind and sun, and here we set up our camp.

Jebel Qeili is about 120 m high and perhaps 150m in diameter, and is mainly granite – huge slabs of rock and many rounded boulders of various sizes piled on top of each other. Nearby are other smaller jebels and patches of rocks. Thick grass was able to grow in cracks between the rocks and a few brilliant green-leaved *Balanites* trees managed to flourish around the base of the jebel. It was quite easy to scramble over and around the rocks, and I spent the first afternoon doing this while setting my live-traps for catching mice (more about this later). It was hard hot work going up and down the jebel, and I was exhausted by the time dusk fell. Thankfully the air cooled quickly once the sun had set.

There were about twenty wells around the jebel. The wells were very old; they were about 75 feet deep, and lined with stones for the top 15 feet. There was no protection around the top of any of the wells, so it would be easy to fall in by mistake! At first light, cows started to arrive at the wells for their morning drink, and there was a continual succession of cows coming and going all day. Water was drawn from the wells by the nomadic tribemen using a sheepskin bucket; the bucket was attached by a rope to a donkey or a cow which walked to and fro, alternately lowering and raising the bucket. The water was poured into large troughs. Nearby, camels crowded together, standing aloof from the other animals. The camels had a habit of wandering away, and only came back when called by a piercing staccato cry from one of the nomads. All day long, we heard the shouting of the nomads and the moaning of the camels around the wells. By 4:30 in the afternoon, silence fell and the last animals wandered away along the many tracks into the surrounding grasslands. As the sun set, bats emerged from their roosts deep inside the wells and flew away over the plains; evidently they stayed there all day in spite of the noise, the swinging buckets, and the spilt water.

I was surprised and delighted to find some rock art (engravings) on the jebel.[2] I knew about the wonderful rock art from some regions of the Sahara, but I did not expect to find any here. The large boulder at the base of the jebel where we camped had some engravings, but they were very faint and difficult to decipher. While I was climbing over the rocks, I found some better engravings. One was a group of eight giraffes. These rock engravings must have been drawn many thousands of years ago when this area was woodland savanna and a suitable habitat for giraffes.

In this climate, it is essential to organise the daily schedule carefully to reduce the effects of the heat. I recorded a typical day in my diary:

My day starts at 5:30a.m. when I get up, have a cup of tea, and start the rounds of checking my mouse traps. This finishes by about 7a.m. when I return to camp. Every mouse that I caught had to be identified, weighed, measured, and carefully examined for other characteristics. At 9a.m., there is a pause for breakfast – grapefruit, porridge, bread and marmalade, and many cups of tea – all brought from Khartoum. By this time, it is already hot and it is tempting to do nothing; however, on most mornings I had further work to do that normally lasted until lunch. After a snack lunch – it is too hot to eat much – I have to go round my traps again, return the ones that I had removed in the morning, and make ecological notes on trap sites and vegetation. Each time I do a 'trap round', I have to climb about 300m up and then 300m down, over and around boulders. By the time I return to camp I am ready for yet another cup of tea. Then, as the temperature is falling, I write notes or read a book. Supper, cooked by Awad, is at 6:30 or 7p.m. By now I am ready for bed. A wind begins to rise about dusk, and it blows for most of the night. Compared with the daytime, it is gloriously cool and comparatively cold! I am glad that I have my pyjamas, sheets, and 'Icelandic' sleeping bag – the same one that I used in Canada in 30 degrees of frost.

Often, local nomads came to find out what we were doing. They were very respectful, and sat a few yards from our camp. Naturally they were intrigued by anyone who was catching mice, and they told me they were plagued with mice in their houses. (I suspect these were the Common House Mouse *Mus musculus*, an introduced species.) These semi-desert nomads are fine people. Some of them must be very wealthy – as measured by the number of camels, cows, sheep and goats that they own. All these nomads were friendly, and it still amazes me what seemingly happy lives they lead, yet (to a Westerner) they have so little. One little boy came to our camp on his way home from his school in the village about a mile from the jebel. He was carrying his satchel of books, and he proudly showed me the cardboard wrapping from a pair of stockings; on the outside there was a picture of a white woman in her underwear showing her legs and stockings. He thought this was tremendous – probably, I suspect, because such a picture is quite contrary to the strict Muslim outlook on life. Another young fellow who visited us came from the Rufaa tribe; his black fuzzy hair stuck out in all directions from his head, his eyes were dark and large and hawk-like, and he had a brilliant engaging smile. His dress was simple and made of three parts: very baggy trousers extending down to just below the knee, a sort of smock also reaching to the knee, and a waistcoat with arms and pockets. His clothes were made of cheap strong '*damureah*' cotton cloth; they were dirty white in colour because of constant contact with animals and the fine desert dust. He carried a stick, a kind of all-purpose instrument. I assumed he was a herder, constantly on the move with his animals.

The Butana Plain is an area with a very ancient history and has been much influenced by ideas and religions that have spread south along the

Nile Valley from Egypt. The Butana Plain is situated at the southern end of the Kingdom of Kush, one of the important kingdoms of the Sahel, which existed from about 1000 BC to 300 AD. This kingdom is famous for its pyramids at Meroe, 200km north of Khartoum; the pyramids are not as large or as well preserved as the pyramids in Egypt but, nevertheless, are very impressive. For many years, they were hidden under the sand and only recently have they been excavated and studied in detail. Later, as Coptic Christianity spread southwards from Egypt, the Butana came under the influence of Christian Nubia which had its centre and cathedral at Faras beside the Nile river, just south of the modern Sudan-Egypt border. More recently, in about 1500 AD, Islam came to the Butana, probably from the north. And, at about the same time, the Butana was invaded by the Funj Dynasty from the south. The Funj established their capital at Sennar (south of Khartoum on the banks of the Blue Nile). At the time, the Funj followed a traditional religion, but as the dynasty spread northwards, it encountered and embraced Islam and became known as the Funj Sultanate of Sennar. It was a very successful Sultanate that ruled from about 1500 AD until 1821 when Egypt invaded northern Sudan. Thus briefly from 1821 to 1899, the Butana became the southern-most part of the Ottoman Empire. Camping beside Jebel Qeili, it was difficult to realise that the Butana was witness to so many great events in this part of Africa. In spite of this, the herders and nomads that I met at the jebel were probably living much the same lifestyle as that of their ancestors many millennia ago.

About 140km west of Jebel Qeili, along a sandy desert track, is the city of Khartoum, the capital city of the Sudan. Here the Blue Nile and the White Nile rivers join to form 'The Nile'. After the remoteness of the Butana Plain, it is a shock to find a place full of people, lights, shops and houses. Khartoum, as I discovered, is a fascinating place...

5

KHARTOUM IN THE 1960s

When I was a small boy, I thought of Khartoum as a place like Timbuktu… situated in the deserts of Africa, miles from anywhere, shrouded in mystery and intrigue, the sort of place that I could never hope to visit and which would remain unknown to me for ever. I associated Khartoum with the epic history of General Gordon and 'the Relief of Khartoum'… and that was the extent of my knowledge. So when I was offered the chance to live in Khartoum for three years, it was an opportunity not to be missed. Hence, Khartoum became an essential part of my journey across Africa along the 15°N latitude. I was so pleased because it meant that I would be able to study jerboas (small hopping rodents) in the desert, and dragonflies along the banks of the Nile.

The Nile Rivers

Khartoum is situated at the junction of the White Nile and the Blue Nile ([1, 2]). Here, the waters of the White Nile flow northwards having travelled about 1,500 miles (2,500km) from their source in Uganda. At Khartoum, the White Nile is joined by the waters of the Blue Nile flowing westwards from their source in the highlands of Ethiopia. Hence Khartoum is bounded by the White Nile on its western edge and the Blue Nile on its northern edge. These rivers are the 'life blood' of Khartoum and the neighbouring towns of Omdurman (west of the White Nile) and

Khartoum North (north of the Blue Nile). The country around Khartoum is semi-arid Sahel Savanna – almost desert – characterised by a very hot dry climate, low and unpredictable annual rainfall, and sandy soil. The landscape is flat and monotonous with a sparse covering of bushes and few trees. The irony is that the Nile rivers provide an abundance of water in a desert environment. After the White and Blue Niles have merged, they become (simply) 'The Nile' which then flows northwards through northern Sudan to Egypt and finally into the Mediterranean Sea. The ancient civilisations of Egypt and Nubia have been dependent on the waters of the Nile for millennia.

One of the most fascinating features of the Blue and White Niles at Khartoum is the seasonal change in the height of the water level and the volume of water that passes down the rivers.[3] The water in the White Nile originates in the high country around Lake Victoria and in the smaller lakes and rivers along the Uganda-Congo border and in Rwanda and Burundi. As the river flows northwards, it passes through the Sudd (the great swamps of southern Sudan). In the Sudd, the river spreads out over the vast swamplands and there is considerable evaporation of water. However, at Malakal just north of the Sudd, large amounts of water from the Bahr-el-Ghazal and the Sobat rivers flow into the White Nile and, as a result, the volume of water in the White Nile just north of Malakal is similar to that leaving Lake Victoria, both on a monthly basis ($2km^3$ – $4km^3$/month according to season) and annually ($29.7km^3$/year at Malakal and $28.6km^3$/year at Lake Victoria). Only a small amount of evaporation occurs as the water flows northwards from Malakal to Khartoum. The White Nile is not actually white in colour; rather it is greyish or pale chalky-blue due to the fine particles of clay suspended in the water. The flow of water in the White Nile is sluggish because the river falls only 170m over a distance of c. 1,380km between Juba (c. 550m a.s.l.) and Khartoum (c. 380m a.s.l.).

The Blue Nile is very different to the White Nile.[2] This river has a huge catchment in the highlands of Ethiopia, and this region has a much higher rainfall (typically about 1,100mm/year) than at Khartoum. Many streams drain into Lake Tana (1,788m a.s.l.) from where the Blue Nile descends in a big U-shaped bend through waterfalls and gorges to the plains of the eastern Sudan near Rosieres (c. 500m a.s.l.). Additionally, other streams and rivers contribute water to the Blue Nile as it flows through the highlands before reaching Roseires. In contrast to the White

Nile, the Blue Nile experiences a large variation in the monthly flow of water because of the seasonal variation in rainfall in the Ethiopian highlands. The 'wet season' in the highlands is from May/June to September and during these times, there is an increase in the amount of water leaving the lake and in the many other rivers originating on the highlands. The Blue Nile reaches its maximum flow in July and August. This increase in flow is evident, some 4-6 weeks later, by the rise of the level of the river at Khartoum. Likewise, the decrease in flow at the end of the wet season is followed by a fall, some 4-6 weeks later, in the river level at Khartoum. At the driest time of year in the highlands, the monthly flow is 1km³ or less per month. At the wettest time of year, in August and September, it is 14-15 km³/month – at least fifteen times as great as at the driest time of the year. The Blue Nile at Khartoum flows very fast during the wet season because the large volume of water cascades down from the high altitudes in Ethiopia to the much lower altitudes in Sudan. The effect of these annual changes is that, during the dry season in Ethiopia, the water at Khartoum is confined within the 'dry season banks' and the exposed flood-plains on either side of the banks can be used for growing crops. In contrast, during the wet season in Ethiopia, the water spills over the 'dry season banks' at Khartoum, floods the flood-plains and flows away from the river as far as the 'wet season banks'. At this time, the Blue Nile looks immensely wide. Later, as the wet season in the highlands comes to an end, the flood-waters at Khartoum recede, the river level goes down, and eventually is contained within its dry season banks again.

The flood-waters of the Blue Nile are rich in silt derived from the erosion of basalt rocks in the highlands. The silt is deposited on the flood-plains, replenishing the soil nutrients every year. During the floods, the waters are no longer blue but muddy brown due to the suspended silt. The annual deposition of silt takes place all along the Blue Nile, and along The Nile downstream from the confluence of the Blue Nile and the White Nile, wherever there are flood-plains. Even after the Nile enters the Mediterranean in northern Egypt, there is a brownish tinge to the sea because of suspended silt. During the floods of the Blue Nile at Khartoum from July to October, the waters of the fast flowing Blue Nile and the sluggish White Nile form two 'streams' where they join to form 'The Nile' – the stream from the White Nile is whitish grey and that from Blue Nile is muddy brown; eventually the two streams merge and mix and continue their way downstream. The annual rise and fall of the rivers at Khartoum (particularly the Blue Nile and 'The Nile') is one of the most interesting biological features of Khartoum.

The Climate

The climate at Khartoum is well known to be hot and dry. The yearly cycle of the climate is determined by the movement of the Intertropical Convergence Zone (ITCZ); for most of year the ITCZ is south of Khartoum and the climate is dry, but when the ITCZ arrives over Khartoum from the south, it brings the wet season which lasts from July to September (see chapter 2 for more details of the ITCZ). One classification divides the year into four divisions: the winter dry season (December to March), the advancing monsoon (April to June), the wet season (July to September), and the retreating monsoon (October and November). [4] During the advancing and retreating monsoons, there is usually no rainfall, so the effective dry season lasts for nine months (October to June). There is no rainfall at all between November and April, but there may be small falls of rain in March to May and again in October (<5 mm/month). The 'wet season' is July, August and September; in these months the average rainfall/month is 46mm (July) to 75mm (August), tapering to 25mm in September. Thus the average annual rainfall is only about 160mm/year (six inches), but it varies greatly from year to year; in some years there may be less than 70mm (or even zero), in most years there is 70-230mm and occasionally there is 230-350mm. [5] During the wet season, rain falls on only 2-7 days each month; sometimes there is very little rain on a particular day, and on another day 70-80mm may fall during a single storm. The pattern of rainfall and the amount of rain is very unpredictable – as is typical of desert environments – with huge monthly and yearly variation and between localities (even those only a few kilometers apart). In the dry season, especially between December and April, when the winds come from the north, there are sandstorms (locally called 'haboobs') when the air is laden with very fine particles of sand, and visibility is often greatly reduced. The blown sand forms drift along the edges of houses, fences, bushes, and railway lines, and it fills up the depressions made by vehicles on the sandy roads. The fine particles seep into houses, and dusting of furniture is required every day.

The temperature also shows strong seasonal variation.[4] In the 'winter' months, the temperature [given here as mean value (minimum – maximum)] is relatively cool [typically 24 (16-32) °C]. As the monsoon approaches, the temperature rises [typically 34 (26-42) °C] and it is very hot during the daytime. The wet season brings slightly cooler weather [30 (25-36) °C]. The temperature rises again during the retreating monsoon [33 (25-40) °C] and then declines again prior to the 'winter' season. The low rainfall and the high temperatures mean that the relative humidity is low for most of the year (daily range 15-30%, although higher in the wet season). During the daytime, except when it is raining during the wet season, the sky is blue, the sun is bright, the air is clear, and mirages are common in the desert. Of course, for all animals and plants (including humans) living in this climate, it is the combination of high temperature, low rainfall, low relative humidity, high evapo-transpiration, high solar radiation, and high winds (leading to sand storms) that make survival difficult and challenging.

Religion

Before Islam arrived in the northern Sudan, it is assumed that there were a number of traditional religions derived from the pharonic religions of Lower and Upper Egypt. Certainly the pyramids at Meroe suggest that the Egyptian influence spread southwards along The Nile valley. At a later date, after the establishment of the Coptic Christian church in Egypt (some 600 years before Islam came into being), Christianity spread southwards through Upper Egypt into Nubia (now northern Sudan). Many beautiful Coptic churches were built beside The Nile, richly painted with wall murals depicting the life of Christ and his disciples. The best known of these churches is the Cathedral at Faras, built in the early seventh century. It remained as a cathedral for many centuries until about the fourteenth century when Islam became the dominant religion of the region. Thereafter it was abandoned, and during the following years it disappeared under the drifting sand until it was excavated in the 1960s prior to the building of the Aswan Dam. The Coptic religion is still recognised in the Sudan, but only about 1% of the population is Coptic Christian; most of them live in the large cities and towns in northern Sudan.

At the present time, Islam is the official religion of present-day Sudan, and the vast majority of Sudanese are Muslims. Islam has a strong influence on all facets of daily life. The conversion of northern Sudan to Islam was a gradual process which took place during several centuries. The influence of Islam into Coptic Christian Nubia probably began, in a small way, in the seventh and eighth centuries when Arab travellers came south along the Nile Valley and from the ports on the Red Sea. Over the following centuries, Islam became more established and the influence of Christianity declined (chapter 4). There are many mosques – Muslim places of worship – in Khartoum and neighbouring Omdurman, and also in most towns in northern Sudan. Mosques are often beautifully and elaborately decorated with Koranic scripts (in Arabic), and painted in brilliant colours, and they are frequently the most impressive buildings in a town.

Islam is noted for its regular daily worship. Five times each day, the muezeen of the mosque calls the faithful to prayers. Prayers are said kneeling on a special mat that is placed on the ground facing Mecca. The prayers are ritualised and take only a few minutes. It is a common sight in the Sudan to see people praying in the open – beside the Nile, on the irrigated farmlands, or wherever happens to be convenient; my steward, for example, always placed his prayer mat on the sand just outside the kitchen door at prayer times. Friday is the day of rest in the Muslim calendar (just as Sunday is the day of rest in the Christian calendar), and offices, schools and shops are closed. There are four special celebrations of Islam each year (each of them a Public Holiday), but unlike the special celebrations in the Christian calendar, the dates on which these are held vary each year because the Islamic calendar is based on the phases of the moon. The most important and long-lasting event of the Islamic year is Ramadan which celebrates the first revelation of the Koran to Mohammad in the year 610 AD (in the Gregorian calendar). During Ramadan, which lasts for thirty days, Muslims are not allowed to eat and drink between dawn and sunset; this can be a very stressful time, especially when Ramadan falls in the hottest months of the year. The end of Ramadan is marked by Eid-al-Fitri – a time of great feasting and celebration.

The countryside around Khartoum

The countryside around Khartoum is mostly flat and sandy. Because of the hot dry climate, there is very little vegetation and all the perennial plants are adapted to heat and lack of water. In most places, bushes and trees are sparse although in some regions, especially near the khors (old stream beds), there may be a few trees. Several species of *Acacia* trees and a shrub *Capparis decidua* are the principal plant species, and most of them retain their leaves all year. Goats and sheep browse many of the smaller plants and the low branches of trees. Some of the *Capparis* are browsed to form small dense bushes two to three feet high, and often a mound of blown sand and dry grass fragments accumulates around the base of these browsed bushes. In the dry season, the sand is bare and dry in most places, although close to The Nile the vegetation is denser and greener than elsewhere. From the air, the Nile is seen as a blue or muddy-coloured meandering line bordered on either side by a narrow fringe of green vegetation in an otherwise yellow sandy wasteland. The flatness of the landscape is moderated in places by rocky jebels; some have steep sides, screes and cliffs, and others are just rocks and boulders. Some are small, others are very large; some are solitary, others are clustered in groups. Most jebels have no vegetation although some support a few bushes (and grasses in the wet season). The nearest of these jebels to Khartoum are the Merkiyat Jebels, just to the west of Omdurman; the rocks are reddish-brown or granite-coloured, bare and rugged. A few miles north of Khartoum are the Sabaloka Hills, and there are other isolated jebels nearby. In such a flat land, it is exhilarating to climb up a jebel and have a wonderful view from the top.

A little bit of history

There has probably been some sort of human settlement at the confluence of the White Nile and Blue Nile for millennia. The few archeological remains that have been found are difficult to date. Multi-barbed bone spear-heads, microliths (made from quartz pebbles) and grinding stones may date from 4500 – 3000 BC. Other early records of human habitation are potsherds and bone hairpins thought to date from *c.* 2000 BC; and there are also potsherds found in burial graves from the Meroitic Period (350 BC – 350 AD) when the Kingdom of Kush had its capital at Meroe.[6] These early records are from sand banks well above the present level of the Blue Nile (roughly in the centre of the present city of Khartoum) which suggests that the level of the Blue Nile was higher than at the present time. After the fall of the Kush, as a result of the spread of the Axumite Kingdom from Ethiopia, three Christian Kingdoms were established along the Nile in

Nubia. The two northern Kingdoms were called Nobatia (with its capital at Faras) and Makuria (with its capital at Dongola). The southernmost Kingdom was Alodia, with its capital at Soba on the Blue Nile, just east of Khartoum. Alodia survived from *c.* 600 AD to c. 1500 AD. Little is known about this period. During these times, Islam slowly extended southwards from Lower Egypt (mainly due to conquest by Arab armies). Nobatia and Makuria were conquered and converted to Islam by the end of the 1200s, but Alodia remained a Christian Kingdom until 1504 AD.[7]

Khartoum as we know it today was established in 1821, when the Khedive of Egypt, Muhammad Ali Pasha, decided to enlarge his empire. He despatched one of his armies, commanded by his son Ibrahim Pasha, to establish a base at Khartoum where it became a trading post for goods and slaves. In 1873, General Charles Gordon – a British General – entered the service of the Khedive who sent him to Khartoum as Governor-General of the Sudan. At the time, the Egyptian administration of the Sudan was poor and slavery was rife. Gordon introduced major changes to the governance of the Sudan, and he managed to eliminate slavery. In the early 1880s, there was a major upheaval in Sudanese affairs: Mohammad Ahmed, the self-styled Mahdi, began an uprising to expel the Egyptians from the Sudan. The deteriorating situation came to a head when the Mahdist forces surrounded Khartoum. It was at this time that Khartoum became well known in Britain because of the 'Siege of Khartoum'. The outcome was the assassination of General Gordon, and the expulsion of all Egyptians.[1] The Sudan was governed by the Mahdists until 1899 when a relief expedition, commanded by Lord Kitchener, defeated the Mahdists at the Battle of Omdurman fought in the desert to the west of Omdurman. Subsequently, the Sudan became an Anglo-Egyptian Condominium, which was effectively a protectorate ruled by the British until Independence in 1956. When Kitchener arrived in Khartoum, the settlement was mostly in ruins, although the Palace, where Gordon was killed, was still standing. Kitchener reorganised the street layout so that there were roads running east-west, roughly parallel to the Blue Nile, and north-south. There were also some diagonally orientated roads so the overall street plan looked like the British Union Jack. Many trees were planted along the main roads. The central part of Khartoum in the 1960s looked very similar to Kitchener's design of 1900, but by this time there were many new buildings, the limits of the city had expanded, and the trees planted by Kitchener were now fully mature, casting welcome deep shade along the streets.

Omdurman is on the west side of the Nile, close to the confluence, and is a more traditional Sudanese town. A single bridge across the White Nile links Omdurman with Khartoum. The Mahdi used Omdurman as his military base, and after his death, his large ornate tomb was built in the centre of the town.

Khartoum as I remember it[8]

The central part of Khartoum is rather grand – a legacy of the colonial days. Nile Avenue runs along the southern bank of the Blue Nile, rather like the Embankment runs along the Thames in London. On the river side, there is a walkway with large mahogany and banyan trees, and on the landward side there are elegant stone buildings: the Palace, some of the Ministries and the Grand Hotel. Further away, and parallel to Nile Avenue, is Gamma Avenue (University Avenue) with the University, the Natural History Museum, the Ethnographical Museum, and the Post Office. Further back still is Sharia el Gamhuria which is one of the main shopping streets. All these major avenues have tarmac surfaces, but some of the little roads in between are just sand. Barlaman Street is one of these little roads; at the end is the Parliament (Barlaman), but for most of the time when I was in the Sudan, the country was under military rule and the Parliament was closed. Further away, the same pattern of criss-cross streets continues; here are many local shops, and the market (*suq*) for meat, vegetables, fish and a multitude of other everyday items. I found it quite easy to get lost in this maze of little streets. All the shops are single story buildings and look superficially similar without any major landmarks. At the southern periphery of Khartoum is the Ring Road (a sort of by-pass road) from which other roads lead off into residential areas. In central Khartoum, it does not seem like being in the middle of a desert. South of the Ring Road is the "New Extension" where many new houses were being built; in the early 1960s, it was a dull and unattractive area and totally bare of vegetation. The houses were mostly large, usually single-storey with a flat roof, and built of concrete and brick. Each house was surrounded by a tall concrete wall with iron gates. Because the houses were being built on desert sand, there was no good soil for making a garden. The little streets were just sand, with a few electricity

38

poles, some of them with a light bulb that gave a dull glow at night. Many of the labourers who were building these houses were very dark-skinned tall thin Nuers, Shilluks and Dinkas from the south of the country; they lived in little shacks of corrugated iron, wood and cardboard, usually placed against a concrete garden wall. I always felt very sorry for these people – they had so little money, so few material possessions and no security. The semi-desert surrounded the edge of the New Extension – just boiling hot sand, glaring sun, small stunted bushes, and a few goats which browsed on the sparse vegetation.

Life in Khartoum

The daily routine in Khartoum is governed by the climate. When I lived there, the shops opened at about 7:30a.m. and closed at 1:30p.m., and then re-opened again from 5p.m. to 8p.m. Most people began work at about 7 a.m., had a break for breakfast from 9-10, and then continued work until 1:30 or 2p.m. The afternoon was spent indoors, resting or sleeping because it was too hot to work or to be outside. Some people returned to work in the cool of the evening. There were many variations on this daily pattern, which changed according to the season. Houses were built to shield the occupants from the harshness of the climate. Most houses had verandas, high ceilings, and huge ceiling fans which rotated slowly with a soft "whosh-whosh" sound. Windows had shutters to keep out the heat and glare of the sun, or – in local mud-brick houses – the windows were very small. Many roofs were flat – which seemed odd to me at first because I thought a large 'dead-space' between ceiling and roof would provide insulation; but, in fact, the flat roof is an extra living space for eating and sleeping when the temperature drops markedly after sunset and the evening breeze brings relief from the heat of the day.

The hot dry climate of Khartoum (and northern Sudan) makes it a difficult place to live in for humans reared in the temperate regions of the planet. The heat tends to sap one's energy, especially in the afternoon. It is imperative to wear the correct sort of lightweight clothing and to live a lifestyle which minimises exposure to the hot rays of the sun. It is essential in this hot dry climate to drink a lot of fluid (especially water) in order to replace the fluids lost as sweat. I drank litres of fluid every day (mostly water, tea and *'lamoon'* – a delicious local drink made from limes and/or lemons) and yet I rarely needed to urinate during the day. Strong Turkish/ Arabic coffee was a favourite drink for many people; it was served in small cups and was very strong, but it did not provide much fluid. Keeping cool at night was always a problem except during the so-called 'winter'. Sleeping clothes were kept to a minimum. The huge ceiling fan rotated slowly, and the windows were wide open to let in the cooler night air. Only in the 'winter' did I turn the fan off and snuggle under a single top sheet. The winter nights can be comparatively cold, i.e. a low of about 16 °C.

Most commodities were available in Khartoum if you could find them and were prepared to pay the price. It was very easy to live satisfactorily on what was available here. Everything – with a few exceptions – was more expensive than in Britain. Fruit and vegetables were purchased in the local markets but more or less everything else was found in the many little shops, many of them owned by Greeks. [At this time, the currency was pounds and piastres (S£1 = 100 piastres [PT]) and the exchange rate was GBP £1 = S£1]. Typical prices in the early 1960s were: meat – 10PT/lb; 8 oranges – 12PT; tomatoes – 7-10 PT/lb; six small eggs – 10 PT; butter – 30- 40 PT/lb; one grapefruit – 3 PT; imported packet of biscuits – 10-12 PT; tin of fruit – 20-14 PT; and one bar of Lux toilet soap – 14 PT. Most of the available furniture was locally made. It was possible to buy imported goods from all over the world (all of which attracted expensive customs duty); for example, paper and envelopes from Sweden, aluminum foil from America, china from Britain, toilet paper from Austria, mouse traps from Czechoslovakia, refrigerators from Japan, and writing ink from Germany. Other shops that appealed to foreigners were bookshops – mostly selling paperbacks – and a music record shop.

Travelling around Khartoum was relatively easy. There were buses and lots of yellow taxis; most of the taxis were Hillmans (a popular British car at the time) because a local dealer offered a flexible long-term hire purchase plan which appealed to taxi drivers. In the 1960s, not many people owned their own cars – they were too expensive and unsuitable for roads outside Khartoum and Omdurman. Instead there were many blue Vespa scooters, but because of their small wheels, they were rather unstable on sand. There were many times when my Vespa scooter skidded on a sandy track and fell to one side, depositing me on the sand – thankfully with little (or no) damage to me or my scooter. Within Khartoum, goods were often carried by donkeys and in donkey-carts.

Khartoum is situated at a crossroads in Africa, and humans have moved through the area we now call Khartoum for millennia. One of the 'roads' runs north-south along the Nile valley which enabled Egyptians and Nubians to travel southwards, and for dark-skinned Africans to travel northwards. The east-west road enabled Arabic peoples from Arabia to travel towards Khartoum and further west, and for peoples from Darfur and further west to travel towards Khartoum. As a result, there is a huge mixture of people in Khartoum; there has long been inter-marriage, although some tribes have maintained their ancestral identity. Walking through the streets of Khartoum, it was very difficult for the non-expert to identify the ancestral history of passers-by although dress, colour of skin, facial characteristics and the language often helped with 'identification'. The Sudanese, especially the Sudanese Arabs, wear dress that is very suitable for the hot sunny climate. The men wear a long loose-fitting white garment called a *jelabiya* that covers the body from shoulders to ankles and has long sleeves. The *jelabiya* is worn over the top of special white trousers or Western-style trousers and shirt. Some men wear a small white hat (rather like a skull cap), others may wear the traditional turban made of a long length of white cloth which is wrapped several times around the top and sides of the head; it is rather like the turban worn by Sikhs but not nearly as neat or formal. Young men or workmen wear a whole range of practical clothing such as shorts, T-shirts, and long trousers. Businessmen wear typical Western clothing – suit, white shirt and tie. Women wear the traditional *tobe* (*thoub, toob, tiab, tyab*) – a long (5-6m) piece of cloth which is wrapped around the body in a rather complex manner, including over the top of the head. *Toobs* cover all the body except for the face and fall to the ankles, but leave the hands free. *Toobs* may be pure white or highly coloured and patterned. The skin colour of Sudanese Arabs in Khartoum is very varied, ranging from pale yellowish-brown typical of Egyptians and Nubians to the much darker brown of people whose ancestry comes from further south and west, and from Ethiopia. There are also very dark-skinned people with obvious African origins; these include the Fur from Darfur, the Nubas from the Nuba Mountains, and the tall thin Nuers, Shilluks and Dinkas from the southern Provinces[9] bordering on Uganda and the Democratic Republic of Congo.

Work, including extended field trips away from Khartoum, took up most of my energy and time, so there was not much leisure time. Many expatriates joined the Sudan Club which had buildings and grounds near Nile Avenue, but I preferred to enjoy my garden and local field excursions when not working. Reading, listening to music (long-playing 33 rpm vinyl records), seeing friends, having Arabic lessons, and small evening dinner parties were favourite occupations. Occasionally there was a film at a cinema on Nile Avenue.

Nothing ever happened quickly in Khartoum, especially when it involved bureaucracy. Anything to do with forms, visas, income tax, travel and bank arrangements were long and drawn-out processes. For example, when visiting an office with a simple request, such as a signature on something or purchasing a ticket, a typical reply was 'bukra' (tomorrow) or 'bukra insh'allah' (tomorrow, God willing), or 'bada'a bukra' (I will attend to your request tomorrow and maybe it will be ready sometime after this). Such a reply means that one has to return to the office on the following day and maybe on a number of days thereafter. One had to have infinite patience! During Ramadan, the month-long commemoration of the revelation of the Koran to Mohammad, the pace of life slows down (not that it was ever fast) and businesses and governments work much more slowly and inefficiently – particularly when Ramadan falls in the hottest months of the year.

In the 1960s, one was quite isolated from the rest of the world, but that did not seem to matter – there was no alternative. I never used a telephone anywhere in the Sudan, and I did not have a telephone in my office or at home. The main means of communication with other people was by letter, or by telegram or, if they lived locally, by physically going to see them. (There was no internet, email, mobile phones or satellite phones at this time.) I was able to write to my family and friends overseas by airmail post. Mostly I wrote airletters (aerogrammes); these were made of thin blue paper, about 24.5 by 20cm in size, and one could write on all of one side and on half of the reverse side. When finished, the airletter was folded into four quarters and sealed by two sticky tabs. The overseas postage was only 4 PT. For a larger letter, there was lightweight thin paper, and airmail envelopes that had a red, white, and blue pattern around the outside edge [postage 55 PT]. For news about the outside world, I listened to the BBC World Service that broadcast regularly to the Sudan, and occasionally friends had an English newspaper which was passed around. Lack of news was something that did not worry me unduly – the isolation of the Sudan was, in fact, a rather soothing feeling. In the years before air travel, the only way to reach Khartoum was by boat and rail from Egypt, or by boat to Port Sudan on the Red Sea and then by train to Khartoum; both were long and hot voyages. In contrast, in 1963-1966, it was easy to fly from London to Khartoum, with stops in either Rome or Cairo, or both. Flight times were arranged so that planes arrived in Khartoum during the night when the cooler air made it safer and easier to land and take off. At this time, BOAC (British Overseas Airways Corporation) used de Havilland Comet 4 jet aeroplanes, the first airliner to use jet propulsion. It was remarkable to be transported from the temperate green cool climate of Britain to the dry barren blistering heat of Khartoum in only a few hours.

The Pink Palace

I was lucky enough to live for two years in a little cottage attached to the 'Pink Palace' on the southern bank of the Blue Nile, about two miles east of central Khartoum. The Pink Palace was so named because it was painted pink. Its main claim to fame is because Emperor Haile Selassie lived at the Palace in 1940–1941 just before he returned to Ethiopia after being in exile for five years during the Italian occupation of Ethiopia (1936 to 1941). The Pink Palace was a single story building with a large entrance hall and rooms around the sides – very simple and humble for an Emperor. My cottage – one of a number in the grounds of the Pink Palace – was small; just a living room, a bedroom, a bathroom, a kitchen and a small veranda. The toilet was a small room in the back garden; it contained a bucket (with a seat) that was emptied each night by the 'night-soil man'. The cottage was sparsely but adequately furnished with a table and chairs, bookcases, wardrobe for clothes, and an *angareeb* – the local Sudanese bed. This simple rectangular bed is made of four horizontal wooden poles (which form the sides and ends), wooden legs about two feet in height, and a net of thick woven rope attached to the horizontal poles. A thin cotton mattress is placed on the ropes. Sleeping on an *angareeb* is surprisingly comfortable and very suitable for a hot country where bedding is not needed. Each cottage had electricity for lights, stove, fans, gramophone and radio. One of the joys of living at the Pink Palace was that it was cooler than in other parts of Khartoum because of the big trees and hedges around the Palace and its proximity to the Blue Nile. Here it was possible to have a small garden with a lawn and colourful flowers. Gardening in a desert may be thought of as challenging, but when there is water, the results are spectacular. The lawn in my garden was completely surrounded by a low mud wall, about eight centimeters high, as were each of the shrub and flower beds. Every week, water was pumped from the Blue Nile, firstly on to the lawn (which temporarily looked like a flooded swamp) and then on to each of the other garden beds. The gardener directed the water to where it was required by breaking a small section of mud wall to allow the water into a particular bed, and by closing other walls. This simple form of irrigation has been used to grow crops on the flood-plains of the Nile for thousands of years.

Living at the Pink Palace, and close to the Blue Nile, allowed me to follow the fascinating seasonal changes of the river and its effects on river life, especially the annual cycle of the flooding and drying of the flood-plains. When the floods receded, local farmers were able to plant crops in the fertile soils of the flood-plains. The land was divided into small fields, separated by irrigation channels, and each field was surrounded by a little mud wall so it can be flooded as necessary with water from the irrigation channels. Most of the crops were grown from October or November (after the floods had receded) to June or July (just before the annual floods began and when the temperature was hot or very hot). The crops had to be irrigated by water from the river because there is no rainfall at Khartoum at this time. The water is raised to the level of the flood-plain by a *shadoof* (*shaduf*); this is a bucket (usually made of leather) on the end of a long pole while at the other end is a weight equal to that of a full bucket. The long pole is attached to a horizontal pole which acts as a fulcrum. The sequence of lowering the bucket into river, using the weight and the fulcrum to raise the bucket to the flood-plain, tipping the water into a large irrigation channel beside the *shadoof*, and finally twisting the bucket so it can be lowered again into the river, goes on for hours at a time. Farmers use this simple method very efficiently; the regular low-pitched squeaking of the *shadoof* is an oft-heard noise on the flood-plains during daylight hours. Farming on the flood-plains is possible for seven to nine months each year – until the river begins to rise again and the flood-plains are flooded. It was a favourite occupation of mine to walk along the Blue Nile in the evening. Often there was a cool breeze, and the fading sun cast a translucent light. When the river was high, I walked along the upper bank where there was a fringe of grass and reeds; when the river was low, I could walk along the edges of the irrigation channels on the exposed flood-plains, past the *shadoofs*, and between the little fields of green vegetables.

The Revolution of 1964

The Sudan has had rather a turbulent history since Independence in 1956, partly as a result of its many ethnic groups. The government of the country has alternated between democratically elected parliaments, and military rule. When I arrived in 1963, the country was under the military rule of General Ibrahim Abboud and was mostly peaceful. However, there were disturbances in the southern Provinces due, in part, to disputes between the Arab Muslims of the north of the country and the African Christians of the south. In October 1964, tensions were rising because of the 'southern problem', the declining economy, and rising prices. The discontent exploded on 21st October with strikes and demonstrations in Khartoum, followed by curfews, the closure of shops, schools, the University and government offices, the cancellation of trains and air travel, and suspension of some forms of communications. The police and army tried to keep order: tear gas was used to control the demonstrators, and armed soldiers were conspicuous all over Khartoum. The following week was one of intense political activity; it ended with the formation of a transitional government led by Al-Khatim Al-Khalifa and the promise of elections in the near future. In June 1965, a new democratic government of Ahmed Mahgoub was elected, and this lasted until just after I left the Sudan.

I remember the days of the 'October Revolution' very well, although at first I was unaware of the political upheaval. On 21st October, I had been invited to dinner with some friends who lived on the other side of Khartoum. I set off on my Vespa scooter along University Avenue just after dark and was surprised how quiet it was – there was no traffic and also no people! When I arrived at my friends' house, they said: "Good heavens, what are you doing here? Didn't you know there has been a revolution and there is a curfew?" "No," I replied, "but I did wonder why it was so quiet everywhere." "Come inside, and have some dinner now you are here," they suggested, "and you can stay the night if you wish". I had a pleasant evening, but at 10p.m. I decided it was time to go home because I had a lecture at 7a.m. the next morning. I set off on my scooter; all was quiet and the streetlights were working. As I reached the

University, I saw lots of soldiers, so I slowed down and turned off the headlight. I was stopped by a group of soldiers who wanted to know who I was and what I was doing. I explained and they, in turn, told me about the revolution. We parted on the best of terms – they bade me goodnight and I continued on my way. The following morning, I did not have to give a lecture because the University was closed, and so I was able to listen to the recent news about the Sudan on the BBC World Service… which confirmed that there had been a military revolution. During the following week, nothing much happened in Khartoum; I spent my time going to my study sites and watching jerboas and dragonflies. Political unrest and change continued, spasmodically, after the revolution for the remainder of the time that I lived in Khartoum. One major event during these tumultuous days was the closure of the southern Provinces to travellers, and consequently there were no longer any backpackers and safari vehicles passing through Khartoum on their way south to East Africa. I, too, was unable to visit the south.

Favourite places in and near Khartoum

Moving away from Khartoum was difficult because most roads outside of the three towns were just tracks in the sand. Travel beyond Khartoum required a 4-wheel drive vehicle or powerful truck with big wheels. The only exception was a new tarmac road on the eastern side of the Nile. This was called the 'American Road' (because it was being built with American Aid money) from Khartoum North to Atbara. However, when I lived in Khartoum, it extended for only about ten miles and then stopped; why this was so was unclear – one view was that American Aid was short of funds, and another was that the diplomatic relations between the USA and Sudan had deteriorated because of the military coup in 1958 and the Americans refused to provide any more funds. I was lucky because I had the use of an old Land Rover belonging to the Arid Zone Research Unit for my research on jerboas and gerbils (desert rodents), and I could also use the large Ford Mercury truck of the department (see Chapter 4). Each week, I drove the Land Rover up the American Road at dusk, and then turned eastwards on to a sandy track to the village of Halfayat el Muluk.[(10)] This village was just a small number of square closely-spaced single-storey houses built of sand and mud bricks; their sandy-brown colour was similar to that of the landscape so as to make them, in some lights, almost invisible at a distance. Here I met some young Sudanese friends – Hussein, Sadik, Ali and Mohammad – and we continued eastwards into the flat semi-arid desert towards my study site where I could observe jerboas and gerbils with the aid of a torch and the headlights of the Land Rover. If we wanted to catch some jerboas, we had to locate an individual and chase it until we were close enough to place a big "butterfly net" over the top of the animal. It was hard and exhausting work, and we failed to capture many of the animals that we chased. Jerboas can hop extremely fast on their hind limbs, just like kangaroos, and can twist and turn with great rapidity (see below). The gerbils, similar in size and proportions to a large house mouse and without any long hind limbs, ran over the sand and frequently disappeared into the entrance hole of an underground burrow (see also below). The expeditions were great fun. After 3-4 hours, we went back to the village and drank lemonade or Fanta that had been kept cool in a kerosene refrigerator – there was no electricity in the village.

Another interesting place was the Sunt Forest situated on the east side of the Nile, just south of the confluence of the Blue Nile and the White Nile. The forest was dominated by *Acacia nilotica* trees; they are attractive trees, about five metres tall with a rather open canopy and small leaves; they are well spaced as in a wooded savanna. The ground slopes very gradually down to the White Nile, and it is just bare packed mud. It was cool and shady under the trees, and it was easy to walk there because there was very little ground vegetation. When not flooded, I enjoyed walking through the forest to the edge of the river where I was able to watch birds and record the species and numbers of dragonflies. During the floods, walking was impossible because the flood-water submerged most of the trees so that only their crowns were visible.

To the west of Omdurman, reached by crossing the Nile bridge, are the Merkiyat Hills which consist of several isolated jebels. After reaching the periphery of Omdurman, there were no roads towards the jebels, so I just navigated to where I wanted to go; usually I was unable to go in a direct line because I had to avoid the scattered bushes and dry stream beds. The Merkiyat Hills are beautiful in a wild rugged sort of way. They are mostly flat-topped with sloping sides covered by orangey-brown rocks, some small, some large. In places there are steep cliffs especially near the base and near the top. In some of these cliffs there are caves where we found some very special bats. There are no trees on the jebels, but after rains, many grasses sprout from between the rocks so that from a distance the jebels assume a hazy green colour that turns to bleached beige as the grasses wither. It was very hot scrambling over these jebels; in the daytime the rocks were hot and radiated heat like an oven. In the evening, as the sun was setting, there was often a breeze and the grasses swayed and rippled like waves on the ocean.

Just north of Khartoum North, was the University Farm at Shambat where Sudanese undergraduates are given practical tuition in agriculture. Here there are always some fields that are irrigated, and hence there is a mesic environment for animals somewhere on the farm during every month of the year – a situation that does not occur on the banks of the Nile. One of the rodents that I found at the farm was the Nile Rat (*Arvicanthis niloticus*); this species requires moist food and water at all times and therefore can only live in places like the farm and along irrigation ditches. It is never found in the desert.

Another favourite place was the Sabaloka Hills. It was always pleasing to be near the Nile because of the beauty of the river, the cool breeze, and the magnetic effect of water in a desert. At Sabaloka, the Nile is bordered (particularly on the eastern side) by bare rocky hills, and in one place the water flows over a series of rocky ridges (collectively called the sixth Cataract) which prevent large boats from travelling up and down the river. The hills are formed of huge broken rock, and are mostly bare of vegetation. On the edge of the river, there is a narrow strip of sand with grasses, reeds, bushes and a few *Acacia* trees, all of which are covered during the floods. Further away, on both sides of the river, the country is flat and sandy with scattered bushes and a few *Acacia nilotica* trees. The only relief to the flatness is a few shallow dry river beds. I camped at Sabaloka on several occasions, sheltering in the patchwork shade of the acacias; but it is impossible to find deep shade and it is always hot. One exciting find at Sabaloka was a species of gerbil (*Gerbillus campestris*) that had not been recorded in the Sudan previously.[11] It was a beautiful animal which lived amongst the rocks overlooking the river; it was soft beige in colour with a very long tufted tail.

South of Khartoum, between the Blue Nile and the White Nile, the countryside was completely different. After leaving Khartoum, the road towards Wad Medani passes through the 'Green Belt', a strip of fenced land which stretched along the southern boundary of the city. It was fenced to keep out goats so that the local vegetation could flourish and form a barrier to prevent sand blowing into the city. The road runs close to the Blue Nile and after a few minutes it reaches the irrigation channels and fields of cotton of the Gezira Scheme. These irrigation channels extend southwards to Wad Medani and Sennar, and westwards towards the White Nile. The Gezira Scheme was begun in 1914 with the construction of a huge dam at Sennar, but work was suspended during the First World War and did not recommence until 1919. The dam diverts some of the water from the Blue Nile into wide irrigation channels; at regular intervals, there are sluice gates and side-channels which reticulate the water into the cotton fields many miles away from the river. The irrigated area is vast – 8,800 square kilometres (3,400 sq miles). The road itself runs beside, or along the top of, a huge earth bank bordering a wide irrigation channel full of water. At some times of the year, huge piles of pure white cotton are stacked in the fields awaiting collection. Although cotton was (and still is) the major crop (mainly for export), maize is also grown for local consumption.

Rains and temporary pools in the desert

The average annual rainfall at Khartoum is 160mm (see above) but as in all desert and semi-desert environments, there is huge variation from year to year. The records for the period 1900 to 1980 show that, in most years, there is a range of about 100 – 230mm/year, although there were very few years when the rainfall was much lower (50mm or less), or much higher (250 to 350mm) than the average. I was fortunate that in 1963-1966, two of the years had average annual rainfalls, and one year – 1964 – had much higher than average (290mm). In each of these years, the desert 'flowered' so that the countryside looked like a green savanna for a few months, and pools of water – some as big as small lakes – formed in low-lying parts of the desert. The year 1964 was a particularly magical year: the grasses were dense and verdant and the tall waving grasses reached to just above my knees. The annual rainfall, and hence the vegetation, determines the biology of the whole ecosystem until the following year. In the years with below average rainfall, the lack (or limited production) of grasses has a detrimental effect on all desert life.

As a biologist, I found the transformation of the desert quite miraculous. I would never have believed that the dry bare arid desert could be transformed into a green 'savanna' with waving grasses, small flowering herbs, and lovely fresh buds and leaves on the bushes. During the 'wet season' (July, August and September) there are only about fifteen rainy days; when it rains, the storms are magical, often heavy, and there is a sudden fall in temperature. Comments in my diaries provide an interesting snapshot of what it was like during the wet season, and the difficulties of working at this time of year. In 1964, I wrote:

14th August 1964: It is fascinating to see all the green grass in the desert, and the large pools of water. The desert beside the airport is very green and there are large sheets of standing water. The sand is very sticky when moist and it is then difficult to walk on it. Yesterday I collected some small crustaceans from these pools; they hatch from eggs that have been dormant and buried in the sand since the end of the last wet season (even if several years ago). They live for only a short time, and have to grow and mature and lay eggs before the pool dries up.

20th August 1964: We have had a tremendous migration of dragonflies today – literally they were as thick as locust swarms. The Nile has flooded; there are many small tadpoles in the flooded areas where the water current is not too fast. In the desert, everywhere is incredibly green, and I was walking in knee-high green grass and slushing through puddles.

11th September 1964: The Nile has started to go down now, and huge mud flats are exposed. As soon as the flats dry, the local farmers will be planting their crops. There is still a lot of insect life about, especially mosquitoes and bugs indoors, and butterflies and dragonflies outside. But practically no locusts which (I am told) is unusual. There are lots of amphibians about now. Little frogs are hopping about in my garden and even in my house. There are four geckos that live in the roof of my veranda. I enjoy watching them each evening when they come to the light to catch insects. Last night one of them managed to eat a huge hawkmoth.

And in 1965, my diaries record:

30th July 1965: It is difficult getting into the desert now that the rains have started – the sand is permanently sticky. There have been several storms, and the desert is already partly covered with patches of short emerald-coloured green grass. On Saturday it rained at about 5p.m.; the sky was pitch black and lightning flashed everywhere. Because of the sticky sand, the Land-Rover had to be in 4-wheel drive; even so it was not very manoeverable. In the course of the evening, the headlights became weaker (an electrical fault?) and then the engine stopped. A passing desert bus got me started again (minus headlights), and by then it was raining hard. The Land Rover stopped completely fifty metres from home. It was very late.

6th August 1965: The Blue Nile river has started to rise rapidly, and the lower bank has been submerged. Soon all the flood-plains will be submerged. Changes in the wind – now mostly from the south – have brought many dragonflies, butterflies, locusts and birds to Khartoum from the south.

14th August 1965: It is rather hot and humid even though there has been so little rain. There was a strong wind today in Khartoum and on my study area. The desert now has a short green 'fluff' on it, and it is unlikely that the growth will be as luxuriant as in 1964; this may mean fewer animals (of all sorts) during and after the wet season.

21th August 1965: I tried to go to my desert study site today. When I was halfway there, it poured with rain so hard that I had to stop, and then it was impossible to continue on into the desert. But not a single drop of rain fell in Khartoum. Rainstorms here are so local. There have been several rainy days with dense dark clouds. Thursday was particularly dramatic: when I visited the mesquite plantation south of the airport, there were black clouds and white clouds all mixed up, high winds and lines of rain falling in the distance. After so much blue sky and heat, this is lovely!

At first, the pools in the desert seemed to be lifeless. But after a few days, ripples and bubbles on the surface of the water indicated that there were living organisms below the surface. I collected some of these, and identified them as various species of crustaceans (the group that also contains crabs, shrimps, crayfish, and many others). As I discovered later, twelve species of crustaceans have been recorded in temporary pools near Khartoum.[12] The largest and most visible are 'tadpole shrimps' (*Triops*) which look rather like amphibian tadpoles because they have a large carapace on the anterior part of the body and an elongated tail. There are also several 'fairy shrimps' (*Streptocephalus*), lightly built creatures with fan-like paddles on their undersides; and also I found 'clam shrimps', water fleas and copepods. As the water seeped into the sand at the beginning of the rains, the eggs of these animals, buried in the sand since the end of the previous wet season, were stimulated to hatch into larval forms. While buried in the hot sand, the eggs are in a state of diapause; experiments have shown that the eggs of *Triops* can withstand temperatures of 80°C and also dessication – and still remain viable![13] Indeed, desiccation may be essential to break the diapause and enable development. Within a short period – just 16-20 days after the pool is formed – the larvae have developed into adults and produced eggs. In dry years, the larvae and/or adults may not complete their life cycle and there may be no eggs (or few eggs) for the following year. In a 'wet year', the full life-cycle will be completed, and hundreds and thousands of eggs will be produced and will remain dormant until the next wet season. It is rather sad, as the pools dry up, to see so many crustaceans concentrated together in ever-smaller volumes of water; they die when all the water has evaporated, and their remains are blown far and wide by the desert winds.

Birds, Jerboas and Dragonflies

Birds. Khartoum was a wonderful place for bird-watching! There are many 'resident' species of birds which can be seen close to the Nile and in nearby deserts and jebels. These include waterbirds such as swamp hens, jacanas, pelicans, kingfishers and ducks; there are also many waders such as herons, egrets, storks, sandpipers and plovers. In gardens, and bushes along the river, weavers, finches, warblers, doves, mousebirds, bee-eaters, and wagtails are common. Scavenging kites are always flying in the skies above Khartoum looking for food, and in the nearby desert, there are sandgrouse, larks and wheatears.

The species of birds recorded in Khartoum may be divided into four categories depending on whether they are resident or migratory. The 'resident' species live all year round in or near Khartoum and never migrate; the 'local migrants' move up and down the Nile Valley depending on the local conditions; the 'African migrants' fly north and south along the Nile valley in relation to dry and wet seasons and seasonal changes in temperature, but always within Africa; and 'Palearctic migrants' fly south along the Nile to their wintering grounds in central Africa, and north again to their breeding grounds in Europe and western Asia (see Note 14 for details).

The Nile river is one of the major 'corridors' for the Palearctic migrants that migrate between Europe and Africa. In October to November, thousands of individuals of these migratory species pass through Khartoum on their way south, and then return again in April and May on their way back to Europe. Because of the harshness of the desert environment, the only way south on the eastern side of Africa is along the Nile river where there is water, food, and places to shelter. Most people in Khartoum are unaware of this migration, especially since many species fly by night and are not seen. My friends Tony and Sally Pettet had permits to mist-net migrating birds and to place a small metal band around one leg. Each band had an individual number and the name of the organisation which kept the banding records. If a banded bird is caught again at a different place and at another time – something that happens quite often – a great deal of information is acquired about the movements, speed of migration, life history and lifespan of that individual. During the appropriate months, we erected the nets in uncultivated riverine vegetation where bushes, small acacia trees and dead grasses were abundant – places where there was plenty of cover for small birds. Early in the morning, many birds were flying around between the bushes and skulking in the grasses, and if one of them crossed a gap in the vegetation where we had placed a net, it was caught. We immediately removed the bird, and it was identified, weighed, sexed, and measured as quickly as possible. If it already had a band, we recorded the number; if not, we banded it with one of our bands. The bird was then released to continue its migration. Sometimes identification was difficult and problematic. Many small birds have rather similar plumage; other species have colourful plumage in the breeding season (especially males) and then moult to a drab winter plumage before the migration, and young birds still have their juvenile plumage. We referred to such birds as LBBs (little brown birds), and we often had to consult our guide – *Birds of the Sudan*[15] – for help with identification. It was possible to net and band birds only during the first two to three hours after sunrise; after that it was too hot and the birds could suffer from heat stress – and it was also too hot for us. We banded many of the smaller species during the annual migration, and also saw many of the larger species that are too big to be caught in mistnets. On one occasion, near the Sabaloka Hills, I saw hundreds of hoopoes resting in the trees near the river – a marvellous and unusual sight.

Jerboas. My main research at Khartoum was on small mammals (particularly jerboas) and dragonflies. Jerboas (*Jaculus jaculus*) are small rodents (adult weight 40-60 grams). They have roundish heads with enormous eyes, longish rounded ears and a wide flatish nose. The body is compact and roundish, with an extremely long tail. The most notable characteristic is the elongation of the hindlimbs so that, in a superficial way, a jerboa looks like a sort of kangaroo. The most elongated bone is the 'foot'; it comprises about one half of the length of the whole hindlimb. There is only one bone for most of the length of the foot; this bone is formed by the fusion of the three middle bones of the foot. The two outer bones – those that in a human would be called the 'big toe' and the 'little toe' – have been lost during the course of evolution. There are three toes at the end of the hindfoot, and the underneath of the toes is covered with a dense thick brush of white hairs. The full length of the foot only contacts the ground when the animal is resting. When the jerboa is moving, the hindfeet are raised (as during hopping) and all the weight rests on the toes. Each forelimb, in contrast, is extremely short, and has five fingers, each with a small claw. The tail is almost twice as long as the body, quite thick, and with a black tuft at the end and a white tip. The dorsal pelage on the head, back and sides is sandy-coloured; some of the hairs have a black tip which gives a speckled appearance, and the ventral pelage is pure white. Jerboas are extremely delightful and attractive animals![16]

Jerboas are nocturnal as are all the other small mammals in the desert. During the daytime, they stay in their burrows, some of which are about a metre deep, where the temperature is much lower and remains almost constant during the day and night. After dusk, when the jerboa emerges, it pushes the sand out of the entrance and then, using its hindlimbs, it flicks the sand backwards into the entrance and finally smoothes the sand surface with its flat nose. Before dawn, when a jerboa returns to its burrow, it excavates the entrance, and once inside it blocks the entrance with sand by pushing the sand from inside the burrow with its nose. Thus the burrow is sealed from the outside air and the entrance becomes invisible.

As well as watching jerboas in the desert (which was extremely difficult), I kept some in my walled back garden (which was just sand!) and also in some very large observation cages (*c.* 5m long, 1m wide, and 70 cm tall). Here I was able to watch them move, feed, groom, and interact with each other – things I could not observe in the desert. When sitting quietly on the sand, the heel and the toes touch the ground and the tail rests on the ground. When alert, the jerboa raises itself on to its toes and the tail is arched with only the tip resting on the ground – thus acting as a third 'leg'. There are four methods (and speeds) of locomotion. When looking for food on the ground, the hindlimbs and forelimbs are on the ground and the animal has a 'quadripedal gait' which is very awkward because of the different lengths of the fore- and hindlimbs; the tail is dragged behind. The three other gaits are performed with only the hindlimbs while the forelimbs are held close against the neck and throat – these gaits are 'slow jumping or pottering' with the hindlimbs acting in synchrony, 'medium speed' which is a fast bipedal walk with the tail held out behind as a counter weight, and 'fast speed' when the hindlimbs, acting in synchrony, provide a tremendous thrust which propels the animal forwards; the tail is held out almost horizontally behind the body. When in the desert, the fast speed is very fast (13-14 m.p.h. according to the Land Rover's speedometer) but also very manoeuvrable. I was amazed how quickly a jerboa could zigzag and alter direction when being chased. Jerboas spend a lot of time grooming, using their forepaws to wash the head, flanks, ventral surface and rump. The tail is carefully held by the forefeet and groomed by the claws of the forefeet and the tongue, beginning at the base and ending at the tip. Jerboas also love to sandbathe; a little depression is scraped in the sand and the jerboa lies on its side with the hindlimbs stretched out to their full length; it then wriggles its body back and forth several times, and finally the hindlimbs are brought forward so the toes are near the head enabling the jerboa to get up. Jerboas are fairly social animals; although they were mostly seen singly in the desert, some were seen in twos, threes and fours. In captivity, when individuals met, they crouched down on all fours, shut their eyes and made nose-to-nose contact for a few seconds. Jerboas do not need to drink water; they obtain adequate water from their food and they conserve water by producing dry faeces and very concentrated urine (one of the most concentrated of any known mammalian species!). I never tired of studying and watching jerboas – they are some of the most engaging of small mammals![17]

Dragonflies. Most people probably do not associate dragonflies with deserts. In general this is correct because the larval stages of dragonflies require water for their development. However, if there is permanent water (as along the Nile valley and in oases and swamps), dragonflies can flourish. The banks of the Blue Nile, close to where I lived at the Pink Palace, were an excellent place to study dragonflies throughout the year.[18] The adults perched on the grasses, reeds and small bushes, lining the river. When the river was low, they were found along the low-level bank, on the flood-plains where local farmers were growing vegetables, and also on the high-level bank further inland. When the river flooded, dragonflies were found only along the high-level bank. My observations were very simple because most species were easily recognisable by their size, colour and patterning, and behaviour. I was able to count the number of individuals of each species on a one kilometre transect along the river several times each month. Whether my observations were on the low-level bank and the flood-plain, or only the high-level bank, or both, depended on the level of the river. Thirteen species were recorded in Khartoum, but only four species were abundant or common. Adult dragonflies were generally uncommon during the wet season (July to August), common after the rains (September to October), rare during the (relatively) cold season, and absent during the subsequent very hot weather in March and April (and perhaps May). Each species showed a different seasonal pattern in its abundance; some species were always rare and only seen for a short period of time, other species were seen for six to eight months although varying in abundance each month. It is a mystery as to where the dragonflies develop and emerge as adults. Some larvae live in the Nile (their remains have been found in the stomachs of some species of fish), but at certain times of the year, the Nile is fast flowing and is not a suitable habitat for dragonfly larvae. There are a few swamp-like habitats that may be suitable for larvae. In one year, I found dragonfly larvae in temporary ponds in the desert, but these pools did not last long enough for the life-cycle to be completed.

Some species of dragonflies are migratory, and it is highly likely that the dragonflies seen at the beginning of the wet season had developed and emerged further south and then migrated northwards as the ITCZ moved northwards. On several occasions in August and September, huge numbers of one species (*Pantela flavescens*) arrived at Khartoum just after the beginning of the rains; there were so many of them that they were like swarms of locusts. Their arrival was accompanied by wind and rain from the south, which probably assisted them in their northward migration. A few days later, they had left Khartoum and moved further north as the ITCZ moved northwards towards Nubia and Egypt. I wished I had had more time to answer so many intriguing questions about these dragonflies. Besides the enjoyment of watching dragonflies, the study enabled me to have many quiet walks along the river in the evening; I could follow the seasonal changes in the levels of the Nile, and enjoy the pleasures of the cool Nile breezes and the luminous pale light and glorious sunsets of the desert environment.

6

KHARTOUM TO WESTERN SUDAN

To the west of Khartoum are thousands of miles of Sahel and Sudan savanna – an immense dry semi-arid region – most of which is rather unknown and 'off the beaten track'. For a long time, I had wondered whether anyone had travelled westwards from Khartoum, or at least beyond the western boundaries of the Sudan. I assumed that since the establishment of Islam, pilgrims must have travelled from West Africa through Khartoum to Mecca. But I never found anyone in Khartoum who said it was possible to travel overland from Khartoum to Nigeria. This seemed all the more reason why I should try! My friends and colleagues in Khartoum thought I was crazy to embark on such a trip; they thought that they would soon see me back in Khartoum having been forced to turn back – or they would never see me again (lost, presumed dead!). Another possibility, they suggested, was to take the weekly Ethiopian Airlines flight from Khartoum to Lagos; my reply was simply that, if I flew, it would defeat the main object of my journey – to see the countryside.[1]

Paul, a colleague in Khartoum, drove me to the railway station after lunch on 29th March 1965. He was the last English person I saw until I reached my destination in Nigeria. It was very hot and six months had elapsed since the last rains fell. It was a relief to find that my reservation was in order and that my name in Arabic script was on one of the First Class compartment doors. I did not have much luggage, just a small suitcase with suitable clothes for Europe (I was on my way for three months leave in the UK), and a small turquoise-coloured carry-on BOAC bag with a shoulder strap in which I kept my passport, tickets, camera and washing things. I also had a tin of rock cakes and a pot of strawberry jam given to me by Paul's wife, Margaret, just as the train was leaving – she thought some sustenance might be useful on the journey. My initial thought was, "What shall I do with these – I can't possible carry them across Africa," but they proved to be lifesavers later on in the journey. The train did not have any sleeping accommodation and the kitchen was a minute compartment where the cook prepared the food on a filthy charcoal stove. Just before the train departed, I was joined by Mohammad Osman, a second year medical student at the University who was travelling to Nyala to visit his father. He was a pleasant companion and we had the compartment to ourselves.

The train was long with about ten carriages. It was pulled by a steam locomotive which belched lots of smoke and steam. The locomotive was powered by coal – which I assumed was imported from overseas. The carriages were painted white and arranged in the conventional way with compartments, each with facing bench seats, opening onto a corridor on one side. The seats were upholstered but very hard. In first class, the windows had glass panes that could be opened at night to let in the [relatively] cool night air. The windows were partly covered on the outside by a canopy that extended vertically down from the roof of the carriage to about halfway down the window opening; these provided protection from the sun but allowed some light to enter the compartment. It was rather spartan but quite adequate. The train left at 2:30p.m. I was feeling excited and exhilarated because, if all went well, I would not stop moving, except temporarily, until I reached Zaria in northern Nigeria. But there was also a feeling of apprehension because I did not know whether I could travel overland to Nigeria, and I had no wish to return to Khartoum having failed to complete my journey. The train passed through the "Green Belt" – an area of low growing *Acacia* trees which acted as a barrier to desert encroachment at the southern limit of Khartoum – and slowly chugged southwards towards the Gezira (see chapter 5). The sight of green cotton fields stretching to the horizon is a magnificent sight after the parched sands of Khartoum. Some of the cotton bushes were still in flower, and there were huge piles of cotton bales at many of the stations. It was very warm in the train and dust was blowing in through the cracks, but the slight breeze helped us to feel a little cooler. Soon after 6p.m., we reached Abu Usher where we met the northbound train – the railway was single track all the way to Nyala except at the stations where there were two or more tracks. By now, the sun was setting and the cooler air was refreshing. After dark, I just lay on my seat listening to the creaking of the train and wondering how fast the miles were slipping by. (The distance was about 120 miles, so our speed was ± 20 m.p.h.) We passed Habahasha at 9.15p.m., and at 10:50p.m. we arrived at Wad Medani on the bank of the Blue Nile – one of the largest towns in the Gezira and an important centre for the cotton industry. We descended to the tracks, which are just visible above the sand (there are no platforms, and the railway sleepers are covered by sand); we stretched our legs and walked over to a bar near the station for a cold drink. The station was thick with jostling people carrying bed-rolls, boxes, suitcases and baskets of food. I could not understand what they were shouting about (my Arabic was not good enough for that!); at times it seemed a bit threatening. There was that indefinable smell – a mixture of sand, sweating bodies, warm air and *tamia* (a favourite snack made of chickpeas, onions, bread and spices rolled into a ball and then deep-fried) – a smell so very characteristic of these regions and which gave an additional piquancy to my journey.

From Wad Medani, the railway travels westwards, firstly south of the Gezira to the White Nile and then, after crossing the Nile bridge, to Kordofan Province and finally to Nyala in Darfur. I fell asleep as soon as we left Wad Medani, and did not wake again until the train reached Rabak on the eastern side of the White Nile. The sun had not risen but it was already light enough to see when we crossed the Nile bridge to Kosti; the bridge is an impressive steel-girder swing bridge about 530m long, built in 1909-1910. In Kosti, we walked into town to where Mohammad Osman had a house; it was deserted but a cook (?) made us some tea. I was afraid of missing the train but Mohammad assured me it would stay for at least an hour – time in the Sudan is a very flexible commodity. The temperature at this time of the morning was pleasant, but for me it was spoilt by the thought that soon it would be unbearably hot. At the station, I first noticed how many passengers there were in Third and Fourth Class carriages. They were crammed in like the proverbial sardines and, because the windows did not have glass, there was no protection from the glare and the wind. At the end of the 'platform', there was a faded notice beside the track: 'TO

THE STEAMERS – VERS LES BATEAUX'. I wondered how long it had been there.

Beyond Kosti, continuing westwards, there was no more cultivation… only dry *Acacia* scrub and occasional long drifts of *qoz* which are extensions of the desert sand dunes further north. Grasses and a few shrubs grew on the *qoz,* and sometimes there were a few trees. After some time, my interest in this new scene waned – the countryside was flat, monotonous and dull. Wisps of ochre-coloured grass covered the sandy soil, and the *Acacia* trees looked as if they were dead. So I started reading one of my paperback books and tried to ignore the rising temperature.

There was no dining car on the train, so meals were served in our compartment. Considering the difficulties, the cook did surprisingly well. For breakfast we ate an omelette with fried fish, and later for lunch we were served stewed meat with *bamia* (the Sudanese name for ochra – a nutritious vegetable) and rice, followed by 'Sudan Railways blancmange'. I had some oranges and grapefruits (bought in Khartoum) which Osman and I consumed during the course of the morning.

The train stopped at many local stations and people came with baskets loaded with goods to sell to the passengers. There was *tasali* (melon seeds sold in small paper packets), handkerchiefs, plate covers, *bamia*, hard-boiled eggs, sweet potatoes (cooked), cheese, bread, fruit and 'tooth sticks'. These sticks (sometimes called 'chewing sticks') are cut from the twigs and small branches of particular species of shrubs. They are rather fibrous and when the end of the stick is chewed (often for many hours at a time), it opens to form a sort of toothbrush at the chewed end. Tooth sticks are remarkably effective at cleaning teeth, as evidenced by the beautiful white clean teeth enjoyed by most Africans; additionally, a diet lacking free sugar must also contribute to healthy teeth of Africans. Most stations also had stalls with a wide range of tinned foods: pineapple, tuna, sardines, and tomatoes seemed to be the most popular. While everyone was buying their food, the local women went to the locomotive with their water cans to collect hot water.

In the early afternoon, while we were still passing through very arid acacia savanna, I saw a *haffir* full of water. Many cows and goats were being herded towards the *haffir* for their evening drink. A few miles further on, we came to Er Rahad, an important cattle town and where passengers may change to the branch line to El Obeid. Here we wandered into the market and looked at grass mats, baskets, all sorts of metal work, and stalls of food.

We had coffee at a small restaurant, sitting on rough-hewn benches while flies buzzed around the spilt food and drinks on the tables. By now I was getting used to being looked at (in the politest sort of way); I suppose the local inhabitants do not often see a single white male travelling by train these days. After buying mangoes (2 Piastres each, about two English old pennies), we returned to the train. Because my plimsoles had thin soles, my feet were almost burnt by the scorching sand.

As the sun was setting, we passed the remote station of Shaykan where, according to Mohammad Osman, General William Hick's army of 10,000 men was defeated at the Battle of Shaykan (or the Battle of El Obeid) by the forces of Mohammad Ahmed (the Mahdi) in November 1883. Shaykan is an important place in recent Sudanese history, and the defeat of Hick's army set in train a series of events that culminated in the capture of Khartoum by the Mahdi, the assassination of General Gordon in 1885, and later the defeat of the Mahdi by Kitchener's army at Omdurman in 1898.

The train chugged slowly on into the night. The stars were wonderfully clear and brilliant in the desert air. Mohammad Osman told me that in the Sudan, the constellation of the Plough is called *angareeb* – the Sudanese name for a bed. The four bright stars represent the four legs of the *angareeb* carrying a dead man, and it is followed by the man's three daughters (the three smaller paler stars behind the bright stars): the first is not married, the second has a small child (a faint star at the side), and the third is pregnant and so she tarries behind the others.

During its journey from Khartoum to Nyala, the train stopped at many places that were not stations. At first, I did not know why this was. On the second or third stop, I went to the carriage door and discovered that many of the men were disembarking from the train carrying their prayer mats. They unrolled their mats on the sand beside the track, and then knelt on their mats, facing Mecca, to say their prayers. The train driver also climbed down from the cabin of the locomotive, and placed his mat on the ground to say his prayers. At the end of prayer time, the driver sounded the train's whistle, checked that everyone was on board, and the journey was resumed. I never discovered whether these stops were sanctioned officially by Sudan Railways, or whether the driver himself took the initiative. I found it rather moving that a whole train could stop in the middle of nowhere so that people could say their prayers.

I woke at about 7:15a.m. on our third day in the train just as we passed the 950 kilometre sign from Khartoum. The 'bush' was thicker here and the trees were larger, but everything still looked dead and there was an air of desolation. Surprisingly, there were a few trees with new green leaves; it seemed incongruous to see this refreshing colour in such a dreary countryside. At breakfast time, the train reached Babanusa; here the railway divides, one line goes westwards to Nyala and the other line goes south to Wau. There were many tall dark southerners – Dinkas, Shilluks, Nuers – at the station. Most of them were dressed in rags and tattered clothing, and they looked very dark beside the northern (mostly Arab) Sudanese. Here – yet again! – Mohammad and I went to the market. Newly planted mango trees were surrounded by stockades of thorns to protect them from the wandering herds of browsing goats. It was warm and cloudy, and the railway officials told us that we would not reach Nyala until about 2a.m. tomorrow – about nine hours late! This did not worry me at all – after all I had no fixed plans and no schedule to keep to.

Here, in Darfur, the countryside is very different to the arid semi-deserts of eastern Kordofan. As we travelled further west, the trees became more numerous and larger in size. Some species of trees showed the signs of "spring"; one species was covered with cream and orange flowers which, when they had fallen, formed a halo around the base of the tree and on the nearby dry sand. Other species were just bursting into leaf and looked as if they were festooned by apple-green cobwebs. Most startling of all were the pink flowers of *Adenium* clustered in masses on the leafless grey bark of the branches. I doubt if there had been any rain here for months… what is it that starts this surge of life in the parched wilderness? One region was rather different from the rest: here, tall stately trees were spaced out as if in parkland with only dead grass underfoot. Later on, we passed many neem trees (*Azadirachta indica*) carefully spaced out in rows. Neem trees are native to the Indian subcontinent and are grown widely in Africa because of their medicinal properties and for the deep shade provided by their thick dense deep green foliage. As we travelled westwards in Darfur, we started to see baobab trees. These strange, almost unworldly, trees look as if they have been planted upside down because the upper branches look more like roots than branches. Baobabs have enormously wide trunks; these often have natural cavities in them, and are sometimes hollowed out by local people to provide a place for the storage of water.

This train journey took place six months after the end of the wet season and as a result there were very few birds. I saw only a few Rollers, Long-tailed Doves, Green Bee-eaters, Little Bee-eaters, Black and White Hornbills and a solitary Hoopoe. A small live gazelle was on sale at Sharif station for 20 piasters – a pathetically small amount for such a lovely animal. After leaving Babanusa, the train continued its slow progress through Bakheit, Dar es Salaam, El Gallabi and El Da'an. Here we had arrived in Umbaruru country: members of this tribe have their hair plaited into pigtails one of which hangs down over the forehead. The Umbararu are often employed as household stewards for ridiculously low wages. As earlier on this journey, the women came to the locomotive to collect water to fill their water cans whenever we stopped. At one station, I saw a small child who continued sucking on his mother's breast while she collected the hot water. Gourds were growing in many villages beside the track. Mohammad told me that in Gallabat, the locals place a hard-boiled egg inside a gourd to catch monkeys (serious pests of crops in some places); the monkey takes the egg in his hand but is then unable to extract his hand, and is then caught and killed.

As the sun was setting, it was still very hot, and we were dusty and tired. The vegetation closer to Nyala was patchy: dense 'bush' alternated with parkland. Although the scenery was still seemingly monotonous, there were always slight changes in vegetation and topography – often barely noticeable unless one was looking carefully. We had our last supper on the train and paid the bill for our two and a half days food – just one Sudanese pound and 64 piasters. Since we were not due in Nyala until 2a.m., we got permission from the guard to stay in the train until the morning. Everyone else had to leave; if we had been told to leave, we would have had no idea where to go in Nyala at that time of the night.

Nyala is a small town in rather flat country. On its southern side is the Wadi Nyala which receives its water from the foothills of Jebel Marra, a huge dormant volcano to the north-west of Nyala. At Nyala, the wadi is wide; for most of the year, it is either a series of large pools or completely dry, but after the rains it becomes a substantial river. Nyala was well stocked with shops and there is a colourful market with an over-whelming variety of things to buy. The town is much more African than any of the towns further east, and is much less Arabic. Most of the inhabitants that I saw had dark skins, flat wide noses and wide lips (and I assumed belonged to the

KHARTOUM TO WESTERN SUDAN

Fur tribe), although there were others who had a mixture of African and Arabic blood.

Jebel Marra is one of a series of mountains in the Sahel and the southern Sahara. It is much less well known than, for example, Tibesti or Ennedi which are huge rocky mountains in northern Chad, famous for their arid grandeur and rock art. I had the opportunity to spend nearly two weeks on Jebel Marra in December 1964, just before this journey to Nigeria; so before continuing westwards to Nigeria, the next chapter is about this very special mountain.

7

JEBEL MARRA

Jebel Marra is a vast extinct volcano northwest of Nyala. It has extensive foothills that radiate out from the crater and covers an area of about 12,000 sq km (= about 100km by 100km). Because it is so large, it is sometimes called Marra Mountain to distinguish it from the much smaller rocky protrusions (jebels) found elsewhere in the semi-arid regions of the Sudan. The highest point, on the rim of the crater (caldera) is just over 10,000 ft (3,088m), and about 7,000 ft (2,000m) above the surrounding plain. Jebel Marra is a comparatively young volcano and is the highest mountain in the Sudan.[1] It was formed about 3,500 years ago, and the ash and pumice from the eruption scattered all over the underlying basalt rock. The caldera is about 5km across and has steep walls; in the centre there are two lakes fed by hot water springs as well as by rainwater. During the eruption, large streams of lava flowed down the mountain leaving ridges of pumice and ash that are still present today. On the northern foothills, there are extensive 'badlands' – huge erosion channels up to 200 ft deep dissecting the already hilly country.

The vegetation shows a marked zonation with altitude, although not to the same extent as on the larger taller mountains of Africa. On the foothills (below about 4,000ft), there is Sudan Savanna with many sorts of savanna trees. In places, especially in valleys with streams, the trees form dense woodland. Higher up, on Jebel Marra itself, there are three vegetation zones known as the lower, middle and upper zones.[2] The 'lower zone' has a community of trees (different to those of the Sudan Savanna), as well as dense and tall 'gallery forest' in the valleys. In more open areas, there are many grasses that manage to survive amongst the rocks and pumice. The 'middle zone', with a different community of trees, is more open and there are olive trees and willows beside running streams, and many grasses. The 'upper zone' (above 9,500 ft and including the crater) is grassland with scattered olive trees, wild lavender, grasses and bracken. The vegetation of the mountain is very green and lush compared with the arid lands of the Sudan Savanna. In places, plantations of exotic trees have been established.

Climatic information for Jebel Marra is scarce. According to one report, rainfall is about 800mm/year, mostly falling between June and September. This is high compared with the rainfall at the nearby towns of Nyala (398mm/year) and El Fasher (212mm/year). Because of its high altitude, the top of Jebel Marra is cold in 'winter' with frost on the coldest nights. The combination of comparatively high rainfall, temperate climate, perennially running streams and good volcanic soil (in places) has enabled humans (primarily of the Fur tribe) to settle and survive on the mountain, probably for millenia. However, the mountain is inhabited only in a few places, and during most of my visit we saw very few people. The Fur people are nominally Muslim and some of them carry small pieces of the Koran with them; however, I never saw any of them kneeling towards Mecca and saying their prayers.

One of the many fascinating aspects about Jebel Marra is that it is an 'island' of temperate climate and vegetation in a 'sea' of semi-aridness. Like true islands, the flora and fauna shows some differences from other similar 'islands', and there are some species (or subspecies) that are endemic to the jebel. Interestingly, the flora and fauna show links with other nearby 'islands'. Jebel Marra is not well known biologically, and so I, with some colleagues from the University of Khartoum, visited the mountain in November 1964 – hoping to increase our knowledge of some aspects of its biology. Because there were eleven of us, and a lot of equipment for our work, we had to hire lorries and donkeys for some sections of our travels. The Provincial Commissioner provided us with a 3-ton lorry to take us from Nyala to Golol. Hussein, the driver, was an enormous Fur; he was an excellent driver and he had two 'mates' who did whatever they were told! (They were rather like a captain, bosun and mate on a ship!) The road was very bad and it had not been graded since the rains, months previously. It was so bad that the 100 miles from Nyala to Golol took about eight hours; we did not see the mountain until about halfway to Golol.

Most of us sat in the back, on top of our luggage, exposed to the hot sun, dust and passing prickly bushes. The grass all around was parched and arid, but the trees were still green. The flowers of the 'fish poison' tree (Adenium) *formed vivid splashes of pink colour among the predominately pastel greys and greens of the countryside. We saw only a few people during the bumpy drive, but when we passed the occasional dura* (Sorghum bicolor) *plantation we saw the local villagers harvesting the crops. Most of the people here live a subsistence lifestyle, and they seemed more friendly than the Arabic Sudanese. The women were naked to the waist, a sure sign of primitive conditions – a situation that is rapidly disappearing throughout Africa. Kas was the only village we passed through – we stopped for tea – and then headed towards the mountain. Tall grass, up to 8 ft tall, hemmed the rocky track, and tall green trees stretched away over the hills. I was amazed that the truck could cope with these rigorous conditions – it creaked and groaned all the time and sounded as if it would fall apart. (These suk lorries are made from imported engines and chasses (a Bedford in our case) and the superstructure is made locally. A conventional lorry would not last for more than a few weeks under Sudanese conditions.) The track led up the side of a valley towards the mountain and, below the track, the Golol River gurgled and fell from the higher slopes. At Golol, there is a large Forestry Department nursery, and we were given permission to stay in the resthouse during our stay. It was practically dark when we arrived. The UN – FAO officer in charge, Gunnar Polsen, a Swede, met us and later we went to his house that he built himself. A little bit of civilisation in the wilds! Gunnar has a magnificent battery-operated record player, many books, colourful carpets, and a wonderful supply of drinks – the advantages of diplomatic immunity! He grows roses and strawberries in his garden. We drank iced beer and ate strawberries and listened to Strauss music. It all went down very well after nearly a week of travelling from Khartoum.*

The resthouse at Golol was perched on a little hill; below (on both sides) were small valleys, one of which had a little stream at the bottom. There was a delightful waterfall near the resthouse; I went there at 6:30 each morning for a wash, and again after the morning's work for a swim. It was wonderful to experience cool clear fresh flowing water; the stream banks were thick with green grasses, and dense non-arid shrubs and trees grew on the slopes above. To the north of Golol, I could see more valleys and the top of the mountain, and to the south the forested hills were lost to sight in the mists of the plains. Everywhere was green and luxuriant. Baboons, monkeys, ground squirrels and rock hyraxes were quite common. Higher up, some of the slopes have been terraced, a feature still seen all over the mountain. Humans have lived here for centuries; but most of them have gone now and their abandoned terraces have become covered with grass and bush. The streams at Golol, and elsewhere on the mountain, are interesting because they contain several species of fish. One study[3] identified 16 species of fish (in five families) on Jebel Marra. Of particular interest is the fact that most of the species have widespread distributions, some to the Chari river catchment (and ultimately to the Niger river catchment far to the west), and others to the Nile river catchment (far to the east). The many isolated fish faunas of today throughout the Sahel and semiarid regions indicate that there was a widespread system of rivers during the early years of the Holocene (c. 12,000 BP).[4]

Golol was delightful; we spent four full days there and it was with regret that we moved on. We loaded the truck again and proceeded to make a detour around the mountain to Beldong, another Forestry Department nursery with a resthouse. The rolling downlands towards Beldong were covered in grass and bushes, and from the top of the truck we had an uninterrupted view all around. In places, groves of exotic trees – eucalyptus and three species of conifers (Mexican Cypress *Cupressus lusitanica*, Mexican Weeping Pine *Pinus patula* and Monteray Pine *Pinus radiata*) – engulfed the countryside but they did not seem to distract from the beauty, wildness or tranquillity of the country. It took three hours to reach the point where our 3-ton truck could not go any further; we off-loaded our equipment into a smaller truck that was able to negotiate the steep ascent to Beldong.

Next morning at 6.30a.m., our donkeys arrived for our trip to the top of Jebel Marra and the caldera. We had sixteen donkeys and sixteen donkeymen. My diary continues:

As we were to learn only too well, the donkeymen had no idea about loads, loading or tying, and apparently they had never been to the crater before. The saddles were bad, and they constantly slipped and broke. We divided our luggage into donkey-sized loads, one load on each side of a donkey. The donkeymen were a motley crowd, some of them children who could not manage to fix the loads when they fell off; mostly this task of re-saddling the donkeys fell to Tony and me. We left Beldong at 9a.m. and were told we should reach Kronga by 12 noon; in fact we did not arrive until 6p.m. because of the many interruptions with the luggage. It was a long, but not difficult walk, although it was rather hot. We passed many cultivated fields of dura and several villages; in other places, there were just tall dry grasses and bushes. At all times, we could see the huge massif of the volcano towering up on our right side. We plodded into Kronga and found that the 'resthouse' was only a racouba – a shelter built of rough wood and grass erected for us only one week previously. Kronga is a small village on the edge of the 'badlands', and the water for the village (and us) was collected from a stream in a ravine close to the village. The place hummed with flies. After supper, I was so tired that I went to bed.

On the following morning, we did not leave until 9a.m. because it took so long to get everyone and the donkeys organised. The walk to the crater was supposed to take seven hours, but it took us 9-10 hours. As on the previous day, we spent a lot of time re-adjusting the loads on the donkeys. The path often wound through narrow clefts in the pumice rock, only just wide enough for a donkey without its load. So each donkey had to be unloaded, pushed through the cleft, and then re-saddled again on the other side. This was tiring and exhausting work. After many hours, we had navigated the worst of the ravines, and started to toil up the gentle slope towards the crater rim. Dark clouds were gathering, and much to our surprise it started to rain and then to hail. It was so cold!!! The light was failing as we scrambled round the rocky screes to the rim of the crater – pulling our donkeys with us. The view from the top was truly stupendous. The crater floor was 300-400 feet below us and surrounded by steep irregular cliffs, now dark and sombre in the slanting evening light. Far below, the two crater lakes – known as the Deriba Lakes – appeared cool and mysterious. The larger lake lies on the floor of the crater and is irregular in outline. The smaller lake is situated in a small volcanic cone within the crater, and is almost round in shape. The guide who was with me pointed out where our racouba was built – it was still a long way to go. We were very thankful that the

Provincial Commissioner had ordered the rakoubas to be built – here and at Kronga. The path followed the rim of the crater and then dipped down where the cliffs were less precipitous. We reached the racouba by about 8p.m. Thank goodness there was a full moon otherwise we would not have known where to go. After supper, I had to go out to set some of my mousetraps in the moonlight. So it was about 10 p.m. when I crawled into my 'Icelandic' sleeping bag. I slept well – everyone else complained it was too cold.

The daily movement of the sun and clouds caused a constant changing pattern of light and dark, of sunlight and shadows, across the crater rim and the waters of the large lake. At times, it was bright and beautiful; at other times it was dark and foreboding. The floor of the crater was covered by grass, now dry and brownish-orange in colour, and small olive trees. There were many little ridges within the crater separated by small valleys and ravines, and many boulders of pumice stone. Our racouba was built on one of these ridges; behind there were more ridges extending as far as the base of the crater rim. As elsewhere, there were lots of pieces of broken pumice and soft pale volcanic ash. The large lake from a distance was blue-green, and when I walked along the shore, I saw lots of green algae in the water and green algal scum blown by the wind into the reedy shoreline. Thousands of flies were emerging from the water and the scum – all scrambling over one another while trying to become airborne. The two lakes have very different characteristics: the large lake is shallow (no more that 11.5m) and saline (1.6% sodium chloride, cf. 3.0 – 3.5% for seawater); the small lake in the volcanic cone is deep (108m) and less saline and sometimes called the "fresh lake" (0.17% sodium chloride).[5] The large lake has very few invertebrates (just the flies mentioned above) but the small lake has many sorts of invertebrates including water beetles and dragonflies. Bird life in the crater was disappointing during my visit – only a few species and individuals: a grebe, Sacred Ibis, Stilt, Greenshank, and some unidentified ducks. I had a magnificent day pottering around the large lake; it was warm with a pleasant breeze. However, as soon as the sun disappeared below the crater rim, it became cold again (49°F, 9°C). The donkeymen kept warm, or tried to keep warm, by huddling around a constantly burning fire in the open.

The following day, we walked to Taratonga:

We set off by 9a.m. and made our way along a winding path to a 'cleft' in the crater wall on the opposite side to where we had entered. The walk to Taratonga was supposed to be about five hours, but again it took us nearly eight hours. The loads on the donkeys had to be continuously checked and re-adjusted. Thankfully there were no ravines to pass through. Some of the country, after we had left the crater, was similar to 'downland' – undulating hills, with few trees and lots of grass. Maybe this was the area that Lynes and Lowe (who collected on Jebel Marra in 1921) called the 'South-east Downs', but no one seems to know exactly where these 'downs' might be. The soil, if one can call it this, was powdered pumice, grey-white in colour and very dusty. We stopped for lunch – sardines, Ryvita and oranges – and pushed on. It was overcast by now and the passing clouds added extra feeling and grandeur to the scenery. Walking on 'downland', high up, with wonderful views, was very exhilarating and I really enjoyed the day's walk. We first saw Taratonga, at a distance over the downs, as a group of conical thatched houses surrounded by terraced hillsides and plantations. Looking back, we could see the whole of our route, including the cleft in the crater rim. We had not walked very far – perhaps 6-7 miles – but it took a long time. This is not the sort of scenery to rush through; it is good to tarry and to have time to enjoy such a magical place.

Taratonga was another Forestry Department centre. A tiny stream runs down the valley beside the stone-built resthouse, and radiating up the hillside from the stream were many small terraced fields – a fantastic patchwork of green among the rugged wild hills. Some parts higher up the valley were also terraced; many of the terraced walls, built of boulders and lumps of pumice, were overgrown with clematis and grass. Immediately on arrival, I set some of my mousetraps in the grasslands and along the walls; these walls reminded me of the old stone walls of rural England except that these ones were made of huge lumps of volcanic pumice. The village houses were rondavels with beautiful ridged conical thatched roofs; despite their beautiful African ambience, they must be unpleasant to live in – inside they were dark, grimy, smelly, and dusty. Everything was rather chaotic, and holes along the mud and pumice walls of the rondavels were evidence that rats and mice also lived in the houses. The Forestry workers were pleased and amused that I wanted to catch mice, so they were most cooperative. It was colder in Taratonga than in the crater and rather windy.

We had one full day in Taratonga. It was a beautiful place to stay because of the openness of the landscape, the mixture of grass-covered hills, boulders, streams, deep green vegetation in the valley, little terraces, beautiful African conical huts, and pleasant helpful people. I had time to walk on some of the nearby hills, take photographs, and visit another stream where I observed and collected dragonflies. Here, the vegetation was thick and lush, and the water (presumably freshwater) glistened and rushed past the boulders and through isolated clumps of grass. High on either side were the pumice cliffs, mostly pale in colour, and with scattered grasses and bushes hanging to their sides. It was still and quiet beside the stream, with no hint of the open windswept downlands above. It was a cold night again.

I was sad that we were leaving the mountain so soon; I wished that I could have had many more weeks here. There were donkey problems as usual! As we travelled further down the mountain, the country turned to scrubland and the temperature increased. We stopped beside a stream for lunch and paddled in the waters to cool off. The last part of the walk, into Kallokitting, was unpleasant – boiling sun, soft sand, little shade, and no water in the stream beds. The waters that flow off Jebel Marra have, by December, drained away into the sands. Water will not flow again until the next rains, and for a month or two afterwards.

My interest in Jebel Marra, apart from the adventure and fun of climbing the mountain, was to survey the small mammals and dragonflies. The only survey of mammals prior to my visit was by Rear Admiral Hubert Lynes and Willoughby Lowe during the Darfur Expedition of 1921-1922.[6] These collectors recorded thirty species or subspecies of mammals on the Jebel Marra, twelve of which are endemic. Most of the endemic species and subspecies are rodents, and not easily seen. The most interesting species that I encountered was Lowe's Gerbil *Gerbillus lowei*. This delightful beautiful gerbil has long silky dark brown and chestnut fur on the back and pure white fur on the underside. The tail is very long with a long dark tuft at the end. The species is endemic to Jebel Marra, and is known only from the crater and from Taratonga (where it lives in the pumice stone walls). This species was not known to science until it was first collected by W. P. Lowe in 1921 (hence the name), and no other individuals had been found since then until I caught several during this trip. (This was simply because no-one interested in mammals had visited

Jebel Marra since 1921.) It was pleasing to know that small populations of this species still live on the mountain, but because they are rare and occur in only a small geographical region, their long-term survival is uncertain. [7] My studies on dragonflies were equally rewarding, especially because there were no previous studies of these insects on Jebel Marra. I collected fourteen species from nine localities, all of which were known from other parts of Africa. On Jebel Marra, six species were widespread, three others were only found at Golol, and four species were found only in the crater.

Jebel Marra is a truly fascinating place: it is like an island surrounded by a 'sea' of unsuitable habitat for those species of plants and animals which have evolved in a montane environment; it also contains widespread species showing that, in the past, it was not an island because it shared habitats and climates with large areas of this part of Africa.

Now to return to my journey westwards into Chad…

8

WESTERN SUDAN

Perhaps the train did arrive at 2a.m., but when I awoke the train was not moving and we were surrounded by goods wagons. Mohammad Osman was awake and, after I had washed and dressed, we took a taxi into town, some two to three miles away. We found our way to a general store owned by a friend of Mohammad Osman's father where we left our luggage. Nyala did not look as attractive as it did in the previous December (after the Jebel Marra expedition); now there was rubbish in the streets and flies everywhere. After breakfast of fried liver, eggs and bread in a little restaurant, we walked to Mohammad Elmina's house where I had a much-needed bath. The house was typical of many Sudanese houses, with a central courtyard and rooms arranged around the sides. The bath, built of concrete and looking like an Egyptian stone sarcophagus, was in a little room on its own. Two buckets of water, a towel, a bar of soap and a mug were placed there ready for me. The family employed an Umbururu woman who was grinding millet in a wooden mortar in the courtyard. We were given another breakfast of *ful musri*, tomatoes, lettuce and bread.[1]

I paid a visit to Abdel Hafiz Osman, the Executive Officer, who had been so helpful to us last December. He had arranged that I could stay in the resthouse in Nyala, but since I hoped to leave that evening, I decided not to stay. (In retrospect I wish I had stayed a few nights, but at the time I did not know how long the whole journey to Nigeria would take, and eventually I had to get to the UK.) I learnt from Abdel that, since we left

Khartoum, there had been a postal and telegraph strike and that Sudan Airways had cancelled all flights. The government had changed – for the third time this year!

We went to the town square where all the *suq* lorries assembled before leaving for their destinations. I was suddenly greeted by a ragged figure whom I recognised as one of Hussein's helpers when we went to Jebel Marra. He told me that Hussein was in the market – "over there under the trees." I found Hussein and we had a good chat and he told me that he would probably be going to Geneina tonight. I learned that all the *suq* lorries go to Zalingei first and then on to Geneina, and that there would be no need to go to El Fasher. The lorries normally depart at about 4p.m. and reach Geneina by the following day at about 10p.m. (In fact, my lorry took about twelve hours longer than estimated.) I decided to buy a local palm-woven basket, some fruit, bread, tinned sardines and jam for the journey – to supplement the rock-cakes which were, by now, the consistency of rock. I did not know then whether I would be offered any Sudanese meals on the way.

We returned to Mohammad Elmina's house at 12:30; it was hot and we were ready to lie down on the *angareeb* beds placed on the veranda. Later, lunch was brought on a huge tray covered by an equally huge brilliantly-coloured tabag. We were given meats, spinach, salads, lettuce, bread and *kisra* (made from unleavened sorghum flour, not unlike *injera* in Ethiopia); to end the meal, we were offered (tinned) cherries and tea. It amazed me that so much fresh fruit and vegetables were available in such a dry place; I assumed that they came from the irrigated gardens nearby.

Mohammad Osman and I went to the square just before 4p.m. There were about twenty-five lorries, six of them bound for Geneina. Hussein decided that he would not be going until tomorrow so I transferred to a different lorry driven by Ibrahim whom I had met earlier in the morning. The square was crowded with people and their belongings. Many of them were Chadiens returning home after their pilgrimage to Mecca. Most of the lorries were loaded with sacks (of millet, sorghum, etc.), and the local people sat on top peering down at the comings and goings – and at me. There never seems to be any hurry and everyone was quite happy to wait for hours, knowing that the lorry will leave sometime soon – getting used to 'Africa time' can be somewhat frustrating to a Westerner used to strict schedules. There were all sorts of things to buy from itinerant vendors –

dresses, lengths of sugar cane (for chewing), perfume, and drinks. Darkness fell, and we still had not departed! So I transferred to a third lorry, this time a very comfortable 'Thames Trader' driven by Beshir Ibrahim, a jovial Fur. Eventually we left the square at 7:30p.m. and started on the road to Kas. There were about forty people perched precariously on the top of the sacks and luggage but there were only three of us in the cab: Beshir the driver, a young woman Hadir Mohammad who was returning to her home in Geneina, and myself. The lorry was typical of the many lorries that plough across the sands of the Sudan – very solid and reliable.

We stopped at a wayside café and found several other trucks already there. The café was only a wood and grass thatch shelter. Tea was being served, and I had a light supper of bread, tomatoes, an orange and a rock cake. I was soon to learn that throughout this journey my meal times would be very erratic; I never knew what might be available (other than rock cakes), and sometimes meals were missed altogether. The village of Kas was passed just before midnight, and a few miles outside we stopped for what I thought was a five-minute rest. However, it turned out to be a stop for the night. There were recumbent bodies lying all over the place, inside and outside the little grass huts. Two of the grass huts were brightly lit with pressure lights, and tea was being served. I drank a glass of tea and then found a rickety old *angareeb* in another hut and gingerly lowered myself on to its sagging rope 'mattress'. In spite of the chattering and aromas coming from the white heaving lumps around me – white because the locals were wrapped up in their white robes – I soon fell asleep. The bumping and swaying of the cab, and the cool night air had made me very tired. So ended my first real travelling day. I was surprised how easy it had been, and my not-very-good Arabic had enabled me to organise the transport and buy the supplies I needed. There were many more lorries on the road than I imagined, so my apprehensions about whether I could travel to Nigeria were allayed. During the night drive, I was disappointed that we saw hardly any animals on the road – just one hare, two jackals or foxes, one gerbil, and some bats flying overhead.

I woke during the night feeling very cold, even though I had changed into long trousers for the night. It was pitch black and I could not see anything; however, the chattering, snoring and spitting reminded me that there were many people lying on the ground, unseen, near my *angareeb*. At 5a.m., while it was still dark, the drivers shouted to wake everybody from their slumbers. I found 'my' truck and clambered into the cab. The air rushing past the cab was bitterly cold – there are no doors on these *suq* lorries – and I was shivering. I had come unprepared for such weather. Hadir lent me one of her blankets which I wrapped around myself. The purring noise of the engine and the vague shapes of Beshir and Hadir in the cab were reassuring. I had no idea where we were, and I only knew that we would, hopefully, get to Zalingei one day – a place I had not heard of before and I did not know what lay beyond. The road – a sandy track that does not deserve the title of a road – was very rough and uneven because we were travelling over the lower slopes of Jebel Marra. A hyaena and a mouse shot across the road just before dawn. Soon after it became light, Beshir stopped the lorry so he could make some adjustments to the engine. I was very impressed by the quality of drivers and the amount of care that they give to their vehicles. Later on, the road joined a wider flatter one and we spun along through an enchanting panorama of rolling hills. At 8:45a.m., we descended into a large dry wadi where a group of racoubas lined the road. We got out and stretched our legs; and the people on top clambered down the wooden struts that form the sides of the truck to the road below. We all bought some tea and I ate some bread and jam and fruit from my palm basket.

I really enjoyed the drive from the wadi to Zalingei. Hornbills and Mourning Doves flew among the trees, and there was a continual chorus of bird songs. The country was very dry and brown, but here and there some trees were in leaf – a glorious pale larch-green that is so surprising and unexpected in a semi-arid region. Some areas were densely vegetated, other areas were park-like, and some were just wide expanses of burnt grass. It was difficult to work out why some trees were in leaf and others were not – I suspected that it depended on the species, the soil and topography. As the road descended away from Jebel Marra on to lower ground, the large trees became less common and the 'desert effect' became more apparent.

Wadi Zalingei is very wide and after the road had crossed over its sandy bed, it climbed up the river bank towards the town. At this time of year, the wadi was dry (except for big pools of water in places). 'Zalingei' is an attractive name, but it did not come up to expectations. It was a straggling town with a large prison. On the outskirts of town there were fruit orchards and tobacco plantations surrounded by hedges of euphorbia plants (presumably to prevent goats from browsing and damaging the crops).

The lorry stopped under a big tree near the central square. By now, the heat was intense and oppressive. Beshir and I ate some liver, omelette and custard for lunch (an odd combination, but much enjoyed by travellers) and I resigned myself to an uncomfortable afternoon sitting under a big tree. Beshir tried to find a mechanic because one of the bolts on the chassis had broken and he did not want to go on until it was mended. After a few minutes, he took me to the home of a friend of his, Belel Mohammad Alamin, and I was given a bed to lie on. There were several other Sudanese there who were also travellers. The heat and flies made sleep impossible! At about 3:30p.m., we were served another lunch, which we ate sitting on a huge mat on the veranda. By now I was used to eating with my fingers, and reaching into the huge communal tray as is the normal custom in a Sudanese house. I wished I had not eaten an earlier lunch! The food was protected from the flies by a beautiful *tabag* (similar to the one I saw in Nyala). I then drank a glass of tea, and had a shave and a 'bucket bath'. I felt so much better! The Sudanese whom I met during the journey were so kind and hospitable, and all of them helped me in every possible way.

Beshir decided to stay in Zalingei so he could repair his lorry, so I transferred to a Bedford lorry. I was sorry to say goodbye to my two travelling companions, but I felt I needed to push on – I had no idea where, or whether, I might be marooned for several days at a time. In the Bedford was the owner, Geli Tahar, who was taking sugar, tea, cloth and millet to Geneina. In addition, there was the driver Fadl Mulah, another passenger Abdelbagi Ahmed, and myself. On top of the lorry, sitting on all the sacks and bales, were another ten passengers. We left Zalingei at about 5p.m; the road meandered over low hills and small wadis. We passed many Fur walking along the road, and saw many swarms of locusts which were stripping some of the trees of their leaves. The road eventually reached another part of Wadi Zalingei and where it ran along the edge of the wadi. There were large dead trees standing among abandoned plantations, and the road was at times no more than a cart track. Several times we crossed the wadi again, ploughing 200 yards through the soft sand and up the bank to the other side. Along the edge of the wadi there were simple irrigation schemes, each with a shadoof (similar to those along the Nile river in Khartoum). The only crops I saw here were onions; the tall green leaves of the onion plants were a wonderful contrast in colour to the dry yellows and beige colours of the countryside. After the village of Sulli, darkness fell and the road deteriorated. My wooden seat in the cab seemed even harder, and in the headlights I was able see that the country was over-cultivated and over-grazed. At about 11p.m., we stopped at the village of Murnei, a regular lorry halt with numerous stalls lining the 'central street'. I bought some coffee and some cooked chicken, and changed into warmer clothes. I stretched out along the seat of the cab – the others had disappeared somewhere – and had a very comfortable night.

Again, it was bitterly cold when I woke at 5a.m., and I think I shivered for the first hour or so until the cab was warmed by the heat of the engine. The sandy road now wandered through open bushland where most of the dry grass had been eaten by herds of domestic animals. Later, as the sun was rising, we stopped at Wadi Nyuri for some tea which helped to warm me up. The wadi contained *very* soft sand; one lorry had become stuck in the middle of the wadi during the night and had to be abandoned until the morning. Luckily all the passengers were helping to get it moving again, so we were not delayed too much. It would have been impossible for us to cross the wadi except along the single track of lorry-hardened sand. Francolins and sandgrouse frequently flew across the road, but apart from these, little animal life was evident. The road was still descending into the plains, and steep wadis and rocky intrusions were becoming less common. The view to the west – the direction we were travelling – was a perfectly flat plain dotted with bushes and trees until all was lost from sight in the blue haze of the horizon. Somewhere in that blue haze was Chad – a completely unknown country to me. Suddenly, there were many more people walking along the road and I saw convoys of camels. I realised that Geneina was not far away. At 9a.m., we crossed an imposing stone bridge leading to the entrance of Fort Geneina. We had to stop at the Police Post (where I was not allowed to photograph the bridge), and then continued along a road bordered by hedges and fruit orchards for a further five miles to Geneina town. And so I reached the most westerly town in the Sudan, almost in the middle of Africa, on the border with Chad.

It was a strange feeling to be in 'the middle of Africa'. Because the continent is such an irregular shape, it is difficult to know exactly where the middle is situated. If you take an old-fashioned compass (the sort used at school to draw circles), and place the point on Geneina (or nearby), it is about 1,700km south-west to the coastline in the Gulf of Guinea near Doula (Cameroun), 1,700km north to the Gulf of Sete in the Mediterranean

(Libya), and 1,700km east to the Red Sea close to Massawa (Eritrea). It is the only place in Africa where it is 1,700km in *three* different directions to *three* different oceans. To the south, the 1,700km circle stays permanently on land through the Congo basin, East Africa and Ethiopia. As far as my journey is concerned, I had now travelled about 1,680km from Massawa (if measured as a straight line) and there were still about 4,000km to Dakar.

The Western Sudan is a very remote region of central Africa, little known to the outside world. So it was surprising to learn that it was the centre of an important kingdom in the past.[2] The earliest records indicate that the Daju people (who are thought to have originally come from the Nuba Mountains and central Kordofan) established a small state in the southern part of Jebel Marra. Later, the Daja amalgamated with the Fur who were agriculturists living in the northern parts of Jebel Marra to form the Kingdom of Darfur. The Darfur Kingdom extended all around Jebel Marra and further west into present-day Chad. The kingdom followed a traditional religion and lasted from about 1200 AD to 1400 AD. Later, sometime in the early 1600s, the kingdom was taken over by the Tanjur, an Arabic Islamic group that came from the powerful empires of Kanem and Wadai (see chapter 11) further to the west. The Darfur Sultanate – as it was then called – became an Islamic state, and chose El Fasher, to the north-east of Jebel Marra, as its capital. The Sultanate survived from about 1603 to 1874 when the Egyptians expanded their influence southwards along the Nile Valley and westwards to Darfur. As with the other countries which I travelled through, the Kingdom of Darfur and the Sultanate of Darfur were involved in many power struggles and battles. Travelling through Darfur in the 1960s, with its peacefulness and delightful people, it was difficult to imagine the conflicts of earlier times. Now, there is scant evidence of the existence of these ancient states. However, the lifestyles of the local people, especially the planting of crops in seasonally flooding river beds and the terracing for agriculture on the jebel, probably predates these ancient states.

Geneina, as I saw it in 1965, was a very remote town seemingly neglected by the outside world. The most noticeable feature of the town was that most people were dark-skinned and 'African' (as opposed to Arabic) in appearance. Historically, the Arab/non-Arab divide has been of great importance and the source of conflict in western Darfur. Now, as I arrived, these centuries of conflict and shifting trends in religion and allegiance were difficult to comprehend. The markets were swarming with people selling food, household utensils, clothes and shoes, and fuel. I met a local man, Abdullah by name, and he kindly drove me to the Customs Post, about a mile out of town. I was told that all trucks departed for Abeché at about 1p.m., so this would give me about four hours in Geneina. I left my suitcase with the Customs Officer and drove back to the town. (In retrospect, I am amazed that I was so trusting, or naïve, but at that time strangers were trusted so much more than now as I write this (2017) – some fifty years later.) The center of town is near a large wadi – Wadi Kaja – which runs along the eastern side of Geneina. The wadi was completely dry (April), just a sea of fine whitish sand although I was told that there were still huge, almost lake-sized, pools in other parts of the wadi. It was now about eight months since the last rain fell in the hills around Geneina and in Jebel Marra, but maybe three to six months since there was any water flow. The wadi is part of a drainage basin (officially named as an endorheic basin) in which the water does not end in a sea or a lake, but evaporates or drains into water aquifers below the surface. Much of the Sahara from Mauritania to Egypt, western Sudan and Chad, and north of the Niger-Benue river system, consists of similar drainage basins. As I looked at the dry river bed, I tried to visualise the millions of kilolitres of water that had drained into the sandy soil and which, in time, have filled the huge aquifers of water under the sands of the Sahara.

It was a hot windless day, and since I had not had anything to eat since a bit of chicken the night before, I was feeling rather hungry. I bought some bread and fruit, and another market basket, and found a little café where I obtained some tea to drink. There was so much to buy and to look at in the market; I found a cobbler sitting under a tree in the square who mended my BOAC bag which was breaking at the seams. Abdullah then took me to a government building where I talked to the Executive Officer who gave me an introduction to the Chadian Customs Officer at Adre. By this time, Abdullah had left so the Executive Officer arranged for one of his trucks to take me to the Sudan Customs Post. I was so fortunate that so many Sudanese helped me on my way.

There were no difficulties with the Customs even though my Exit Visa had already expired. (All foreign nationals had to obtain an Exit Visa – complete with the date of exit – in order to leave the country. Likewise, before leaving, foreign nationals had to obtain a Re-entry Visa for their return. This bureaucratic red tape in Khartoum was always a hassle, but no one seems to take anything so seriously in the provinces.) I ate some lunch at the Customs Post and surveyed a number of rickety old lorries parked outside. These were Chadian lorries, very ancient, with high mudguards and wooden seats. I surmised that travelling in Chad was going to be more arduous and uncomfortable than in the Sudan. I paid my Sudanese £2, and was shown a red-coloured Dodge that looked incapable of even returning to Geneina, yet alone of going to Abeché. It was with some relief that later I was taken to a Ford Custom lorry that was taking a Sudanese trader, Karar Al Sheik, to Abeché. (My surmise about the Dodge was correct – it was not going anywhere!) I assumed that Karar had hired the Ford lorry for his own use because he had flown from Khartoum to Geneina, and was then going to fly from Abeché to Fort Lamy. In 1965, there were no direct flights from Khartoum to Fort Lamy, only to Lagos in Nigeria.

In the Ford lorry, we passed through a sort of no-mans-land. To begin with there was no obvious change in scenery and we were still driving on the left side of the road, although mostly the sandy tracks were single lane with no left or right sides. It was flat, hot and sandy and I did not know exactly where the border was situated. The driver sped along the sandy road far too quickly for my liking. After a few miles, we passed a signpost instructing us to keep to the right, and I knew that we were now in ex-French territory. Miraculously the road surface improved and there was a ridge of sandy-gravel along each side of the road indicating that it had been graded recently. Concrete bridges spanned the small wadis so we could maintain a constant speed without bouncing into and out of dry wadis. It took only an hour to reach Adre, the Customs Post into Chad. So now I was in a 'new' African country and I was intrigued to know how 'French' it was after a few years of independence.

9

CHAD

It was 2:30 in the afternoon when we arrived at the Chadian Customs Post at Adre. My diary records:[1]

All the Customs Officers were asleep and we were told we would have to wait until about 5p.m. So Karar and I sat under a big tree – the only shady place nearby. Karar produced lunch which he insisted on sharing with me, including a tin of Heinz Vegetable Salad, a favourite food among wealthy Sudanese. Here we met Zaki Gharib, a trader in Abeché, who suggested that we should stay with him when we reached Abeché. We spent a hot unpleasant afternoon. Eventually the Customs Office opened. I think the Chadian officer was a bit perplexed by my movements, but he was reassured when he saw my Kano-London air ticket. Eventually we left Adre at 5:30. The light was fading as we careered along the road. I was impressed by the smooth surface of the sandy road, and the numerous road signs warning about bridges and steep slopes in the road. The countryside was not especially interesting. The undulating hills were covered by tall dry 'bush'. Severe overgrazing was common around the few villages that we passed, and other parts had been burned extensively. On the road I saw two Ground Squirrels, four Jackals, and three Gazelles (species unknown) – much more than I had seen in the Sudan. It took three hours to reach Abeché, much faster than for the big lorries which normally took six to eight hours. By now it was dark. Outside the town, there was a road barrier, manned by the local police. At first, they refused to let us through, but after some persuasion (in French), they relented and let us proceed to the Police Station nearer the town. The Police Inspectors had already gone home, and so the lorry and its contents – just our suitcases – had to be left in the Police compound until the morning. Apparently the authorities are afraid that illegal merchandise may enter the town at night, so when the sun sets the town is sealed off from the surrounding countryside. We were sure that there were many illegal entrance points but we did not know where these were!

Karar and I walked into town. I carried only my BOAC bag and he had no luggage. It is an odd feeling to walk into an unknown town, with no luggage, no real destination, and no idea where we were going! And when it is a French Colonial town, it is even more strange. The street was lit with streetlamps – quite amazing! – and we walked past some pleasant-looking residential houses of (French?) officials. A few minutes of walking took us to a central square and here we turned into a darkened side street – much more 'local' in appearance. The dirt road was lined by high single-storey brick walls, interrupted in places by huge solid metal gates. We hammered on one of these, and the sound echoed up and down the street. This was Zaki Gharib's house. We were let in by a servant, and found Zaki sitting on a mat in the bare courtyard. We conversed for about half an hour; luckily Zaki's English was good. He told me that because tomorrow was a Sunday, everywhere would be closed and, anyway, few lorries went to Fort Lamy these days. How encouraging – I wondered whether this was where my travels would end! My bedroom was as bare as the courtyard – just an *angareeb* bed and a wooden chair – but at least I had somewhere to rest and sleep. I clambered onto the chair to open the shuttered and barred window high up on the wall so some cool night air might blow in. I was very tired and slept like a log.

The following day I did not wake until 7a.m. The air was cooler. It was rather difficult to know what to do because I had no idea where the rest of the house was. After a few minutes, Mr Zaki appeared and showed me the bathroom – all covered with dust since he had not been in the house for three weeks. I was given a bucket of water and had a leisurely 'bath' and shave. Normally there is piped water in the house; a donkey-man comes once or twice each day with a drum of water that is poured into the 'mains system'! On returning to my room, I found some bread, tea, and six hard-boiled eggs for my breakfast. I learned that Mr Zaki had lived in Abeché for thirty-three years and owned ten shops in the market; his house was at the back of one of the shops.

After breakfast, Karar and I walked back to the Police Station to retrieve our luggage. We had to wait for half an hour, and even then no one looked at our luggage; there had been no point in leaving it in the first place! Later, accompanied by one of Mr Zaki's servants, I went to the main market. It is one of the most fascinating markets I have seen anywhere in Africa. The central *suq* was a square piece of ground, all sandy, about 150 yards along each side and surrounded by a low wall. In the middle of each side was an imposing mediaeval-looking gateway with an avenue leading to the gateway on the opposite side of the *suq*. Ramifying off the central avenues were a maze of small paths leading into the inner recesses of the market. The avenues and small pathways were lined with small shelters made of rough sticks and covered by palm matting. It was very 'rough and ready' and everywhere was covered with sand and dust. The shelters, the people and the camels took up practically every square inch of space so one had to side-step, shove and push in order to get from place to place. The people were extremely friendly, and seemed really intrigued that I was taking such an interest in their produce. I was especially interested to see so many forms of different coloured rock salt – just large lumps of mineral mined further north in the Sahara. There was lots of food – sacks and baskets of dura and dried beans were especially common, all foods that are dry and can be kept for many months. It was disappointing that there was no fruit in the market; I came to realise later that fruit was practically unobtainable at this time of year in Chad. A different part of the market contained metal-workers, another part was dedicated to leather merchants, and another to just camels – dozens and dozens of them. These were probably the animals that I saw walking along the road to Abeché on the previous day. Now all of them were crouched on the ground with their saddles and innumerable leather bags lying on the ground at their sides. I had never seen so many camels so close together. I walked over and around them, taking great care not to tread on the tail of one while avoiding the legs of another. Their huge mournful faces and peering eyes were on about the same level as my eyes, and it was impossible to avoid their inquisitive stare. There were lots of grunts and groans from the camels and the incessant chattering of humans; there was also a very strong smell of indefinable fragrance… a mixture of dry sand, camel, human sweat, cooking fires and food.

Abéché (Abecher) was the capital city of the Wadai (Ouaddaï) Empire or Sultanate, one of the most important and long-lasting of the empires of this region of Africa. The sultanate emerged as an offshoot of Darfur in about 1630 AD, and over time extended its influence westwards to the region of Lake Chad and southwards into the savannas. The capital of Wadai was originally at Ouara but after the wells dried up in the 1800s, the capital was moved some 50 miles to the south to Abeché. Both Ouara and Abeché were geographically situated at the crossroads for trade going east and west, and also northwards across the Sahara Desert to the Mahgreb. The Sultanate survived, in spite of numerous battles, until the French conquered Chad in the early twentieth century. The many camels that I saw in the market suggested that these beasts were still used extensively for desert travel, and for bringing many sorts of goods into the local markets.

At the time when I visited Abéché, it was about eighty years since the German explorer Dr Gustav Nachtigal arrived in Abéché. Nachtigal – a medical doctor – travelled extensively across the Sahara desert and Soudan between 1869 and 1875. He had a sympathetic attitude to the local people regardless of their status in life, was very intelligent and observant, and was able to make friends with many people whom he met on his travels. In these respects, he was different to most of the explorers of his day. On his return to Germany, he wrote several fascinating volumes about his impressions and observations.[2] Nachtigal travelled with many camels and horses and a retinue of helpers – all necessary because of the many supplies he had to carry. When he arrived near to Abéché, he was relieved that he had actually managed to get as far as Abéché, but also depressed because he did not know whether King Ali, the Sultan of Wadai, would receive him. King Ali had a reputation for fierceness and a dislike of Christians. Eventually, after a wait of several days, Nachtigal was summoned for an audience at the Royal Palace – a large building with a courtyard, many rooms and verandas. He was surprised to find that the King was sitting alone on a mat, wearing simple clothing and with a tarbush on his head. He was very impressed by King Ali's assurance of safe passage through the Kingdom, his intelligence, his interest in Nachtigal's travels, and the King's "simplicity, dignity and self-assurance." But he also realised that the King had "sound common sense, little feeling, boundless energy, and a powerful – even cruel – sense of justice." And a strong desire to increase the power of Wadai abroad. At the time, Abéché was rather a wild place with a population of 10,000 – 15,000 people; there were often many drunken people in the streets, and rough justice was given to those who did not obey Koranic law. Nevertheless, Nachtigal felt safe walking around and having excursions away from the town because of the protection afforded by the king and his staff. Abéché was a great trading centre in those days, with trade routes across the Sahara and to the east and west (as it still is today).

Nachtigal stayed in Abéché for two months and he was able to observe many aspects of life in the town. He visited the Palace frequently because the King wanted to learn more about neighbouring Kingdoms; he was deeply interested in "gunpowder, manufacture of cannons and guns, steamships," and other issues of state. Nachtigal recorded that the King had brought many slaves from the Kingdom of Bagirmi, a small Kingdom south of Lake Chad. These slaves were a great asset to Wadai because (in contrast to the local people) they were good craftsmen and good servants, and the young girls made good wives for the local men. Nachtigal was very aware that he had to be diplomatic in his dealings with the king's followers and supporters. At the time, it seems that there were many intrigues and rumours circulating in the town, and Nachtigal had to ensure that his name was not associated with any such intrigues and rumours. Sensibly, he occupied much of his time being a medical doctor and surgeon – he performed many operations (in spite of the lack of anaesthetic and medical equipment). He commented that butter was widely used as an embrocation for a variety of internal and external maladies, and that this treatment was obviously thought to be effective by the local people. Diseases were common, especially during the 'wet season' – 'fevers' (presumably malaria) were prevalent (mostly among the Arab population) probably because the seasonal presence of water in rivers and swamps close to Abéché provided suitable breeding grounds for mosquitoes. Guinea worm was another horrible tropical disease; it was treated (as I saw it treated in Nigeria in the 1960s) by carefully pulling the worm by its head as it emerged through skin, making sure that the whole length of the worm was removed. On one occasion, Nachtigal attended the festival after some of the princes had been circumcised. Festivals were magnificent and luxurious: there was dancing by upper-class girls wearing gold necklaces (imported from Egypt and Sennar), silver bracelets, and strings of coral. Nachtigal also recorded that he saw "graceful dancing" when men danced with women – an interesting observation considering that such dancing was not allowed in most Muslim societies.

King Ali died one year after Nachtigal left Abéché, and the kingdom was taken over by his brother. In subsequent years, the independence of the kingdom declined; there were internal power struggles, invasion by the Turco-Egyptian authorities in Darfur and, later, by the Mahdi (see chapter 5). Finally, Wadai and all of Chad was invaded by the French and became part of French Central Africa. Nachtigal's diaries, therefore, provide an excellent record of Abéché (and Wadai) just before the Kingdom ceased to exist.

Not far to the north of Abeché is the southern-most part of the Sahara Desert. The transition from the Sahel Savanna Zone to the desert is gradual and there is no clear-cut dividing line. Several millennia ago, Abeché (if it had existed) would have been surrounded by lush wooded savanna with plenty of water. The savanna extended throughout most of the present Sahara Desert. The rock paintings and engravings of Tibesti (800km northwest of Abeché) and Tassili (part of the Hoggar Range) depict elephants, hippos, giraffes, antelopes, cheetahs, ostriches, lions, and humans with their cattle.[3] These rock paintings are considered to have been drawn 4,000 to 9,000 years ago, and are strong evidence for the existence of these animals near to these sites. Other evidence about paleoclimates, underground water sources and the presence of many rivers flowing from the high plateaux suggest that the African Humid Period enabled an East-African-like flora and fauna to survive in these now arid regions. Perhaps even more amazing is the presence of fishes in some isolated regions within the Sahara. Fish can only be present in such places where (at one time) there has been adequate water and inter-connecting waterways.[4] Not many species of fish have the ability to survive the vicissitudes of the Sahara, but their presence, like that of the rock art, is strong evidence that the Sahara was green, lush and humid in the not-so-distant past.

Also in this region, just to the north of my route and south of Tibesti, is the Durab Desert. This is an area rich in fossils of fish and mammals. One of the most interesting fossils found in this area in recent years (actually in 2001) is *Sahelanthropus tchadensis*, an early hominid who lived in the

Miocene epoch, about seven million years ago.[5] The habitat that supported *Sahelanthropus* must have been savanna-like, which would also have supported many of the creatures (or at least their progenitors) portrayed by the rock art much later in history. The exact relationship between *Sahelanthropus* and other hominids is uncertain and strongly debated, but it seems that this creature lived at a time when the chimpanzee-human line began to diverge from that of other primates. This fossil was found about 2,500km from the well known sites of more recent fossil hominids in East Africa, and suggests that hominids were much more widespread in Africa than previously thought.

The locals – or were they nomads? – in the *suq* at Abeché had very dark complexions. Most of the women wore wraps of deep blue indigo cloth, often very faded by the intense sunlight; many did not wear anything on their heads. The men mostly wore white cloth, and some also had a white turban. Many had short beards and moustaches and friendly twinkling eyes. None of them minded being photographed – such a contrast to the Sudan.

Surrounding the central market was the rest of the square bordered by other shops. A wide covered veranda supported by thick brick pillars ran along the length of the shops providing deep shade and protection from the sun. The locals slept, sat and talked, drank tea and watched the many tailors making clothes on their ancient pedal-operated sewing machines. Colourful Japanese cloth and Nigerian enamelware were particularly evident.

After the noise and bustle of the market, I ambled along some of the other streets. They were wide, sandy and spacious, and lined by low buildings, and all of them were named "Rue de… " just as in France. The Police, apart from their dark skin-colour, looked just like French gendarmes with their distinctive uniforms. In an African sort of way, I liked Abeché. It had none of the cramped feeling of a town like Omdurman.

I decided to find the Chambre de Commerce because I had an introduction to Madame Luisiano, the Secretary of the Chambre. I did not know what sort of person to expect, but I did not expect to meet such an extraordinary personality. My first view of the Chambre was a mass of locals who appeared to be trying to get into a side entrance. Somebody suggested that I should push my way through, and after a few minutes I reached the gate to find a white woman wearing sunglasses. She was clad in a black blouse, billowing Eastern trousers (the sort that I have always associated with harems and Scheherazade) and a black headscarf. We introduced ourselves and I followed her into the courtyard of her house. I was completely taken aback when I saw three gazelles, an ostrich, and masses of chickens and rabbits strolling around the yard and through the door into the living room! Then she showed me her two lions which lived in a large enclosure next to the house; it was these animals that the locals at the gate wanted to see. Madame has kept lions for nearly twenty years. The lioness came to the barred window of the living room, was sprayed with disinfectant to keep the flies away, and allowed me to stroke her. There were also two warthogs in another enclosure ("rather troublesome animals") and two caracals (?) in the bathroom!

Madame was rather disappointed that she did not know that I was coming – she said she would have prepared a large lunch. However, we talked while drinking cold beer (a real luxury after many days of tepid muddy water), and she showed me some of her photographs. One particularly interesting one was of a lion resting beside a warthog – a most unnatural state of affairs. She told me that during her twenty-four years in Abéché, the number of wild animals in the region has gradually decreased and that now you have to look really hard and long to see any of the larger species – the same situation that occurs throughout the rest of this part of Africa. Madame offered me lunch – salad with red wine, followed by coffee; it was so much better than dried bread and rock cakes with jam. While we were having lunch, my eyes strayed around the room and I counted the rabbits; there were twenty-seven of them – some on the floor and others on the bookcases and chairs. After this excellent lunch and the most extraordinary couple of hours, I returned to Mr Zaki's house. On the way I passed an arcade in the *suq* full of beautiful camel-hair carpets, all of them with wonderful designs and bright colours. How I wished I could have purchased one!

During the morning, I noticed a bus near the central square and discovered that it would be leaving for Fort Lamy in the evening at about 5p.m. This was marvellous, especially since I had been told that there was very little road transport to Fort Lamy these days. So at 4:30p.m., I walked to the bus with my luggage and a cardboard box of food that Mr Zaki had given to me. I was told that it would take fifty-two hours to reach Fort Lamy and the fare was the equivalent of Sudanese £4. Here I encountered my first problem with money; I recorded in my diary that:

Travellers Cheques can be changed only in Fort Lamy. Chadian money (CFA francs) is not available in the Sudan, and officially a traveller can take only Sudanese £10 out of the country. In fact, I had less than this. Mr Zaki changed £6 for me at the rate of CFA 500 to the Sudan £1.00, not the official rate of CFA 680 to the £; so I got some CFA francs and could pay for my bus fare and he made a profit! No wonder he is a successful businessman and owns ten shops!

The bus was quite respectable, a much better means of transport than I expected in central Africa. It was a French-made Citroen diesel bus owned by the 'Union Tchadienne de Transport'. Painted along one side, in large capital letters, were the words: UNITCHADIENNE. There were a lot of people around the bus; thankfully most of them were saying goodbye to friends and not coming themselves. It was quite a surprise that the bus left on time at 5p.m. and I nearly missed it while I was taking photographs. There were only six passengers: a policeman and his wife and two children going to Fort Lamy at the end of his leave in Abeché, a tall thin fellow with a cowboy hat going to Mongo, and myself. As the sun set, our driver Abdu Abaka stopped the bus so he could get out and say his evening prayers. The 'bush' here was very uniform and rather dull. By this time, in the headlights of the bus, the trees looked grey and lifeless. I was rather tired and dozed some of the time. The warm air blowing in through the open windows was very hot, the countryside was flat, and there was nothing special or remarkable to see. Occasionally swarms of locusts appeared in the headlights.

Just after 9p.m. we stopped at Oum Hadger, the first town of any size since leaving Abeché. Oum Hadger, like so many towns in this semi-arid landscape, is situated on the banks of a wadi, now without any water. The town is laid out in a series of parallel roads forming a rectangular pattern. Within each square or rectangle are a series of small tracks leading to the little houses, all built very close to each other in a seemingly haphazard way; there were few trees (if any) and no gardens. At the stop, I had some tea – always available at the lorry and bus stops – and some rock cake and jam. It was too hot to eat anything else. During the last few days, I had been drinking more and more water because of the heat and dry air from which it was impossible to escape. Sensibly the drivers always carried lots of water, and I had been able to drink as much as I wanted. Mostly the water was dirty and tepid and nasty to taste, but it was either this or nothing. I decided that I would drink as much as I could whenever I had the chance regardless of what it was like. Luckily I did not get any tummy upsets during the whole trip despite the quality of the water and variety of foods I ate. We drove on, westwards, for another 60km to Anset, a small village of grass huts which is not shown on any maps. I could not see anything in the darkness except for a few racoubas beside the road. A number of local women were waiting by the rakoubas selling grass sleeping-mats and food. The hair of the women was cut in a different fashion compared with the Sudan; some parts were left long and other parts were cut short. The women wore terra-cotta coloured or dark blue cloths around their waists with their breasts bare, and the small children were completely naked. Strings of coloured beads encircled their necks, and some had a gold (or gold-coloured) ring in one nostril. There is no regulation here that clothes must cover all of the body as there is in most of the (Arabic-speaking) Sudan, and there was no embarrassment about being totally or partially naked. It was still hot but I expected and hoped it would be (comparatively) cold in the morning. Eventually I found a secluded corner in a rakouba where I unrolled my grass mat and settled down for the night. The ground was hard, but I was so tired that I did not stay awake for long.

I woke at 5a.m. feeling stiff and cold. It was Monday 5th April, exactly a week since I left Khartoum. On most days, I lost track of the date and time except when I wrote my diary. I walked away from the village into a barren area of *Callotropis* bushes for my morning toilet. This was another problem on the journey; I never knew when or where the transport would stop or whether there was any suitable place for ablutions. Needless to say, there were no public lavatories or toilet paper in most of the places that I visited or passed through during the whole journey. After my toilet, there was just time to eat an orange and clean my teeth before we set off again.

My route continued westwards, but I wished that it had been possible to go north towards the oases and rocky hills of the Sahara. These fascinating areas of sand, rock, and volcanic craters have an amazing fauna and flora adapted to the harshness, heat and lack of water of the Sahara. In some areas, after rainstorms, there are rock pools, flowing water, new leaves on the few trees and bushes, green grass and flowers. But there was no public transport, and so I was unable to go. Perhaps I could have hired a camel and travelled like a nomad… maybe another time!

The countryside west of Anset was dry and open, with scattered trees and bushes which became more numerous and dense along wadis and drainage lines. Round grass huts with conical grass roofs clustered together among the bushes. The scenery was enlivened by huge flocks of Guinea-fowl feeding beside the road in the morning sunlight. The driver stopped at one village to buy a sack of millet; during the journey from Abeché to Fort Lamy, he accumulated many sacks of produce which, no doubt, he sold at great profit in Fort Lamy!

We arrived at Ati at 8a.m. There was a long central street lined with flat-topped mud houses and shaded by large *neem* trees, very reminiscent of the Sudan. The deep shade under these trees was a popular place to sit, and the shady parts of almost every tree was crowded with people reclining or sitting cross-legged. We stopped outside the office of the 'Cie Tchadienne de Transports'. I asked where I could buy some coffee or tea, but there was no café here. The official in charge of the office kindly offered to get me a pot of tea, a teapot of milk, and a glass. I sat on the steps of the office overlooking the road – not much happened, it was too hot for any human activity. When I thought we were about to leave, the driver and I were invited into the courtyard at the back of the office for breakfast. I did not expect such hospitality in such a remote and poor part of Chad. The first course was a huge joint of cold meat which was torn apart with almost animal ferocity. Then came two dishes, one of meat curry, and the other of millet and water mixed to a glutinous mass like cold porridge – which I found rather unappetising. Nevertheless, I was now full and ready for what the day would offer.

As the day wore on, it became hotter and hotter as every hour passed. The blistering sun beat down on the shadeless bush. I did not have a thermometer with me but I found out later that the average daily maximum in April is c. 40°C. The inside of the bus was like a furnace and the hot air fanned us like a fire. It was too hot to take in the view, and my one hope was that it would soon get cool. I longed for the sun to sink below the horizon. To begin with, the countryside was flat and desolate, but later it became slightly hilly and I saw some marvellous purple-coloured rocky jebels in the distance. Suddenly we stopped under two enormous trees – so unexpected in this countryside – and were surrounded by people. Under these great spreading trees, there was a little market and all the available shade was solid with women and children. As at Anset, the women wore only a cloth around their middle and were adorned with beads and nose-rings, and the children were naked. They were very friendly and unashamed, and were rather surprised to see me. Probably very few white people came there those days, and even fewer talked to them. At midday, the bus stopped again under another group of large trees – I realised that the driver knew the location of every shady place along this road. Each of us found a patch of shade and had lunch. I enjoyed some chicken, tomatoes and bread that Mr Zaki had given me. As soon as we arrived, women and children appeared, and the driver sent some of them off to get water and local produce. He then settled himself down with an enormous hamper of food and listened to western pop songs from Radio Kaduna in Nigeria! As I lay on my mat trying to get cool (almost impossible!), I was surrounded by small children – they looked so ebony black in the deep shade. The small boys, as elsewhere, wore nothing and the girls only wore a string of beads round their middles. A few of the older children wore battered dirty *jelebeas*. The heat was oppressive and the flies prevented sleep. I washed and shaved in about half a pint of water to pass the time, and was quite glad when we moved on again.

In the late afternoon, we arrived in Mongo, by far the most pleasant small town visited so far. The two main streets formed a 'Y' and were lined with mud-built houses and large trees. The town is built at the base of a large jebel which dominates the town on the western side. As I got out of the bus, one of the crowd watching our arrival greeted me with 'Bonjour', and I asked the usual question: "Il y a un restaurant ici pour le thé ou le café, si'l vous plaît?" Rather than answer my question, he suggested that I accompany him to his house and, since I was told that the bus would not leave for one and a half hours, this seemed a very good idea. I learned that Sergeant Mahadjir had just retired from fourteen years in the French Army, yet he was only a little older than I was (i.e. twenty-nine years). During his service he had been posted to France, Saudi Arabia, and Indo-China during the long war. It was strange meeting such a well-travelled person in such a remote place. In some ways this was not surprising because France considered all its colonies as 'La France d'Outre Mer', and the citizens of the colonies were regarded as French citizens. Sergeant Mahadjir retired because the French Army had just been removed from Chad, and now he was going to set up a business in Mongo. We reached his house, only a few minutes walk from the bus stop, and I was escorted into the courtyard. First, he thought I would like a bath – an offer gratefully accepted. A small portion of the courtyard was screened off with matting and this was the toilet and area for a bath. I was given a bucket of water, soap, towel and even shaving things. It was a lovely feeling to take off all my dusty clothes, and pour the cool water over my head and let it trickle down my body. Cleaned and refreshed, I sat with Sergeant Mahadjir in the yard drinking peppermint tea, and then his wife produced curried chicken, rice, and coffee. The air was cooler by now, and I felt wonderfully rejuvenated and able to continue the journey. Eventually it was time to walk back to the bus which was gradually filling up with more people; we continued chatting until about 6p.m, when I had to say goodbye. It was getting dark as the bus drove off into the setting sun. After these two days in Chad, my French was becoming more fluent (helped by the little French-English Dictionary I was carrying) and it was not too much of a strain to maintain a conversation for an hour or two.

The bus had not travelled for more than a mile or so from the town before the driver stopped for his evening prayers – and they were rather long prayers on this occasion. For the rest of the drive, it was dark and I was in a semi-stupor. The heat, the hot air, and now the effects of a bath and good food lulled me to sleep, and only the chatter of people when the bus stopped brought me back to life. I got out at Bitkine, sat on some sacks, and nearly missed the bus since I was half asleep. One stop was particularly noisy because all the drums in the village were being beaten (for no apparent reason it seemed). At each halt, I helped myself to the driver's supply of water; this was kept in a vast fifty-litre glass flask looking like a Chianti bottle that was kept beside his seat in the front of the bus.

At 10.45p.m. we stopped for the night at a small village that the driver called 'Abou'tchat'ak'. As for last night, we all settled down on our grass mats on the sand amid the chatter of the local women who were selling mats, water and food. Once I had found a reasonably comfortable place to lie down, I soon fell asleep. It was just light when I awoke, feeling stiff and thoroughly chilled. The alternation between being incredibly hot and tired during the day, and then cold, stiff but not so tired at the end of the night, was a feature of my travels in this semi-arid country. The local people must be very resilient to cope with this every day, as well as the continual deprivations of food and water. I got up and walked along the road to get some exercise and to get warm. Beside the road were several trees with bright yellow flowers (*Cassia*?) shining like jewels in the early morning sunlight. Later I ate a mango, cleaned my teeth, and then we set off again. It was comforting to know that we should arrive in Fort Lamy during the evening.

The first stop of the day was at Bokoro. The road was sandy but moderately good. We passed many jebels and rocky hills which added a lot of interest to the drive, but the countryside was mostly bare and parched, with scattered trees and bushes. Bokoro was an unattractive place. The large square was littered with broken-down lorries and deserted market shelters, and there were flies and rubbish everywhere. There were four 'hotels' in the square, each with a small grass-lined shelter and makeshift tables and benches outside. The first was not able to offer anything to drink, and the second had only black coffee. The tables were dirty and stained, and the tabletops were solid with flies which flew up in clouds when I sat down.

The morning's drive was hot and monotonous. There was little change in the scenery from mile to mile – rather uninspiring bush, rocks, inselbergs and intense sun. We stopped once to do some repairs to the springs, and passed several broken-down lorries by the roadside. At each, there were some locals in ragged clothing lying down in the shade waiting for a mechanic to come, or maybe for some spare parts to be delivered. Some of the lorries were extremely large and overloaded and, judging by the number we passed, not as reliable as the *suq* lorries in the Sudan. I was very glad that I was travelling in this bus; it would have been very uncomfortable and frustrating to be travelling in one of these lorries and to be stuck in the middle of scorchingly hot Chad for even a day. At 1p.m. we stopped for lunch under some large trees. This was a popular stopping place, and there were six other vehicles parked under the trees. As usual, local women brought food and water for sale. It was here for the first time that I noticed that some of the women were wearing silver Maria Theresa dollars around their necks. I examined some of these – some were so worn that the picture and writing were almost obliterated; others were newer so I could read the 1780 date.[6] Later on, I realised that many of the women I had seen earlier on the journey were also wearing these dollars, but I did not recognise them at the time.

Our lunch stop lasted for only about one hour because the driver wanted to reach Fort Lamy before dark. There are no proper timetables for these buses; starting and leaving times are vague, and one never knows how long the journey may take, or whether there will be any breakdowns on the way. I just had to accept 'Africa time' and hope that I would arrive sometime in the future. Time is timeless here... During the afternoon, it seemed hotter than ever, and the glare was so painful that it was impossible to look out of the window. (The mean maximum daily temperature at this time of year – April – is 42°C.) By now, I had a headache, a streaming cold from getting so hot in the day and so cold at night, and I was covered with sweat and dirt. The countryside was more open and with less vegetation, and the effects of overgrazing by domestic animals suggested that we were getting near to civilisation. At Massquet, the road turned from sand to tarmac, and so the bus was able to speed along through low very degenerate bush similar to that around Khartoum. Beside the road, there were many stalls selling firewood – which explained why there were few trees here and why the place was so desolate. The road did not go near Lake Chad (which is surrounded by swamps and unsuitable for roads), and on the right side of the road I noticed a sign declaring that the area was a National Park – but I did not see any animals.

Eventually, I saw lights in the distance. We drove around the edge of the airport (where we met another larger bus setting out for Abeché) and entered the mud-house African part of Fort Lamy. There were electric lights, lots of shops, and masses of people – so strange after nearly 1,000 miles of bush country. All the passengers disembarked in a central square, and I got a taxi to the 'Chambre de Commerce'. I did not know where I was going to stay, but since Madame Luciano had given me a letter of introduction to Monsieur Joux and suggested that I stay at the Chambre, I decided to go there first. Luckily M. Joux was at home, but he was rather curt and unfriendly and wanted to know why he had not received a telegram from Madame Luciano announcing my arrival. Anyway he showed me to a bedroom and departed. I was so thankful to see a bed and a bath that I was quite happy to be by myself. By now I was two-thirds of the way to my destination in Nigeria and the most difficult and unpredictable part of the journey was over.

By now, about 8p.m., I was not feeling too good but I had a shower, put on clean clothes, swallowed four Disprins and went to look for the restaurant that M. Joux told me was 200 yards down the road. It was an attractive place with awnings and lights, tables under the trees, and table lamps. I had only 300 CFA (c 10/- in English money) and I thought this would be sufficient but I had a shock when I saw the prices. I suggested that I could pay the remainder in the morning when I had changed my travellers cheques, but the proprietor was an unpleasant Frenchman who implied that if I could not pay the normal 600-700 CFA francs, I should not come to his restaurant. He did not believe me when I told him I had just arrived by bus from Abeché – he said that was impossible!! However, he did change one cheque for me and I was able to order tomato salad, steak and coffee (600 CFA francs). It was very good and refreshed me no end. I was surprised at all the French people I saw. The restaurant was next door to a cinema; I saw more French people during the evening than one would see English people in a week in Khartoum. The men wore very short shorts, had short crew cut hair and drooping moustaches, and the women (at least some of them) wore low-cut provocative dresses or shorts. One woman who was looking at the cinema notices wore a skin-tight blouse and long trousers of flesh-pink (which, at a distance looked as if she was not wearing trousers at all!). So my first impression of Fort Lamy was that it was very French and very expensive.

10

FORT LAMY AND WESTWARDS TO NIGERIA

I hoped I would sleep well, but the heat and the insects (despite being under a mosquito net) prevented a really restful night. I had breakfast of coffee, bread and jam at the Chambre with a French geologist and his wife who had spent a year motoring round the north and west coasts of Africa from Algeria. After breakfast I set out to explore Fort Lamy.[1] If you did not know where you were, and if it were cooler, you would think you were in a well-designed French town, with the streets radiating out from a central square. In some ways, Fort Lamy was like Bukavu in the Belgian Congo (as I saw it in 1959, one year before Independence) – white arcades, lots of shade trees, European shops, and a pleasant clean look – but without the glorious surroundings that make Bukavu so attractive. In Fort Lamy, the African township was confined to one part of the town, and the French part was separate and entirely French. All the shops that I went into were French-owned, and the shop attendants were also French. The streets buzzed with little box-like Citroen cars. I spent the morning happily soaking up the atmosphere of the town. Almost all the buildings were painted white (as in other French Colonial towns). I went to the Post Office (bought stamps), and the Bank (where I exchanged some travellers cheques at 680 CFA francs to the £ sterling), and then to the Customs Office to enquire about leaving Chad. All the officials and secretaries I met were French; there was not a single Chadian in any of these government offices. It was quite obvious to me that the

French were still in control of the country, even though it was officially independent and had a Chadian Head of State.

The 'Museum Prehistorique' had a wonderful display of Chadian artifacts, mostly collected in the last five years. The Director showed me around and despite my inadequate French, I learnt a lot about the history and culture of Chad. There were ancient bowls, copies of drawings of wild animals from the caves near Largeau, and fossilised skulls of hippopotamuses and crocodiles from Koro Toro. This locality is south of Largeau, in an area that is now bare sand and rock. There must have been extensive areas of rivers (and lakes?), savanna trees and grasslands to support such large (semi-aquatic) animals. Besides prehistoric remains, there were also modern bows, funerary jars, papyrus boats (from Lake Chad), clothing (some of it decorated with shells from the West African coast), and fighting weapons. One particularly interesting display was a complete set of the handicrafts used in one village; the museum had purchased a complete village including the houses, to provide a detailed record of all the material possessions and way of life of the villagers in the 1950s.

It felt very tropical in Fort Lamy; it was warm and more humid than in the Sudan. Large orange and blue Rainbow lizards (a common species throughout West Africa) were found everywhere, especially in gardens, on walls, and on warm sunny surfaces. Multitudes of sunbirds flew in and around the *neem* trees.

I decided to go without lunch (too hot, too expensive), and spent the afternoon resting until it was cooler. As the sun was setting, I walked to the Chari River on the western border of Fort Lamy. At this time of year, it was a wide gently flowing river that flowed northwards into Lake Chad. It is the longest river in Africa that does not flow into the sea. Its waters originate on the plateaux and hill country to the south, mostly in the Central African Republic. Radiating out from these hills are the watersheds for three major river systems: to the north is the Chari-Logone river system, to the south is the Ubangi-Congo river system, and to the east is the Bahr-el-Ghazal – White Nile river system. It was fascinating to ponder on the source of each litre of water that flowed in front of me as I stood gazing at the river – it could have come from many parts of central Africa! Just north of Fort Lamy (but a little south of Lake Chad), the Chari is joined by another large river, the Logone which originates in the hills to the west of the Chari, in the Central African Republic and Cameroun. Together the waters of both

101

rivers flow northwards into the swamps around Lake Chad and then into the lake itself. The Chari river at Fort Lamy is hemmed in by steep mud-banks, and on the opposite side is Cameroun. I had thought there was a bridge across the Chari river, but in fact the only means of crossing is by ferry. When I reached the river, a petrol tanker was being ferried across; it did not look very safe and I half-expected to see the tanker fall into the water!

Lake Chad is a freshwater lake situated where Nigeria, Chad, Cameroun and Niger meet. The lake has been known (to westerners) for a long time. A lake is depicted in Bowen's map (Chapter 2) in about the same position as Lake Chad, although it was known by a different name and had a different drainage. Over the course of time, the lake has fluctuated dramatically in area. The Lake Chad basin (that is the whole of the region where rainwater will drain into the lake) is vast – some 2.3 million km².[2] This area covers most of Chad as well as parts of northern Nigeria, Niger, Cameroun and Central African Republic. At its maximum size, during the early Quaternary Period (c. 2.6 – 1.8 million years BP) when the climate was warm and humid and most of the surrounding regions were savanna, the lake is estimated to have covered about 350,000 km² and to have been up to 160m in depth. Some authorities have called this huge lake 'Mega-Lake Chad' and likened it to an inland sea. During the Ice Ages, the area of the lake is assumed to have waxed and waned in area in accordance with the glacial and inter-glacial periods. Not all of Lake Chad is water; it is surrounded by seasonally inundated swamps, and there are many swampy islands within the lake. Besides these major changes in size, Lake Chad also changes its shape and area seasonally depending on the rainfall in its catchment. In more recent times, from about 4,000 to 5,000 years ago, the size of the lake has declined greatly. The greatest decline has been in recent years partly because of the general drying of the Sahara (so that the only water draining into the lake comes from the Logone and Chari rivers in the south) but also because of irrigation for agriculture, the sinking of many artesian bores to provide water for humans and domestic animals, and extensive overgrazing and deforestation in areas around the lake.[2] In 1960, just before my travels, Lake Chad covered about 25,000km²; by 2008, it had shrunk to only 2,500km² and now (2017) it is even smaller. In the 1960s and 1970s, the Fisheries Research

Centre at Mallamfatori (in Nigeria) was on the edge of Lake Chad; now it is many tens of kilometers from the lakeshore and the land in between is old sand dunes, semi-arid scrub and dry reed beds.[3]

In town, I bought some provisions for the remainder of my journey, and marvelled at the French butter, cheeses, meats and wines – all imported from France. I bought some apples (four of them cost 240 CFA francs, about Sterling 8/-), and then found some African street-sellers with melons and grapefruit, none of them very good. I had supper at the same restaurant as last night, and amused myself observing the behaviour and idiosyncrasies of the French people as they passed by in the street. I was glad to be leaving in the morning: Fort Lamy was too artificial and expensive for me.

The customs officials told me to be at their office at 7a.m. It was about one mile from the Chambre, and I walked there with my luggage and basket of food. No one looked at my luggage, and I was directed to Passport Control and the ferry. Eventually I found the ferry, and purchased my ticket (20 CFA francs). Also on the ferry was a Frenchman in a Citroen car, so I asked him about transport to Fotokol; he said he did not know (which seemed very strange because that was where he was going). I was very annoyed when we arrived at the far bank and he drove off in a cloud of dust without offering me a lift, which he could easily have done. Cameroun is very narrow at this northern end of the country – just a small wedge of territory about 120km wide that extends northwards to the edge of Lake Chad. With the other foot-passengers, I walked about 500 yards to where there was a group of cars. There were no buses in this part of Cameroun, so I had to pack myself in with other travellers in a communal taxi (cost 500 CFA francs). The road was well graded and wide, but so dusty that I had to clean my glasses every few minutes. Thick vegetation bordered the road, with tall *Balanites* trees rising above the lower bushes and reeds. On the right, some areas were flooded – and I realised that we were travelling along the southern edge of the Lake Chad swamps. I saw numerous waterbirds amongst the reeds and, in one area, three troops of Patas Monkeys scampered across the road. We arrived at Fotokol, on the Cameroun – Nigeria border at about 10a.m. The border is simply a bridge over a wadi with a large notice proclaiming 'NIGERIA'. The notice also included the caution *'Drive on the left. Tenez a gauche'* because in Chad, as in France, vehicles drive on the right of the road whereas in Nigeria, and in the Sudan, vehicles drive on the left as in Britain.[4] The Cameroun Customs Office had an overpowering smell of bats, and the Customs Officer suggested that I should wait because some petrol tankers should arrive soon on their way to Maiduguri. He told me that during the 'wet season', the roads are impassable and that the Chari River often floods; because of this, all the petrol required in Chad during the wet season has to be delivered during the dry season. I sat by myself under the trees wondering where the other passengers had gone to – apparently, as I learned later, I could have walked about one mile into Nigeria to a village where there were buses. In Africa, as I knew, one has to have infinite patience.

11

NIGERIA

At 1:30 p.m., a Shell petrol tanker arrived. The driver told me that he could take me to Kano, and this sounded fine. I climbed into the cab. Next to me was a Nigerian who was sitting on the engine covering, and next to him, on his right, was the driver. I thought that this means of transport would be excellent, with wonderful views because the cab was higher off the ground than in a bus or a car. However, the next six hours turned out to be the most uncomfortable, unpleasant and hot journey I have ever made. The tanker appeared to have no springs, the engine made so much noise that it was impossible to talk or think, and the metal engine covering inside the cab radiated heat like a fire. In comparison, the 'hot' air outside seemed almost cold! Because the tanker was such a large and heavy vehicle, it was not allowed on the graded part of the sandy road but only on the corrugated sand track at the side. To make matters worse, the driver was not proficient or careful by my standards. After half an hour of this, I decided I would go no further than Maiduguri, and look for better transport there.[1]

I was unable to take in much of the scenery. At first, we passed over black cotton soil. Presumably this was alluvial soil from the time when Lake Chad was much more extensive than at the present. I suspected that all this area was flooded each year during the wet season. Several flights of Crowned Cranes sailed majestically overhead, but at this time of the afternoon there was little animal or bird life to be seen. We stopped for a few minutes at Dikwa, and then continued at breakneck speed (at least for a heavy petrol tanker on softy corrugated sand) because the driver wanted to reach the Customs at Maiduguri before dark. It seemed a strange situation: we were officially in Nigerian territory, yet we had not yet entered Nigeria through a Nigerian Customs and Immigration Post! The driver knew that if he did not pass the Customs Post by dark, he would have to wait at the Post until the following morning before continuing on to Kano. I was hot and sticky and had a headache, and was longing to get to Maiduguri and out of this dreadful tanker. Then, as the thoughts of a quiet bed, a cool wash, and no more bouncing around inside the cab were in the forefront of my mind… the tanker stuck in some soft sand. We had to cut branches to place under the tanker's wheels, and eventually we got going again. By now, I was sure that we would never reach Maiduguri before dark.

A few miles further on, the engine stopped. The unimaginable had happened – the petrol tanker had run out of petrol! In a different situation, this would have been hilarious. The driver assured us that he had more petrol in a spare tank, but, regrettably, he did not have any receptacle or hose to transfer the petrol from the spare tank to the main tank. He told us not to worry – another tanker would pass by soon and then we would be able to borrow a hose and bucket. By now it was dusk and there were only a few minutes before dark. Eventually a bus came and we borrowed a tin and transferred some petrol; but still the engine would not start, probably because there was air in the petrol line. It was only then that I discovered that the driver had no tools, no spare parts, and no drinking water with him. He was undoubtedly the most improvident driver I had ever encountered. The Nigerian who shared the cab with me, Ezekiel Olu Akintola, was also rather fed-up and he suggested that he and I walk to Maiduguri, a distance of about five miles. The driver was against this idea. He warned us… "it is much more than five miles… there are robbers about… and he could not take any responsibility if anything bad happened to us…" Ezekiel and I debated whether we should go; neither of us liked the idea of spending the night here, and there was no assurance that the tanker would start in the morning or whether we could transfer to another vehicle.

So I extracted part of my fare back from the driver, and Ezekiel and I started to walk towards Maiduguri. He balanced my suitcase on his head and we set out along the sand track in the dark. I just followed Ezekiel's obscure form a few feet in front of me. It was a dark night, and the moon had not yet risen. It was good to be walking in the cool evening air. We talked quietly, so as not to draw attention to ourselves, and I learned that Ezekiel worked for the Briggs Transport Company in Maiduguri, although his home was in southeast Nigeria. Eventually, we reached a tarmac road, and turned right. I had no idea where we were going. After what seemed a long time, we saw a light, and were overtaken by a cyclist who was a Customs Officer whom Ezekiel knew. We explained our predicament, and were told to go to the Passport Office. On the way, we passed an enclosure crowded with trucks and people sitting around fires; they had arrived after dark and were waiting there until the morning. We slumped – exhausted – into the Passport Office (now officially closed) and were revived with mugs of cold water.

At last I had arrived in Nigeria but in rather an unusual and unofficial way! One of the Customs Officers drove both of us into the centre of Maiduguri. Ezekiel thought a hotel near the bus square would be a convenient place for me to spend the night. We found the 'Verma', a sort of beer-parlour hotel. In the courtyards, the tables were crowded with Nigerians and empty beer bottles. My room was large and spartan, but tolerably clean. By now it was after 10p.m., and after a beer (which I did not really want), Ezekiel departed, and I had a 'bath'. The hotel 'waitress' brought a large supply of water so I could wash. There was no food in the hotel at this time of night, so I had to be content with some stale cake, and the last of the now-very-hard rock cakes with jam. With the fan full on – even though I had been asked to turn it off before going to sleep – I fell asleep absolutely exhausted.

I was woken by the chinking of bottles – as the hotel staff cleared up the sordid remains of last night's drinking. It was about 7a.m., and I had time for breakfast (salad 1/6d, two cups of coffee 1/-) before Ezekiel arrived at 8a.m. I hardly recognised him for he was now wearing his national costume: a long cream-coloured smock, baggy trousers of the same material, and a small blue pillbox-shaped decorated hat. Together we went over to the bus park and found a 'mammy-wagon' going to Kano. It was a converted Morris truck, full of seats at the back. Painted across the front of the cab above the windscreen were the words BLESSED ARE THE PURE IN HEART. I paid my £2 (Nigerian), said goodbye and thank you to Ezekiel, and then wandered around the Bus Park and nearby market. It was so colourful and vibrant. The market stalls were filled with goods, and the dresses of the Nigerians were aglow with colour and pattern. Everyone was talking and gesticulating; the whole atmosphere was one of animation and life. Arriving in this gaiety after the subdued quietness of Sudan and Chad was such a tonic and a contrast. Numerous itinerant sellers were walking around the bus park selling the odds and ends needed for mammy-wagon journeys – soap, biscuits, miniature loaves of bread, perfume, tea, Brilliantine (hair cream), toilet articles, magazines and torch batteries. I ordered a glass of hot Ovaltine from one seller who kept the milk and water hot on a portable charcoal stove. It was so good that I had a second glassful. No one knew when the mammy-wagon would depart, but I was quite happy to sit on a sack of millet (or something) watching the world go by and the Rainbow Lizards chasing one another and catching flies.

Amid tremendous noise and shouting and waving, we left at 10:30a.m. The cab was divided by a partition, two thirds for the driver and one third for two passengers. Unfortunately, my companion in the cab was an enormous aloof Nigerian who did not speak English. So I found myself sandwiched between the huge Nigerian and the partition. Nevertheless it was quite comfortable, not too hot, and the road was paved all the way to Kano. The driver drove carefully and slowly compared to most mammy-wagon drivers; the wagon cruised along at a regular forty miles per hour, so it was restful to look at the scenery. The countryside was densely covered with bushes and there were many large trees. The vegetation was much greener than in Sudan or Chad and many of the beautiful yellow-flowering trees that I had seen intermittently in Chad formed wonderful patches of colour among the deep greens and browns of the landscape. The single width of tarmac, bordered by wide red-coloured laterite edges, meandered gently up and down the low hills, often in large curves so that as we travelled the road behind us was quickly lost to sight behind the green vegetation.

As I travelled westwards into Nigeria, I realised that I was passing through the lands of another great ancient empire. The Kanem-Bornu Empire extended over Chad and the northern part of Nigeria, where at various times it abutted the lands of the Hausa and Fulani peoples and the Caliphate of Sokoto. The origins of the Kanem-Bornu Empire are unclear. The Kanem Empire was a state founded in about 700 AD on the eastern side of Lake Chad. At that time, the inhabitants followed a traditional religion, but in the eleventh century, travellers from the Mediterranean and Arabia brought Islam to the Empire. The fortunes of the Empire changed during the following centuries: the Empire expanded and contracted, there were many wars, and trade and diplomatic ties were expanded. In the thirteenth century, the influence of Kanem spread westwards into Bornu (now northeast Nigeria) and northern Cameroun. The Kanem-Bornu Empire, as it was now called, attained its maximum size, importance and wealth during the reign of Idris Alooma who was, by all accounts, an outstanding statesman and administrator. Many of the riches of Kanem came from the trans-Saharan trade: salt, horses, silks, glass, firearms, and copper were imported from North Africa, and cotton, kola nuts, ivory, ostrich feathers, perfume, wax, and hides were exported to the north.[2] Thereafter, the empire declined in size and importance because of internal wars and attacks from Ouaddai in the east.

Further west (now north-east and north central Nigeria, and parts of Niger) was the Sokoto Caliphate. The foundation of the Caliphate in the early1800s was a response to the gradual demise of Kanem-Bornu, and the rise of a radical mallam, Usman dan Fodio, who was supported by many Fulani and Hausa Islamists. Dan Fodio established the town of Sokoto as his capital. The Caliphate was a loose collection of about thirty emirates extending from Cameroun, throughout Nigeria north of the Niger and Benue rivers (as well as some areas south of the Niger River near Ilorin), and the eastern parts of Niger. The Caliphate lasted for about 100 years until the advent of the British colonial period in 1900.

Just to the north of the Maiduguri to Kano road was a place called Kukawa – once the capital of the Bornu Empire. At one time Kuwawa was an important and flourishing town, but now it is only a small village (with no evidence of its former glory). One of the notable travellers in Bornu in the middle of the nineteenth century who visited Kukawa was the German explorer Heinrich Barth. In early 1850, Barth joined a British expedition, together with James Richardson and Adolf Overweg, which travelled across the Sahara to Bornu (and other places) in order to establish trade relations between Britain and parts of central and western Sudan (i.e. from the region of Lake Chad westwards towards Senegal). Barth was not only an explorer – he was a scholar, author and artist; he recorded everything that he observed about the landscapes, peoples, climate, agriculture and lifestyles of the places he visited; his detailed writings provide a wonderful insight into Kukawa at a time when the Bornu Empire was declining.[3]

Kukawa was established in 1814 after the former capital, Ngazargamu, had been sacked by the Fulani in the early nineteenth century. When Barth first reached Kukawa in 1851, he was impressed by the tall white thick clay walls surrounding the town, and by a large wood and metal entrance gate. Barth's plan of the town showed that it was about three miles from east to west and about one mile from north to south. It comprised a walled eastern end, where the Sheikh and the rich citizens lived, and a walled western end where the other citizens lived. In between the two walled areas was a motley collection of clay buildings, thatched huts, and many enclosures made of clay or reeds. Surrounding the town complex were numerous little villages, farms, a huge market, a cemetery and – less savoury – an area where rubbish, dead camels and donkeys were left to rot. Water was obtained from wells. Kukawa was a huge and bustling place, said to have a population of 50,000 inhabitants.

Kukawa was situated at the crossroads of important trade and pilgrimage routes. Many people travelling to and from Mecca, and travellers crossing the Sahara, stopped in Kukawa. They brought news, stories and new ideas from far and wide. Barth met many of these intelligent and interesting travellers, and he liked to drink coffee with them and learn of their experiences. Barth was obviously very impressed by Kukawa. When he first arrived, he was greeted by the Vizier, given a small house to live in, and provided with meals and servants. Later he moved to his own house, ironically called 'the English House', in the western town. The house was made of clay and had many small rooms and courtyards. A "splendid korna-tree" provided shade, and in another courtyard there was a "caoutchouc tree". Barth commented that a troop of monkeys lived in the caoutchouc tree, and two squirrels lived in a hole at the base of the tree.[4] In the house, Barth kept (at various times) six horses and five cows.

Within a short time after his arrival in Kukawa, he was taken to the Palace to see Sheikh Umar who was a "kind, liberal and just" man. Barth had many interviews with the Sheikh and, on one occasion, he was allowed to see ancient documents that chronicled the history of Bornu. The Sheikh had a huge retinue of courtiers, concubines, slaves and eunuchs (as was normal amongst the wealthy at this time). Important people in the town were well dressed, often in magnificent robes adorned with gold stitching and their horses wore colourful harnesses. Barth gives a wonderful description of the markets. There was an immense variety of produce for sale: cloths, shirts, beads, building material, mats, leather bags, camels, horses, little boxes for storage, meat, dried fish, dura (and other sorts of grains), and fruits of local trees. (In this respect, the market at Kukawa in 1851 was very much like the market I saw in Abeché in 1965.) The main currency for buying and selling in the market was cowries and Maria Theresa dollars. At this time in its history, Kukawa was a flourishing place, complete with a bureaucracy, tax collectors and a postal system. When Barth was in Kukawa, he was able to send letters to North Africa and Europe (mostly requests for money, and for goods to sell and to give as gifts). The postal system was informal and slow but it allowed a link with the outside world. These were the dying days of the Kanem-Bornu Empire, now reduced to just Bornu. Intrigues and family rivalries were rife (just as they were in Abeché – see Chapter 9). Finally the Empire succumbed when Britain amalgamated Bornu and other regions of the north to form the Protectorate of Northern Nigeria in 1900.

The mammy-wagon stopped at several large villages for ten to twenty-five minutes for refreshments. As soon as we stopped, it was surrounded by villagers selling bread, beans, and fruit. There were also many little restaurants selling roasted chickens. I was impressed by the colour of the Nigerian clothes, especially those of the women. Most of them wore headscarves and they were covered from neck to ankle with colourful wraps or dresses. Sadly, I saw several pathetic cases of leprosy; it is a terrible disease and I was surprised that there were so many victims who had not been given adequate treatment. I managed to get water to drink, or some kind of liquid refreshment, wherever we stopped. At one place, the shopkeeper thought the local water would be bad for me and suggested that I buy a bottle of mineral water instead. If only he could have seen some of the water I had been drinking in Sudan and Chad! As I was leaving his shop, he bade me "Goodnight" and "Long Life and Prosperity". I was speaking English all the time now; French and Arabic were languages of the past – in other countries many miles away to the east.

During this tranquil part of my journey, I was able to reflect on the changes that I had observed since leaving Khartoum. Considering that the distance from Khartoum to Kano is about 2,500 miles, the changes in scenery are slight because I was travelling along the Sahel – one of the vegetation belts (or zones) of Africa. A journey of similar length from north to south would pass through many different zones with spectacular changes in scenery. Apart from the hilly regions around Jebel Marra, there was little change in the vegetation although, in the west, the vegetation was greener and more abundant than in the east. The character of the people was ever-changing: skin complexion became darker, facial characteristics changed from 'Arabic' to 'Negroid', and the white tobes of Sudan were replaced by the blue indigo cloths of Chad and the brilliantly-coloured dresses and agbadas of Nigeria. The languages changed as well: Arabic in the Sudan, French and Arabic in Chad, and English and local dialects in Nigeria. I enjoyed the Sudanese food most of all; it was more appetising and the bread and *kisra* had a pleasant consistency and taste. In Chad, the only 'bread' available was moist, solid, and grey-coloured which I found rather unappetising. In Nigeria, bread was made from yeast and plain flour (and sometimes eggs) and baked to form a soft chewy brick-shaped loaf which was enjoyable to eat. In Sudan and Chad, everyone sat on mats on the ground to eat but in Nigeria every little teahouse and restaurant had tables and chairs. The numerous teahouses bordering the roads in Sudan disappeared completely in Chad, and refreshments were available only in the larger towns. In Nigeria, little restaurants were common even in small villages. The methods of transport also varied. The powerful *suq* lorries of the Sudan were replaced by the decrepit old French vehicles of Chad, and by the mammy-wagons of Nigeria. The Sudanese drivers were undoubtedly the best, and the Nigerian drivers were the worst. The camels and donkeys of Sudan and Chad became fewer in number as the Nigerian border was approached, and bicycles became more common. The road system of Nigeria was much better than that of Sudan and Chad, and consequently more suitable for bicycles. Most of these variations were so gradual as to be almost imperceptible and it would be quite easy to travel on this 'major highway of Africa' without consciously noticing any changes at all.

Kano is about 360 miles from Maiduguri, much further than I expected. It was a shock when I learned that we would not arrive until about 1a.m. the next morning. I knew it would be impossible to find accommodation at that time of night, so I arranged with the driver that I could sleep in the mammy-wagon. From about 6p.m. onwards, when it was getting dark, I dozed and did not see much of the countryside. The road was smooth and so it was easy to go to sleep.

We arrived in the lorry park, outside the old city walls of Kano at 1a.m. It was cool by then and the park was crowded with trucks and buses and people sleeping all over the ground. It was a desolate unfriendly sight, so different from the brightness and colour, and lively chattering people, of the daylight hours. All my fellow passengers disappeared into the night and I settled down as best I could on a hard wooden plank in the back of the mammy-wagon. It was uncomfortable and windy, and I knew that I would probably be woken by about 5:30a.m. as the sun was rising. I was tired and hungry; I had not had a proper meal all day, so I ate an orange and tried to go to sleep.

Early next morning, I woke up and walked around the filthy squalid lorry park, and bought a cup of tea from a wandering salesman. The lorry park was the most disgusting place I have ever been in – there were human faeces and flies everywhere. I decided to get away as quickly as possible.[5] The mammy-wagon driver helped me find a minibus that was going to Zaria, about 80 miles to the south. The drive was rather disappointing. The excellent tarmac road was bordered with cultivation all the way, with a few large trees standing amongst the fields providing shade for the yam plants growing underneath. There were no fences, walls or hedges between the fields, just little pathways which separated one field from another. The driver of the minibus was hopeless; he had his foot hard down on the accelerator all the time and was quite perplexed when steam rose up from the engine. We had to stop several times to allow the engine to cool. Such driving, I was to learn later, is common and widespread in Nigeria. We 'stopped and started' all the way to Zaria; at each stop, some passengers (complete with their baskets, sheep and chickens) left the bus, and new passengers (with even more baskets, sheep and chickens) got on the bus. My friends with whom I was going to stay in Zaria, Hilary and Sue Fry, had advised me to get off my transport at the 'Sokoto junction' where I could find a yellow taxi to take me to their home on the campus of Ahmadu Bello University.[6] To arrive in such civilised surroundings after two weeks of travelling was an immense relief. When I set off from Khartoum, I did not know how long the journey would take or even whether it was possible.

The countryside around Zaria was beautiful. The flattish countryside was punctuated here and there by 'inselbergs' – huge rocky hills made of giant boulders and rocks, in much the same way as 'jebels' in the Sudan. Instead of arid sand between large rocky hills, as in Sudan, there were fields of crops and savanna woodlands. To my 'semi-arid' eyes, it was so green and lush, the climate was warm but not scorchingly hot (as in Sudan), and the ground was soil rather than sand. The bird life was fantastic… so many species and individuals. A special favourite was the Carmine Bee-eater, and on occasions Hilary and I watched these glorious birds at their nesting sites in the steep banks beside a local river. My host was making a detailed study of these birds and, by using special equipment, he was able to watch what was happening at the end of the nesting tunnels deep within the river banks.

The final part of my journey took me southwards. Here, I experienced for the first time how the vegetation changes as one travels southwards towards the Equator, as one vegetation zone gives way into another. My journey until now had been within the Sahel Savanna Zone, where the vegetation was similar across this great expanse of Africa except for minor changes due to altitude, changes in water availability (e.g. in wadis), and the effects of rock and shade. From Zaria to Ibadan, as I drove with Colin Wood-Robinson, we passed through the Northern Guinea Savanna Zone and then into the Southern Guinea Savanna Zone. As we travelled southwards, the trees became larger and more numerous, the species composition of the vegetation changed, and the grasses became taller and more dense. In places, there were cultivated fields of maize, beans, yams and cassava. The people who I saw in villages were very dark-skinned, with typical negroid facial characteristics – wide flat noses, thick lips and black dense curly hair. Brightness was everywhere, from colourful dresses and hats to the brilliance of flowers and birds. We passed over the Niger River bridge at Jebba, and soon arrived in the Rainforest Zone. Near Ibadan, much of the rainforest had been destroyed or modified by human activities over many decades, but the high rainfall ensures that plant growth is fast and hence some sort of green vegetation was present everywhere. My first impression of rainforest, in a Forest Reserve near Ibadan, was one of delight and awe at the size of such massive trees. I was amazed at the vastness of the canopy high above my head, and it was such a joy to breathe such delicious moist air. Some of my delight, no doubt, was because of the enormous contrast with the desert environment (in itself a fascinating and frightening environment because of its harshness) but also because of the softness of the subdued colours in the rainforest.

12

IBADAN IN THE 1960s

When I first visited a rainforest near Ibadan in 1965, I did not know that I would be living and studying in these rainforests by the following year. In April 1966, about one year after I had first visited southern Nigeria, I started a new life in the Department of Zoology at the University of Ibadan. When I first visited Nigeria in June 1965 (Chapter 11), I was overwhelmed by the masses of green luxuriant vegetation – this, no doubt was partly because of the absence of such vegetation earlier in my journey. In the rainforest, the tall trees and shrubs have green leaves throughout the year, and an open piece of land is quickly covered by herbs and grasses – and thereafter by young shrubs and trees. Lawns are green and dense, shrubs are profusely covered with flowers, creepers climb over everything, and wherever there is light, sunshine and moisture there is a riot of vegetation. It was all so exuberant and full of life! Ibadan is situated on the northern edge of the rainforest zone in southern Nigeria. It was (and still is) a huge bustling city, so very different in character to Khartoum.

The Climate

The climate in Ibadan is hot, moist and sticky for most of the time (as is typical of the rainforest zone) except during the short dry season. The timing and length of the wet and dry season is due to the movement of the Intertropical Convergence Zone (ITCZ), as it is in Khartoum (Chapter

2). The ITCZ is the leading edge of very wide band of warm equatorial air and rain that moves from south of the Equator northwards over Nigeria during the Northern Hemisphere summer, and then southwards during the Southern Hemisphere summer. The ITCZ (travelling northwards) arrives over Ibadan in March bringing the first rains of the wet season, and the rains continue as long as the warm equatorial air mass remains over Ibadan. The wet season lasts from March or April to about October; during these months there is rain every few days. The actual monthly rainfall varies; it is lowest at the beginning and end of the wet season (April and October) and highest in the middle (June to September). In August, the trailing edge of the rain band is over Ibadan and there is a reduction in the monthly rainfall (the 'little dry season'). The average annual rainfall in Ibadan is 1,120mm, lower than in many parts of the rainforest zone because Ibadan is close to the rainforest-savanna boundary and inland from the coast. (In contrast, Lagos – on the coast sixty miles south of Ibadan – has an average of 1,500mm/year, and Calabar – on the coast in eastern Nigeria – has an average of 2,700mm/year.) During the wet season in Ibadan, the average rainfall is 125-170mm/month, and in the dry season it is only 0-20mm/month (the actual amount varying from year to year). The wet season continues until the leading edge of the ITCZ returns to Ibadan on its way southwards and passes over the Nigerian coast into the Southern Hemisphere; this heralds the dry season that lasts from November to March. During the dry season, there is usually no rain (although sometimes there maybe a light shower), the air is drier, and the temperatures are cooler (especially at night) than in the wet season. The winds from the north that help to push the ITCZ southwards are laden with fine dust from the Sahara. In Ibadan, in December to February, the presence of this desert dust is known as the "harmattan" (the West African equivalent the "haboob" in the Sudan).

The temperature at Ibadan is high, but not excessively so; the monthly average temperature is 27-33°C, lower in the wet season and higher in the dry season. The daily fluctuation is small, only around seven degrees in the wet season (e.g. July: 21-28°C) and eleven degrees in the dry season (e.g. January: 10-21°C). A very important consideration is the relative humidity: it is always high – e.g. it averages around 71% in the dry season and 78-88% in every month of the wet season. Hence there is little relief from the hot humid weather, and not much chance of being cool at night, except on some days in the dry season. In such a climate, my skin was permanently sticky (except immediately after a cold bath). I sweated a lot, my clothes felt soggy, and mould appeared on everything (especially leather shoes and photographic slides and negatives) unless kept in an air-conditioned room or in an artificially dry environment.

Yoruba land

The Yoruba of southwestern Nigeria – including Ibadan – is one of the largest ethnic groups in Nigeria. The origins of the Yoruba are uncertain. One view is that they are of negroid ancestry who, with other groups (such as the Fon, Ibo and Ewe), evolved and remained in the rainforest where they were protected from raids by the Fulani, Hausa and other Hamitic tribes to the north. One result of this 'protection' is that Islam did not reach the inhabitants of the rainforest zone of southern Nigeria until very recently; even now Christianity and traditional religions remain the principal religions of the south. The physical characteristics of a Yoruba are a very dark skin, short curly hair, flat broad nose, thick lips and well-built body. They also have distinct cultural characteristics such as traditional religions (and latterly Christianity), a gregarious nature, great imagination in the arts and music, and a well-structured social system headed by chiefs. The Yoruba are immediately recognisable by their dress. Yoruba women, in particular, wear wonderfully coloured clothes. The traditional dress for a Yoruba woman consists of a *buba* (blouse) on the upper part of the body, an *iro* (wrap around the waist and legs) and a *gela* (head tie). The *buba* and *iro* may be made from the same material or different materials. There is a huge variety of materials, patterns, and textures so that walking along a pathway in any market provides a kaleidoscope of colour. The *gela*, if worn, is a very long piece of cloth wrapped several times around the head and tied in an intricate manner; often it forms quite a tall 'hat-like' structure above the head. Everyday dress is usually made of some sort of not-too-expensive cotton, but dress for special occasions is made of the most expensive fabrics or silk, wonderfully embroidered, and radiant with gorgeous colours and patterns. The standard traditional dress for men is an *agbada*, a long coat-like shirt, usually with long sleeves, which falls from the shoulders to above the knee, and long trousers. In Ibadan, many men in shops and businesses wear western-style dress, with or without a jacket. For special occasions, the traditional dress for men is as special and colourful as it is for women.

Ibadan – a general view

The countryside in and close to Ibadan is mostly flat with small hills and little streams. All around, at least in the past, was rainforest. Most of this rainforest has been cut down now and, instead, there are isolated forest trees, farmlands, plantations and houses. The old part of Ibadan has been called 'the largest village in Africa' – because it appears to be unplanned and to have expanded in a chaotic sort of way. The old-style houses are constructed of mud bricks, usually two storeys high, with tin roofs which have usually rusted with age. Little roads or lanes run between the houses in a seemingly haphazard way. There are few if any trees, so from a distance the town appears as just a mass of rusty tin roofs. A few major roads, with tarmac surfaces, and often many potholes, weave through the city. At the sides of roads there are deep open drains, necessary for draining the large amounts of water that fall during tropical rainstorms. However, these drains fill with rubbish – rotten food, plastic bags and anything else that is thrown in – and become more like rubbish dumps than drains. Inevitably, these drains produce a strong odour, especially in the wet season. Wooden planks are placed at intervals across the drains as walkways for pedestrians and animals. In the centre of the city, there are local traditional markets as well as western-style shops such as chemists, hardware stores, grocers and drapers, and electrical shops for radios, air conditioners, refrigerators and other electrical goods. There are also high-class general stores (which sell almost anything) such as Kingsway, UTC and Leventis, all of which stock many imported goods.

Surrounding 'old Ibadan' are newer areas, where the houses and offices are built of concrete blocks, with tiled roofs, and surrounded by gardens. These areas are similar in design and ambience to those found in other towns and cities in the wet tropics. The houses are large and spacious, many have air-conditioners, and have large gardens. Growing plants is easy in this warm and wet climate: *Hibiscus, Bougainvillea, Oleanders, Frangipani, Plumbago, Allamanda, Cannas, Ixora, Albizzia, Bombax* and *Caesalpinia* trees, *Aristolochia*, ferns and lilies and many

The harbour at Massawa with the former Imperial Palace.

The Asmara-Massawa train at Nefasit station.

A typical street scene in the old part of Asmara.

The steep rocks on Jebel Qeili with the Butana Plain in the distance.

Rock engraving showing eight giraffes on one of the rocks high up on Jebel Qeili.

A nomad on his camel beside one of the wells at Jebel Qeili.

Passenger coaches on the Khartoum-Nyala train.
The small child is selling tooth-sticks.

The railway station at Er Rahad, Kordofan Province, Sudan.

A market at one of the small stations on the Khartoum-Nyala railway,
with many angareeb beds for sale.

The lorry park at Nyala, Western Sudan.

The main street in Nyala, Western Sudan.

Geli Tahir and friends beside his suq lorry, Geneina, Western Sudan.

The saline lake in the crater of Jebel Marra, western Sudan, with our racouba in the foreground.

The stream at Golol on Jebel Marra, Western Sudan – an unusual sight in an otherwise arid environment.

Taratonga village on the slopes of Jebel Marra, Western Sudan.

Suq lorry piled high with sacks, luggage and
people near Geneina, Western Sudan.

The central square in Geneina, Western Sudan.

The courtyard where I had lunch in Zalingei, Western Sudan.

The Sudan-Chad customs post at Adre on the Chad border; photo was taken in mid-afternoon, it was very hot, and the customs office was closed!

The market at Abeché, eastern Chad. One of the four gates into the market is on the left.

Baskets of food and market stalls in central Abeché.

My bus somewhere in central Chad, stopped so the passengers can say their evening prayers. The countryside is very dry and hot.

A small market somewhere in central Chad. The young girl on the right has a Maria Theresa dollar on her necklace.

The bus stop at Ati, central Chad. There were many small children sitting in the shade under the trees.

My bus ticket from Abeché to Fort Lamy.

'Laisser-Passer'. The official authority allowing me to leave Mali on my way to Dakar. It is intriguing that the authorities recorded my parents' names, my profession, and when and where I was born!

A petrol tanker on the Chari River, western Chad.

The bridge over the El Beid Ebeji River on the Cameroun – Nigeria border. At
this time, traffic in Nigeria drove on the left of the road, and on the right of the
road in Cameroun and Chad.

'My' petrol tanker stuck in the sand on the main road
to Maiduguri, northern Nigeria.

Ezekiel Olu Akinola and the mammy-wagon from
Maiduguri to Kano, northern Nigeria.

A typical Nigerian scene at a bus stop near Maiduguri.

Rainforest at Olokomeji Forest Reserve near Ibadan, Nigeria.

My taxi (an old Peugeot 404) at one of the numerous police checks in Dahomey.

Accra, Ghana, from the Lighthouse, on a cloudy overcast day.

My Ghanaian mammy-wagon on the road towards Axim – running repairs!

The ferry at Half Assini, western Ghana. The ferry was the only means of transport to reach Côte d'Ivoire along the coast.

Forest track in the rainforest near Frambo, Côte d'Ivoire. The lorry and the bus (right) are stuck in the mud in front of the old Peugeot (with lots of firewood on the roof rack).

A street scene in Abidjan with trees, open air bookshops and bicycles (rather reminiscent of Paris).

My bus on the road from Abidjan to Bamako. A large depression on the right of the road is filled with water from a recent rainstorm.

Heavily laden buses waiting at the Côte d'Ivoire – Mali Customs post. My bus is in the front of the photo.

A coffee-house near the Côte d'Ivoire – Mali border.

The Niger River at Bamako with the Niger Bridge and people swimming and washing clothes in the river.

The entrance to the main market in Bamako, Mali.

The Bamako-Dakar train at Kayes, western Mali, at 6p.m. when the temperature was about 40°C.

A small traditional village near the Bamako-Dakar railway in central Senegal.

A small side-street on Goree Island, showing the Portuguese influence on the architecture of the buildings.

Le Pointe des Alamadies, near Dakar, Senegal –
the most westerly point on the African continent.

others, produce a riot of colour and textures throughout the year. In some ways, this is surprising because the soil is not good. The topsoil and many minerals have been leached over the years during the rainstorms, leaving just the poor non-productive laterite exposed on the surface. In my garden, in the University grounds, I had to add lots of homemade compost to increase the fertility of the soil; best of all, I added elephant dung from the zoo which I shovelled into sacks and carried home in the back of my car!

Day to day living in Ibadan in 1966

A typical day began with a small breakfast of paw-paw (papaya), bananas, toast and tea; the breakfast table always had containers containing Paludrine (the daily anti-malarial tablet) and Daraprim (the weekly anti-malarial tablet), as well as Chloroquine (for treatment of malaria). Morning was the best time of the day because it was comparatively cool. Even so, the large ceiling fan turned slowly, providing just enough draught to give a pleasant feel. In my office, I had an air-conditioner; this was essential for keeping books and equipment in good order, and preventing me from becoming too hot and sticky. All houses had mosquito nets over the beds and/or mosquito netting over the windows. Mosquito bites had to be avoided at all costs to minimise the chances of getting malaria.

In many ways, living in Nigeria was easy. I employed a steward and a part-time gardener. Moses, my steward, looked after the house, did the cooking, clothes washing and ironing, house cleaning, and some of the shopping. When I first arrived, news soon got around that I was looking for a steward, and several stewards who had worked for European families in the past came to the house seeking employment. Each had references from former employers. Moses seemed the most suitable and we discussed his monthly wage and conditions of service. In addition to the monthly wage, an employer was also expected to pay for other items requested by the steward, such as a bicycle to go to market, income tax, children's school fees and books, medical expenses, and perhaps even a new roof for his house in his village if required. Also, stewards employed by expatriates had their own living quarters, free of charge. Some people considered that employing staff was a form of exploitation; however, it provided many Nigerians with employment and a level of security, and it was necessary because the standard equipment of a European home, such as vacuum cleaners and washing machines, was unobtainable.

The supply of goods and services was unpredictable. Electricity to my house often failed – sometimes for unexplained reasons, and frequently during major thunderstorms. Likewise, the water supply was intermittent so it was prudent to keep the bath full of water, and I also had six buckets that were full of water. An old electric water heater was attached to the wall above the bath. Candles and kerosene lamps (and matches) were placed strategically around the house. The kitchen was small and basic – an old electric cooking stove, an old refrigerator (both useless during the frequent electricity failures) and a ceramic sink for washing up. Water was boiled in the kettle for drinking, and when dishes needed to be washed.

Communications with the outside world were minimal, as they were in Khartoum. There was a mail service for letters within Nigeria (which was rather slow), and an airmail letter service to and from overseas destinations. Airletters took about one week to reach to England. For anything urgent, a telegram could be sent from the local post office; for example, a telegram to England was delivered in about twenty-four hours. I did not have a telephone at home or in the office. The radio, both Nigerian stations and the BBC, was the best way of knowing what was happening in the world. Although these communications may sound woefully inadequate (as judged by the standards of the early twenty-first century), they did not seem inadequate at the time because no one knew anything else. In fact, it was so much better than during the previous generation when overseas mail travelled by ship, there was no BBC, and when travelling within Nigeria (or anywhere else in Africa) there were no communications at all.

The heat and humidity of southern Nigeria determined the correct dress to wear. Expatriates are not as well adapted to the climate as are the local people, although some level of adaptation may occur after several months or years (depending on the individual concerned). I wore an open-necked short-sleeved shirt, loose-fitting shorts, socks, and either sandals or shoes. When walking in the sunshine, I wore a floppy 'bush hat' and sunglasses if necessary. Sometimes, and always in the evenings, I wore a long-sleeved shirt and long cotton trousers so I was less likely to be bitten by mosquitoes. Most clothes could be made by local tailors, or purchased ready-made. Very occasionally, I had to wear a suit, with a long-sleeved shirt and a tie – not a pleasant experience!

There was plenty of food to buy in Ibadan. I ate locally produced food, and there was rarely any need to buy imported produce. There was a marvellous selection of fruits, such as oranges, bananas and papayas, and also vegetables such as sweet potatoes, yams, tomatoes, spinach, beans, and maize. There was locally produced bread, butter, milk, meat, bacon, jam, tomato paste, tinned meat, flour, and many other items. I bought locally brewed beer (*Star* and *Gulder*), lemonade (to make shandy), and other soft drinks. Many people bought imported spirits and wine (both of which were expensive). Occasionally, Dubonnet (which includes quinine!) was a favourite treat.

Gardening is easy in the tropics because of the warm weather and adequate rains (except in the dry season). I employed a gardener, Lawrence, who was self-trained and very good with plants. There seemed to be a 'gardeners' cooperative' on campus because new sorts of plants arrived unasked-for in the garden; I discovered that these came from gardens nearby (and no doubt plants from my garden went to other people's gardens!). The biggest garden chore was cutting the grass: there were no lawn mowers, so Lawrence held a short stick in one hand which he used as a support for his body when he bent over, and a long thin metal blade (about twenty-four or thirty inches long) slightly curved upwards at the sharpened tip which he held in his other hand. He used the blade in the manner of a scythe with the short upturned tip just above the ground; it was slow work and rather inefficient but the results were good. This method of grass cutting was widespread throughout the country, including on the verges of roads where teams of grass-cutters – sometimes 20 or 30 of them – worked as a group.

A shopping expedition in Ibadan

Every week I went into Ibadan to buy supplies. It was always an adventure! I usually drove in my own car from the University to a car park near the Kingsway department store. The tarmac road was in reasonably good condition; it was flanked by laterite edges and without formal pavements for pedestrians. There were many hazards driving into Ibadan. At this time (1966 and 1967), traffic drove on the left side of the road, although some taxi drivers and lorries interpreted 'left' in a rather flexible way. Taxis, minibuses and mammy-wagons had to be treated with caution because of their unpredictable behaviour. Taxis were painted bright yellow; most were rather old and battered and often carried more passengers than permitted by law. Because of the heat and humidity, all the windows were wide open, and drivers and passengers hung their arms out of the windows to cool themselves. Any pedestrian who wanted a taxi, simply waved at a taxi that was passing by; if there was room for a new passenger, the taxi swerved on to the laterite edge, picked up the passenger and then swerved out again without any warning. Minibuses were equally erratic; the main door on the left side was always open and the 'driver's mate' leaned out shouting for potential customers. 'Mammy-wagons' were large Ford or Bedford trucks with a locally-made wooden superstructure with a roof and benches for passengers; besides people, mammy-wagons were used for carrying chickens, goats, vegetables and other goods to market. Most wagons were painted in bright colours and patterns. Usually, there was a slogan painted above the windscreen or on the back, such as 'Trust in God', 'Safe Journey', 'Praise the Lord', or 'Christ be with You'. There were dozens of such slogans, all of which were meant to give reassurance to the passengers; however, the number of crashes – especially on narrow bridges at the bottom of valleys – suggested that this assurance was sometimes misplaced. There were also many people walking on the sides of the roads: women with huge baskets of produce on their heads, mothers with babies strapped onto their backs, men leading goats or cattle to markets or carrying furniture on their heads, newspaper sellers, cyclists with wicker baskets full of chickens, itinerant tradesmen with trays full of food and other consumables, and children with their satchels coming and going to school. So much humanity on the move!

Often there were white-robed Fulani herdsmen walking sedately with their gentle white long-horned Fulani cattle. They had walked south – on their way to the markets – from the north of the country. These herdsmen had a wonderful empathy with their cattle; they just talked to them and occasionally tapped gently on the flank of an animal to encourage it to move in a different direction. In contrast, if a cow had already been sold to some Yorubas, it was tied with ropes and pulled and pushed along the road and was obviously terrified by the experience.

On some of the main roads there were huge advertising billboards. In the 1960s, advertising for soap, margarine, baby foods, powdered milk, cigarettes, and drinks was particularly common. It seemed that Nigerians were very susceptible to the powers of advertising; this was particularly evident for brands of baby foods that showed a radiant-looking mother with her well-nourished healthy baby. However, it was well known that some mothers who bought these comparatively expensive baby foods did not follow the instructions; their babies were fed diluted food made with contaminated water in unhygienic glass bottles. This was one of the reasons why infant mortality was shockingly high at this time.

The most fascinating parts of old Ibadan were the local markets. There were many markets in different parts of the town, and each had a different name: Mokola, Dugbe, Oje and Mapo Hall to name a few. There was a bewildering mass of goods for sale in these markets: locally grown fresh foods, meat, fish, tinned and packaged foods, electrical goods, clothes, stationery, hardware, plastics, china, enamelware, pots and pans, cutlery, bicycles, kerosene lights, and more or less anything else you can think of. Some markets were 'specialised' and only sold one item, e.g., locally made tie-dye cloth, goats, cattle, basket work, Adire cloth, ju-ju (black magic) objects, beads, or carvings. Most market stalls were owned and managed by women, and the majority of the shoppers were women. The markets were a pageant of colour, not only the attire of the women but also the bright colours of the goods for sale. The market stalls were very simple: wooden poles supporting an old corrugated iron roof, simple wooden tables – dark with age and years of use – and a multitude of baskets, boxes, and odds and ends stored under the tables. For most items, prices were flexible and bargaining for what you wanted was the norm. The buyer bargained with the seller about the price to be paid; if agreement was reached, the buyer paid in cash. There was no formal receipt, and the seller placed the money in a piece of cloth attached to her *buba*. Most purchases were placed directly into the buyer's shopping basket without any wrapping. Occasionally, some items (for example fish and meat) were wrapped in a piece of old newspaper or a banana leaf. This sort of simple trading was much the same as it had been in centuries past.

The markets were full of children. Many of the traders were mothers with a baby wrapped in a cloth and attached to her back; others were breast-feeding a baby while attending a stall (a very common sight in Africa). Older children (perhaps six to ten years of age) often helped at the stalls or ran errands for their mothers. I often thought these children should have been at school but, sadly, not all children attended primary school because their parents were unable to afford the modest cost. At this time, primary school attendance was only 50-70%, and even fewer attended secondary school.

Markets in Ibadan were noisy! Mostly it was the chatter between shoppers and sellers, but sometimes discussions and bargaining became very heated. When this happened, voices rose and (to the non-Nigerian) it seemed as if a fight was about to begin… Yoruba people have loud voices and can be very argumentative if they so wish. Quite often, someone had a radio playing African music and pop songs; the volume was often turned to maximum so that everyone was able to hear, and no one seemed to mind or to object. Certainly the level of noise in the Ibadan markets was much louder than I heard in any other place during my travels.

Traditional Arts and Crafts

Nigeria is justifiably famous for its arts and culture and Nigerians are probably the most creative people in Africa. Each region of Nigeria has its own special art forms so that, for example, the arts and crafts of the north are very different from those of the south. In Ibadan, there were markets dedicated to specific crafts, and often travelling salesmen came to the house with a sack or suitcase of items for sale. There were many sorts of wooden carvings for sale. A well known sculptor in Ibadan in the 1960s was Akin Fakeye; he specialised in carvings, made of mahogany, depicting different Nigerian activities, e.g., a woman carrying a bowl with her baby on her back, a Yoruba man in traditional dress with his talking drum, and a horseman on horseback. All were elaborate and full of fine detail such as a lady's hairstyle, or the scarifications (tribal markings) on each cheek that identify the ethnicity of the person (a practice now discontinued). Sometimes planks of mahogany wood were carved to produce a frieze depicting aspects of Yoruba life. There were also sculptures made from ebony, a black, hard and heavy wood that 'shines' when polished. Many of these ebony sculptures were full size replicas of the famous Benin brasses which date (primarily) from the thirteenth to sixteenth centuries. The hardness of ebony allowed exquisite details to be carved; most ebony carvings are of heads, warriors in their war regalia, and important historical events. Much simpler carvings were made of cream, brown and pink wood from the thorns of two species of forest trees. Thorn carvings are small, beautifully simple and rustic, and depict every imaginable activity of the Nigerians – for example, hoeing the soil, feeding the chickens, reading a prayer board, hairdressing, travelling on a mammy-wagon or a boat, weaving cloth, cooking, and pounding yams. Carvings of calabashes (or gourds) are also a widespread art form. Calabashes are the dried outer case of the fruit of a pumpkin-like plant; they come in many shapes and sizes. After the pulp inside has been removed, the calabash can be used to store water, or cut in half to form a covered container, or cut on a diagonal to form a dish or plate. The outer surface is brownish in colour but just under the surface the colour is white; using these two colours, and sometimes pigment stains, the carver is able to carve intricate and beautiful coloured designs on the outer surface. Many traditional household utensils are carved calabashes.

Dyed textiles are a flourishing art form. Ibadan (and other towns nearby) are famous for *adire* cloth – white cotton cloth which is dyed with indigo. There are several places in Ibadan where large clay pots for dyeing are buried in the ground. The dye, made from the leaves of the indigo plant, wood ash and water, fills each pot and the cloth is 'washed' in the solution. The real art of making adire is the preparation of the cloth so that the indigo stains only chosen parts of the cloth. Before dyeing, the cloth may be tied into knots or folded on itself, or raffia is stitched on to the cloth to make a pattern, or cassava paste is painted on the cloth to prevent the dye from reaching the cloth under the paste. All these methods result in intricate patterns in white or pale blue (the non- or lightly-dyed areas) surrounded by the dark blue background (the fully dyed areas). Although there are some 'standard' designs, each dyer can add her own designs or embellishments so that each piece of cloth is (almost) unique. Many other sorts of cloth, besides *adire*, may be found in the markets of Ibadan. These come from other regions of Nigeria and are made from a variety of fabrics, and are of many colours and textures; some are woven, and others are embroidered. All of them illustrate the amazing creativity and imagination of Nigerians. In recent years, printed textiles have been imported from overseas but none of them have the vibrancy or authenticity of the locally made cloths. Another variation on how to make cloth interesting and beautiful is embroidery on shirts, dresses, *bubas* and *agbadas*; thick brown paper is attached to the underside of the cloth (to make it thicker and easier to work) and white cotton is sewn, usually with a foot-treadle sewing machine, to make patterns which look like crochet or lacework.

Beads are widely used for decoration. Small colourful spherical beads are used to make necklaces and bracelets, or are sewn as ornaments onto cloth. Beads are made of many materials: glass, metal, wood, ivory, bone, seed, stone and more recently plastic, and are available in many colours and shapes. Yorubas and all other Nigerians love colour and show great imagination in creating wonderful bead jewellery. Sometimes in the markets it was possible to find very old beads known as "trade beads"; these were made overseas in previous centuries and were used to purchase goods or to pay for labour. The best known were the wonderfully colourful and intricate millefiore beads made in Murano (near Venice) in the 1800s.

In some markets there was a huge variety of pots made of clay. These are simple and functional, and were mostly made by hand without a potter's wheel. Coils of clay are arranged in circular fashion and then beaten and smoothed before being fired in open wood fires at a low temperature. Some pots were huge and used for storing and cooling water, or for storage of food. Others were very small (lamps, little dishes) and some were decorated with designs, or coloured with strips of red or white clay. There were also wicker baskets made of cane for carrying vegetables, chickens and other produce.

Beside locally made crafts, many other crafts were brought into Ibadan from all over the country. All such crafts show marked distinct regional differences, each easily recognisable. These included woven cloth from Bida and Akwete; blankets, leatherwork and embroidered hats from Kano; and wooden carvings and furniture from Awka on the eastern side of the Niger river. I was fascinated by these crafts particularly because they were traditional, made from local materials, and so enjoyable to use and look at.

Diversity and the political situation in 1966 and 1967

The land that is now the Federal Republic of Nigeria has had many changes in name, political boundaries, and capital towns during the twentieth century while the country was under British rule. Its modern political history began in 1900 with the amalgamation of the 'Royal Niger Company' and the 'Niger Coast Protectorate' to form the 'Southern Nigeria Protectorate' (which included land both east and west of the

Niger river south of the junction of the Niger and Benue rivers). 'Lagos Colony' (which was a large area south and west of the Niger River, and not simply the town of 'Lagos') was added in 1904 to form the 'Colony and Protectorate of Southern Nigeria'. Later, in 1914, the 'Colony and Protectorate' was amalgamated with the 'Northern Nigeria Protectorate' to become the 'Colony and Protectorate of Nigeria'. At first, the colony was divided into two Provinces – Southern Nigeria and Northern Nigeria. When Nigeria gained Independence from Britain on 1st October 1960, the country was split into three administrative Regions: Northern Region (north of the Niger and Benue rivers), Western Region (west and south of the Niger river) and Eastern Region (east of the Niger river and south of the Benue river). Later, in 1963, the eastern part of Western Region was separated from the western half and named as the Mid-Western Region. If this seems complicated, it is nothing compared to the situation in more recent years (outside the scope of this account); at the time of writing there are now thirty-six States and one Federal Capital Territory.

These administrative changes were considered necessary because of the ethnic, linguistic and religious diversity in the country. There are said to be 250 to 300 tribes in Nigeria; some are large and widespread, others are small and live only in restricted geographical areas. Three of these tribes make up about 70% of the population: Hausa-Fulani (29%) in the north, Yoruba (21%) in the west, and Igbo (or Ibo) (18%) in the east. Each of these can be subdivided into smaller sub-tribes. There are about 250 languages and even more dialects. A third layer of diversity is religion; the north is predominately Muslim, and the south – both west and east – is predominately Christian (Anglican, Catholic, Methodist, Seventh Day Adventist, and others) and traditional. Tribal affiliations are very strong in Nigeria and members of a tribe bond very closely to each other; although this is wonderful in one way, it has been the source of much conflict and strife over the years.

Shortly before I arrived in Ibadan to live, I heard on the BBC World News that there had been a military coup in Nigeria on 12th January 1966. The coup had been initiated by a group of rebel junior Army officers. The first Prime Minister of the Republic, Abubaker Belewa, was assassinated,[2] and this led to the President of Nigeria inviting Major-General Aguiyi-Ironsi to form a Supreme Military Council to run the country. Major-General Ironsi's leadership lasted only until 29th July 1966 when he too was assassinated. He was replaced by Lt-Colonel Yakubu Gowan (later General Gowan) who remained as Head of the military government until 1975. The short time between when I arrived to live in Nigeria (1966) and continued on my journey towards Senegal (1967) was one of political turmoil and unrest, the prelude to the declaration by Eastern Nigeria to form the independent Republic of Biafra and Nigerian Civil War that engulfed country from 1967 to 1970.[3]

Animals in my house

The zoology of Nigeria is fascinating – so many species, so much diversity. Several species often wandered into my house and the veranda. There were multitudes of colourful Rainbow Lizards which have blue bodies, bright orange heads and beady eyes, and white, orange and black tails; they often came into the house hunting for insects and other food. At night, large Common African Toads, greyish brown in colour and with lots of warts on the skin, hopped towards the lights to catch insects. Every picture on the walls of my house had its resident gecko; at night each gecko emerged from behind its picture frame and ran up and down the walls chasing its prey. There is an abundance of birds in Nigeria (about 950 species) and many of these have become adapted to towns and gardens.[4] When sitting on the veranda and looking out over the garden, I watched and heard bulbuls, doves, plantain eaters, rollers, hornbills, wagtails, kurrichane thrushes, drongos, glossy starlings, shrikes, weavers, and several species of brilliantly coloured sunbirds. Kites frequently flew overhead. All these animals were a source of great interest and pleasure – a changing daily pageant of fascination each day.

I was studying small mammals, and in order to learn more about some of the animals that I was studying, I kept some of them at home. Often, a local person would arrive with an animal, hoping I would buy it. That is how I obtained two young Gambian Giant Pouched Rats (*Cricetomys gambianus*). These rats are large; the body length is about 35cm and the tail is about the same length. They have rather sparse brown hair on the back and flanks, a relatively large head, pointed nose, small eyes, and large bare ears (all of which gives the animal a rather 'goofy' look!). The long tail is dark on the basal half and pure white on the end half. Their common name refers to the large cheek pouches where the animal stores food while foraging and before taking the food into its underground burrow. These rats, as wild adults, bite ferociously but if handled when small and their eyes are still closed, they become tame and can be handled. My two were babies and at first were fed on warm milk from an eye-dropper; I let them sniff my hands and get used to being held and rubbed. By the time their eyes opened, they did not try to bite although at times they 'nibbled' my fingers in play. When they started to walk around, they explored the main rooms and soon learnt to pick up food (such as carrots, palm nuts and potatoes) and take it to their nest box. They were engaging 'pets', full of curiosity and fun. Moses was remarkably tolerant of them, especially since Giant Rats are widely hunted for 'bush meat' and Nigerians consider them very good to eat. I kept them for several months before releasing them in a nearby forest.

Another 'pet' was a young Palm Civet (*Nandinia binotata*); this is a small beautiful arboreal carnivore, about the size of a domestic cat, with a very long tail, dark brown pelage and black spots. She arrived as a baby in a sack. At first, she was fed on milk but soon graduated to minced meat. She was very active, climbing over the chairs and climbing up the curtains (which soon looked rather dishevelled as the threads were pulled out by her claws). She liked to cuddle up to me when I was reading a book or newspaper, but she was very wary of strangers. If a stranger (to her) came to the house, she immediately bolted into her box and would not leave until the stranger left. Sadly, one weekend when a red-headed friend came to stay, she took an instant dislike to him and attacked him. I had to lock her into a temporary cage, but thereafter, she attacked me too. I do not know what caused this immediate change in behaviour, but it was no longer safe to keep her in the house and, regretfully, I had to move her into a large enclosure at the University Zoo (which was part of the Department of Zoology) where she lived for several years with a male Palm Civet.

The countryside around Ibadan

Much of the countryside around Ibadan has been altered in recent years because of the increase in the human population numbers, the replacement of rainforest by plantations and farmland, and the increase in the size of villages and towns. Natural vegetation was present only in reserved areas, and even these were not truly natural. However, within one to two hours

129

driving of Ibadan, there were four relatively undisturbed places – Gambari Forest Reserve, Olokomeji Forest Reserve, Ado Rock, and Upper Ogun Game Reserve – which I visited as often as I could.

Gambari Forest Reserve

Gambari Forest Reserve was one of my major research study sites and I visited it once every week for many years. The reserve is about twenty miles south of Ibadan. The rainforests in this part of south-western Nigeria are officially classified as either 'dry semi-deciduous rainforest', 'Nigerian lowland rainforest' or 'Guinean-Congolian rainforest – drier type'. These terms are based on the characteristics of the trees and their environment, and by comparison with other rainforests. All rainforest trees have green leaves throughout the year, so they always look fresh and lush; however in those regions where rainfall is relatively low (as near Ibadan), the trees are semi-deciduous – meaning that they shed some (but not all) of their leaves in the dry season. The rainforests in Nigeria are part of the much more extensive Rainforest Biotic Zone which extends from the Congo basin in the east to Liberia and Sierra Leone in the west.

I always had to be in 'my' rainforest at 7a.m., just after dawn. It took about forty-five minutes to drive from home to the forest, first through Ibadan itself and then through cocoa plantations and subsistence farms with their crops of yams, cassava, maize, bananas, and vegetables. There were almost no tall rainforest trees in these humanised landscapes, although – as in rainforest – there was masses of luxuriant green vegetation. Some fifteen miles south of Ibadan, I turned off the main Lagos road onto a smaller road leading to Ijebu-Ode; at the time, this road was being widened and the forest along the edges had been cut and the graders had left wide scars of bare soil. Over several months, I was able to observe how the quick-growing 'pioneer' plant species colonised the bare spaces. Grasses, herbs, creepers and quick-growing shrubs and trees (especially *Trema guineensis* and *Musanga cecropioides* – the Umbrella Tree) soon converted the roadside bareness into a tangle of green vegetation. None of these pioneer species are long-lived; for several years, they provide shade to slower-growing longer-living rainforest species. When the pioneers die, the rainforest species are sufficiently well established that they are able to survive by themselves.

Because of the Nigerian Civil War (see above), I had problems at first getting to my study area on time. There was a night-time curfew, and vehicles were not allowed to enter or leave Ibadan between 10p.m. and 7a.m. Just north of the turn-off to Ijebu-Ode, there was a road block manned by armed soldiers. When I first encountered this, I found a line of trucks and mammy-wagons – several hundreds of them – waiting in front of me. I realised that I might be delayed for a long time, so I drove slowly past the parked vehicles until I reached the roadblock and a line of soldiers pointing their rifles at me. I guessed that the soldiers would be very fed up and bored and that some sort of distraction (like me!) would add some 'spice' to their dull lives. They asked what I was doing, and was told that I should have waited my turn at the end of the queue. I explained what I was doing, that I had work to do in Gambari, and that I had to be there at 7a.m. I asked the soldiers if they had had a good night, enquired after their families and where they lived – the normal polite conversation in African society. I knew that all soldiers smoked, so I offered them some cigarettes which they accepted gratefully. (I always carried some cigarettes in the car even though I did not smoke.) I told them I would be coming every week and asked if it would be OK for me to come to the top of the queue each time. They said that I could do this, and we parted the best of friends. They probably could not understand why a crazy white Englishman was studying mice in the rainforest, and no doubt this made a good story to tell all their friends! For all the years of the civil war, I never had any delays at this roadblock.

The dry semi-deciduous rainforest at Gambari was not dense. Once inside and away from the rampant green growth at the forest edge, I could look up towards the canopy high above my head. Botanists recognise five layers (or storeys or strata) in a rainforest, in the same sort of arrangement as in a four or five storey building. The lower layer comprises the plants growing on the *forest floor* (up to *c.* 30cm). Above the forest floor is the *shrub layer* whose upper branches reach to about 4-6m. Higher up is the *understorey* comprised of smaller trees, but none of these are as tall as the *canopy* that contains the upper leaves and branches of most of the big trees. Breaking through above the canopy are the tops of the *emergent* trees; these do not form a continuous layer because they are well spaced out. Each layer is typified by its own characteristic species and also by the young individuals of other species that will, in time, grow up into the higher layers. On the forest floor and in the shrub layer, the light intensity is low and direct sunshine rarely reaches these lower layers. Looking up through the layers of vegetation, there were only a few places where I could see small irregular patches of sky or cloud high above me. It was quite easy to walk through the forest because of the lack of dense vegetation on the forest floor and because the shrubs have a rather open structure and small leaves. The trunks of the larger trees do not have branches low down; they just rise up like thick poles, and their branches, twigs, leaves and flowers are confined to the upper storeys where there is much more light. Most remarkable of all are the very tall canopy and emergent trees, some of which have buttresses at the base of the trunk; the buttresses flare out forming big struts which support the huge size and weight of the trunk – just like the buttresses on the walls of ancient castles and cathedrals. However, if a tall tree does fall, it creates a clearing in the forest where sunlight is able to reach the ground. At such places, the warmth and light promotes the germination of the seeds of forest plants and very quickly the area becomes dense with herbs and the seedlings of future forest trees. The fallen tree itself dies and is invaded by fungi, micro-organisms and a multitude of other organisms (such as worms, beetles, insect larvae, etc.), and is soon reduced to wood fragments and pulp, and the essential nutrients of the tree are returned to the soil. It came as a big surprise to me to learn that rainforest soils are – contrary to expectations – very poor in nutrients. In fact, the majority of the nutrients of a rainforest ecosystem are in the living structures of the forest and, consequently, the maintenance of the rainforest is dependent on the very slow turnover of nutrients derived from the yearly fall and breakdown of leaves, and the decay of fallen trees and branches. The felling of trees for timber, or clearing the forest for agriculture and plantations, removes most of the organic nutrients from the ecosystem and all that remains is the impoverished lateritic soil. Although this soil may support agriculture for two to three years, exposure to the heat of the sun and leaching by tropical rain reduces its fertility to the point when it is unable to support any more crops. These basic ecological facts explain the historical practice of 'slash and burn' and 'shifting cultivation' when it was essential (and possible) to move to a new place when an older one could no longer be used for agriculture. Thankfully, rainforest has the capacity to regenerate through a slow succession of ecological change if given the chance, but it may take a century or more without any disturbance to reach the climax vegetation again.

It was essential that I checked my traps regardless of the weather, so over the years I witnessed the rainforest in all its moods. In the wet season, it was often raining early in the morning. The rain fell heavily on the leaves high above my head, and at times the noise was deafening; my assistant held an enormous umbrella over me so that any animal that I was examining (and my equipment) did not get wet. On other mornings when it was raining and the clouds were low and dark, I had to use a torch to see what I was doing. On fine mornings, it was delightful; sometimes little flocks of birds flitted through the forest. Leaves from the upper layers fell to the ground every month of the year; the highest monthly leaf fall was in the dry season (November to March) and the lowest in the wet season (April to October). It was quiet walking in the forest in the wet season (when it was not raining) because the surface was just moist brown soil with a few old broken-down soggy leaves, and lots of earthworm castes. In contrast, in the dry season, the leaf litter – dry leaves, fruits and twigs – accumulated because it was not broken down by micro-organisms, and every footstep caused a crackling noise. At this time of the year, the soil was hard and dry and the earthworms had burrowed deep down into the moister levels of the soil. But as soon as the rains began, the soil became moist, the earthworms burrowed upwards towards the surface, and the micro-organisms, fungi and earthworms rapidly decomposed the leaf-litter and the resulting detritus was incorporated into the soil. The speed at which this process happened was amazing, and within about four to five months after the start of the wet season there were hardly any dead leaves on the forest floor.

Once I had arrived at my study area and collected the forestry assistant who helped me, it took several hours to go round my grid of 100 live traps. These little traps were baited with *gari* (flour made from cassava) mixed with palm oil, a mixture that attracted small mammals into the traps. Once an animal was inside, the trapdoor closed and the animal was unable to escape; the solid roof of the trap kept it safe and dry. The object of the study was to determine the structure and demography of the community, how this might change during the year, and how each species (and the individuals of each species) interacted with each other.[4] Every animal was marked with an individual number when it was first captured; during the whole study (four years; 1967-1970), I marked 538 individuals of nine species (seven spp. rodents, two spp. shrews). Some individuals were caught only once and never seen again. Others were caught on numerous occasions (over a period of about eighteen months); these became 'old friends' and I got to know the characteristics of each of them – where they lived in the rainforest, who they were likely to interact with (e.g. others caught in the same trap at a different time and in nearby traps) and when they were breeding and suckling young. It was really fascinating and I always looked forward to encountering these 'old friends' each time I went to the forest. I enjoyed the quietness of the forest; there were only a few soft sounds when a slight breeze rustled the leaves above my head, but sadly I never heard or saw any monkeys and duikers because there was too much hunting by local people. Apart from when there was a rainstorm, the noisiest time was at night when the tree hyraxes were barking and Franqueti's Fruit-bats uttered their loud "cracked bell" call. Both were evocative calls in the stillness of the night, but neither of them was conducive to sleep.

Olokomeji Forest Reserve

Olokomeji Forest Reserve is west of Ibadan on the road to Abeokuta. Its main features are the lovely rainforest, a beautiful freshwater river studded with boulders, rocks and little sandy beaches, and its proximity to the rainforest-savanna boundary. It was a favourite place for Sunday picnics and swimming. The narrow road in the reserve is flanked with grassy verges and tall forest trees whose higher branches overhung the road. As in so many places in southern Nigeria, the vegetation was so incredibly green and verdant. Eventually, the road reaches a bridge over the Ogun river. Here, there was a wonderful view up and down the river. To the north, the river was dense with creepers, shrubs and trees, and it was difficult to walk along the river's edge. To the south, there was a series of rocks jutting out into the river, and little sandy pebbly beaches. In the dry season, when the river was low, small pools were formed amongst the rocks – a lovely place to sit and contemplate and to watch Mona monkeys playing in the forest trees overhanging the water. Nearby was the old government resthouse, built in colonial times, where District Officers, Forest Officers and others stayed when on duty. It was a grand two-storey solid brick and cement building, with wide verandas and a corrugated iron roof. I stayed here on two occasions when conducting surveys. In the olden days, the resthouse was furnished with solid wooden furniture, beds, and mosquito nets. Outside there was a kitchen and accommodation for the staff who accompanied officers when on 'safari'. Even in the post-colonial era, there was still some furniture and the resthouse was a lovely place to stay.

Olokomeji is situated at the present northern edge of the rainforest zone. Near the bridge, a little track runs northwards through the rainforest, and within a few hundred yards, the rainforest gives way to savanna grasslands. Here, it was an open environment, with scattered savanna trees, tall grasses and herbs. The transition was abrupt, rather like leaving the end of a dark tunnel and emerging into the light and sunshine outside. The relationship between rainforest and savanna is complex and dynamic. During each of the Ice Ages, when ice covered much of the northern regions of the world, the rainforests of West Africa retreated southwards so there were only a few isolated refugia on the coast where rainforest ecosystems survived. At these times, the savannas also moved southwards. During the intervening Inter-glacials, when the ice retreated northwards and conditions were warmer and wetter than during the Ice Ages, the rainforests spread northwards. At these times, the rainforest-savanna boundary was much further north than it is at the present time; there is good evidence that rainforests extended north to what is now the middle of Nigeria (i.e. *c.* 10°N). Likewise, the savanna zones also moved north into what is now the Sahara desert. The evidence from pollen cores, the composition and distribution of rainforest trees in different parts of the rainforest zone, and the current distribution of rainforest animals, suggest that there were about eight Ice Ages and eight Inter-glacials during the last one million years. This complex history means that the rainforest is very heterogeneous – not homogeneous as it may seem to be to the casual observer. The structure of the rainforest, and where it exists, is also dependent on soil type, topography, rivers and drainage patterns, geology, local rainfall and altitude.

For example, there is 'riverine forest' along the edges of rivers in the savannas where soil moisture promotes growth and limits the effects of fire, and there are 'relict forests' around the bases of large inselbergs where the rain flows off the rocks and creates a mesic environment similar to that of a rainforest. In more recent times – that is during the last two or three centuries – the rainforest on the rainforest-savanna boundary has been cut by humans to establish plantations and farms. This 'derived savanna' would still be rainforest if it were not for human activities. Likewise, human activities have allowed 'savanna-like' habitats to become established in the rainforest zone, e.g., roads allow grassland to spread into the forest, and clearing of forests for plantations and agriculture results in spaces (like those created when a rainforest tree falls naturally) which can be invaded by non-forest species. Over the last few centuries, the extent of the rainforest has diminished drastically around Ibadan and elsewhere in the rainforest zone. It is a very sad reflection on the destructive nature of human beings.

Many years ago – in 1929 – an experiment was initiated at Olokomeji Forest Reserve to investigate the influence of fire on the vegetation of the "derived savanna". At this time, it was uncertain to what extent fire influenced the plant composition and density of the vegetation at the rainforest-savanna boundary. Three experimental plots were established, each about half an acre in area; at the beginning, each plot was burnt and the trees were coppiced or removed.[5] Annually, in subsequent years, one plot was burned early in the dry season (when soil was still moist and there had been no drying effect of the dry season), the second was burned late in the dry season (when soil moisture was low and the tall grasses were very combustible), and the third was the control plot with no burning at any time. The Early Burn plot developed into a savanna with large trees, there was no scarring on the trees as result of the fire, and there was a rich diversity of plant species. The Late Burn Plot developed into a more open savanna, with only fire-resistant trees and there was a lesser diversity of plants. The Unburnt Plot developed into a dense mass of vegetation with many grasses and creepers, and a mixture of savanna and rainforest trees. The results were much more complicated than this brief description suggests; each plot varied with respect to species composition, growth rates, soil fertility and nutrients, and fire regime. This experiment, and others like it in different parts of Africa, has shown that fire and human influences have been major factors in determining the structure and species diversity of the vegetation (and the animals that live in the vegetation) throughout the continent.

Ado Rock

Ado Rock was another lovely place to visit. It is a huge granite rock (shaped rather like an upturned pudding basin), with a very steep slope on its eastern side. Ado Rock is further north than Olokomeji Forest Reserve and is surrounded by Guinea Savanna, farmlands and plantations. When I went there for the first time – a Sunday excursion with the 'Inselberg Scramblers Club' – we left the cars near a little village and walked through the farmlands to the eastern side of the rock. There were about a dozen of us, two of whom were very good scramblers. One of them quickly scrambled up the slope with a rope – he reminded me of a Rock Hyrax, a rabbit-sized small mammal that lives on inselbergs and has specially adapted feet for running up and down steep rock slopes. The rope was then lowered down the slope so the rest of us could be helped up the rock. The rock was smooth and dry, and there were a few small clumps of grasses and herbs that, amazingly, managed to survive in little cracks and crevices in the rock surface. I managed to reach the top (tied to the rope all the time!). The view from the top was fantastic: miles and miles of wooded savanna, broken here and there by little villages and farmland; but because it was the dry season, the far distance was obscured by the haze of the harmattan. In some places, smoke from grass fires lit by local people to burn the old dead grass stems and promote the growth of new grass, merged into the harmattan haze. The top of Ado Rock is a huge slightly undulating bare rocky plateau, with some patches of grass and, surprisingly, a few big trees. I wondered how the trees managed to get their roots into the rock, and how far the roots penetrated downwards. There was also a 'swimming pool' in a big depression of the rock surface, and also many smaller dry depressions that would have held water in the wet season. By the time we reached the top of Ado Rock, I was very hot and also hungry and thirsty. Much to my surprise, one of my companions opened his rucksack and produced a large pineapple; he cut it into thick slices and we each had a slice – it was so tasty and refreshing! After exploring the rocky plateau, we descended (on the western side) along a small path which meandered around rocks and boulders and eventually arrived at the village where we had left our cars. It was a relief that we did not have to descend the steep eastern slope while attached to a rope! Inselbergs became great favourites of mine, mostly because of the openness of the scenery, the fresh air and the views – all of which were in stark contrast to the darkness and high humidity of the rainforest.

Upper Ogun Game Reserve

The high density of humans in Yorubaland meant that there were only a few places that were untouched by human activities. Hunting for 'bushmeat' was common and consequently there were very few larger species of mammals in most places. Upper Ogun Forest Reserve was the least disturbed area near Ibadan, although grass fires (some early and some late in the dry season) occurred in most years. The reserve straddles the Ogun river, further north than at Olokomeji. The vegetation is Guinea savanna; some areas were mainly grassland with scattered bushes and trees, others (especially on higher ground) were primarily woodland; low lying areas were swampy, and there was riverine forest bordering the Ogun river. The drive into the reserve was along a narrow bush track that gradually descended towards the river. It was very beautiful with lots of variation in scenery. At the end of the track, close to the river, was a cleared area with a hut... and nothing else. On my many visits, I was self-contained with my camp bed, mosquito net, cooking utensils, food, medical supplies, binoculars and camera. Water was collected in buckets from the river. The river here was a series of rocky platforms and boulders so it was easy to cross over to the other side. In the dry season, the river was just a series of isolated pools, some several meters long but, in the wet season, the river flowed all the time. The colours and textures of the vegetation ranged from the deep green of mature leaves to the pale translucent green and gold of new leaves, the beige and ochre of tall dead grass, the bright emerald of newly sprouted grass, and (after fires) the black of burnt wood and charred grass. Walking along the river's edge was delightful, especially in the early morning when the air was cool and there was dew on the grasses. It was quiet except for the songs and calls of birds, the rustling of leaves or grass as an animal passed by, and the flopping splash of a fish jumping in the river. Sometimes there were loud noises – the alarm call of a Kob or a Rock Hyrax, the crashing of some large unseen creature in the undergrowth, or the bark of a Baboon. I walked slowly, placing my feet carefully to avoid making unnecessary noise, and I stopped every fifty meters or so to listen and look around. Mammals which I saw during most visits, but never in large numbers, were Kob (*Kobus kob*), Bushbuck (*Tragelaphus scriptus*), Waterbuck (*Kobus ellipsyprymnus*), Red-flanked Duiker (*Cephalophus rufilatus*), Grimm's Duiker (*Sylvicapra grimmia*), Patas Monkey (*Erythrocebus patas*), Grivet Monkey (*Cercopithecus aethiops*), Gambian Mongoose (*Mungos gambianus*), Ground Squirrel (*Xerus erythropus*), Baboon (*Papio anubis*) and Rock Hyrax (*Procavia ruficeps*) – these last two only on an inselberg known as

Yemosa Rock. One of the many joys of Upper Ogun was that there were no tracks for vehicles (other than the single track coming in) and so one had to walk everywhere. It is much more fun and enjoyable to watch animals in the African bush on foot rather than from a vehicle, but it takes longer and more skill. There were so many birds within a few miles of camp. An ornithologist friend recorded 130 species but I recorded only about 50 species. On one visit, I recorded in my notes: *'There was a pair of African Fish Eagles with their one youngster; they are marvellous birds with a high-pitched piercing cry; there were Senegal Thickknees (a type of Curlew) which have a very characteristic cry which continues throughout the night, and also Hadada Ibises which make an extremely loud drawn-out call (Haa... haa... haa... daa) when alarmed'*. (I was not particularly fond of Hadadas because if one of them saw me as I walked quietly beside the river, its alarm call frightened everything else away!) Many species were very colourful – Kingfishers, Rollers and irridescent Splendid Sunbirds. Others I saw frequently were Bateleur Eagles, Buzzards, Kites, Green-backed Herons, Bee-eaters, several species of Doves... and so many more. Another great joy of Upper Ogun, while still half asleep under my mosquito net, was listening to the glorious dawn chorus as the sun was rising and the bright stars were fading.

Yemosa Rock was a favourite destination from camp. It was only a small inselberg, but it was isolated and the only place nearby to view the surrounding savannas. After crossing the river, the rock was in full view and it was easy to walk directly towards it, and then climb to the top. The rock was almost bare except for irregular patches of grass. There were a few rocky overhangs that shielded small caves where the Rock Hyraxes sheltered. I liked to sit high up on the rock, while having a drink and munching biscuits, and scan the savanna woodland below me; often I could see Kob and Bushbuck, but they were always far away and looked small, even with my binoculars. Quite often, Baboons were sitting close to me on the rock, and Rock Hyraxes were feeding and calling to each other. It was a place of peace and calm.

13

GHANA AND WESTWARDS TO THE CÔTE D'IVOIRE

The third part of my journey to the westernmost limit of the African continent began on 22nd June 1967.[1] I did not have much luggage: the same old blue suitcase, a shoulder bag with documents and camera, and another bag with food and drink. On this journey, I did not have any rock cakes! I travelled from Ibadan to Lagos to stay with a friend for one night before leaving Nigeria. Lagos is not an attractive place. It is built on a swampy area near a big lagoon, and the climate is warm and humid (more so than in Ibadan). The town is very densely packed with houses and humans, it is noisy and vibrant, and the roads and traffic are chaotic. Because my travels would take me through several West African countries, I had to visit several embassies in Lagos to obtain visas; at this time, it was essential to have a visa for each foreign country. Also I wanted to find out where I could find transport going to Ghana.

At 6a.m., my friend drove me to Offin Street, a small street in a dirty sordid part of Lagos near Carter Bridge. There was only one taxi going towards Accra – a decrepit old Peugeot 404 (a very popular make of car in West Africa at the time) that had obviously seen better days. To my surprise, there were no buses travelling to Ghana. Eventually, we left at 8a.m. There were six of us in the car including me: the driver Jean Baptiste De Bonza was from Togo and the others were Nigerians. I sat in the back seat with two other passengers. The springs of the seat were old and un-springy and rather uncomfortable. But despite its looks, the car went well and Jean Baptiste was a competent driver. Our route passed through many miles of typical square African houses made of mud or concrete with rusty corrugated iron roofs. These were interspersed, occasionally, with modern well-built dwellings. Little shops, street sellers, cyclists, pedestrians, and old cars spewing exhaust fumes were everywhere. It took one and a half hours to reach the outskirts of Lagos. From then on, the road to the Nigeria-Dahomey border was tarred and in good condition. There was no rainforest here now; all this area was secondary scrubland with many palm trees grown for their palm oil and palm nuts, and numerous small farms of maize and citrus fruits. At Ota, we stopped to buy some bread. Beside one of the stalls was a man with an enormously enlarged scrotum (visible through his clothing) resulting from the disease elephantiasis; although I knew about the disease from textbooks on tropical diseases, this was the first example that I had seen.[2]

We had to stop briefly at the Nigerian Customs Post at Idiroko; my guess was that the driver knew the Customs Officers and so they did not bother to look at our credentials. One mile further down the road was the Dahomey Customs Post where the Customs Officers looked in all our cases and handbags.[3] They even searched our clothing and pockets! It took a full hour before we were allowed to continue. The tarmac road in Dahomey was full of holes, very uneven, and drifts of sand covered the surface in places... so we had to swerve frequently from side to side to avoid the many hazards. Now, of course, we had to drive on the right-hand side of the road because Dahomey is an ex-French Colony. Later on, the driver left the main road and drove along small sandy side tracks and through little villages hidden amongst the coconut palms; supposedly this was a short-cut, but it also had the advantage that we avoided the potholes in the main road. Eventually we arrived in Porto Novo, the original capital of French Dahomey. Porto Novo seemed to be a neglected run-down place – maybe this was because we wandered through the back streets. The Portuguese founded Porto Novo as a slave-trading centre in the eighteenth century, and there are still some old Portuguese buildings in the town. In 1863, as a result of attacks by the British in Nigeria, the local people sought protection from the French and the country eventually became a French colony. The name, Porto Novo, suggests that it is situated beside the sea; but in fact it is inland and connected to the sea at Cotonou by a series of lakes and channels and many mangrove swamps.

At Porto Novo, the road turned southwards towards the coast – an excellent road through the swamps and lagoons. By now I was getting used to driving on the right-hand side of the road. Cotonou is a pleasant well-laid out town with wide streets lined with trees and large buildings. All the cars here were French-made and many of them were the small Citroen 'Deux Chevaux' which were so popular with the French. Several boys were carrying long loaves of French bread on their heads. As in Chad, I came to realise that ex-French colonies are still very French. We stopped in Cotonou for some unexplained reason, and so I took the opportunity to eat some bread, jam and bananas (my staple diet on these journeys when nothing else was available).

From now on, the road remained close to the coast. We passed mile after mile of coconut palms, their long fronds waving in the winds coming in from the Atlantic Ocean. On our left, we could see the waves crashing on the beach. Lots of small fishing villages lined the shore; the huts were simply made of coconut fronds. The sun and sea had weathered these little homes to the same colour as the sand so they tended to be almost invisible at a distance. Along the beach were piles of coconut kernels and coconut husks, fishing nets hung up to dry, and log canoes pulled up on to the soft sand. In some places, piles of dried fish were heaped up on the sand, presumably waiting for transport to market. We had to stop on the way to Lomé for innumerable police checks, for Customs and Immigration formalities at the Dahomey-Togo border, and to mend a puncture. In Togo, the road runs within a few yards of the turquoise and aquamarine-coloured sea; it was really beautiful and just like a brightly-coloured postcard of the perfect tropical beach. In the late afternoon, we reached Lomé where I said goodbye to our Togolese driver at the Togo-Ghana Customs Post.

We had no troubles at the Ghana Customs Post, and the Ghanaians were most helpful. I was able to change £5 Nigerian for 16 New Cedis (£N1 = NC 3.20); as I realised later, this was much better than the official bank rate (£N1 = NC 2.0). There is a huge gateway at the entrance to Ghana with the words 'Welcome to Ghana' on the entrance side and 'Bye Bye Safe Journey' on the departure side. I had to wait around for some time until I found a green-coloured Mercedes Minibus going to Accra. At the border, travellers gain one hour because Ghana (and all countries further west) are on Greenwich Mean Time whereas Nigeria, Dahomey and Togo are on West Africa Time. I watched the other passengers milling around, each looking for transport to their various destinations. My diary continues:

The country from the border to Accra (and beyond) – but also in Dahomey and Togo – is part of the 'Dahomey Gap', a natural area of grassland which is different to the rest of the West African coastline which is bordered by rainforest and, in places, by mangrove swamps. The presence of grassland is due to many factors – the position and angle of the coastline in relation to the prevailing winds from the Atlantic, the old Precambrian rocks underlying the soil, the current rainfall patterns, and the influence of former climates. As we continued westwards towards Accra, driving on the left side of the road again as in Nigeria, we passed through the extensive grasslands, broken here and there by farmlands and by thick vegetation bordering the swamps and watercourses. By now, there was low cloud and rain; dusk was approaching, and visibility was limited. The road was excellent but, as in Dahomey, we encountered police road checks (five of them) between the border and Accra, a distance of only about 100 miles. We crossed the superb bridge over the Volta river after paying a toll fee, and then entered the 'Accra Highway' (Ghana's version of the M1 motorway in Britain). On our left were the lights of Tema, the new port of Ghana and soon after, I could see the lights of Accra reflected on the low cloud base above the city. On the outskirts of Accra, we passed the airport – a blaze of lights – and the bus stopped at a Mobil petrol station where the driver said I could find a taxi to the University. It was pouring with rain but a kind policeman helped me to find a taxi. By now I was beginning to realise that everything worked much more efficiently in Ghana than in Nigeria, and that Ghanaians are kind helpful people.

The University of Ghana (the oldest University in Ghana) is five to six miles out of town on the road to the north of the country. In recent months, I had been in correspondence by airmail with Professor Ewer, the Professor of Zoology. Since I did not know exactly when I would arrive, he gave me his address on the University campus so I could find my way to his home. I did not know where I would stay, so I was slightly surprised when Professor Ewer's steward showed me to a bedroom in the Ewers' house. The Professor and his wife had gone to a student party, so the steward gave me a much-needed supper. When I learned that the Ewers would not return until about midnight, I decided to write a note announcing my arrival. It was an odd feeling going to bed in a strange house having never met my hosts. I was so tired that I went to sleep immediately and did not meet the Ewers until breakfast.

It was impossible to do justice to Accra in a couple of days, but during those two days I had a happy and informative time. The University is built on the side of a hill so there are wonderful views of the flat countryside around, although for much of the time, the view was obscured by low cloud and rain. The University buildings are built in a uniform 'Sino-African' style – walls are white-washed and clean and the high roofs are terra-cotta or orange-coloured and reminiscent of a Burmese temple. This uniformity is not monotonous – rather, it gives a feeling of cohesion and oneness. The buildings are set in beautiful spacious parkland with many trees and lawns. My impression of Accra is that it is a much more pleasant city than Lagos – better designed, cleaner and neater. Many avenues have large trees, and the curbstones defining the edges of the roads are painted white. The most notable places I visited were the Ambassador Hotel (new and expensive!), Jamestown near the docks, the Lighthouse (which I climbed to see the view over the city), Lighter Point (where passengers from ocean-going liners disembarked from the lighter (a small boat) which ferried them from the liner to the shore), and Christiansborg Castle where the Governor lived when the Gold Coast (as it was then called) was a British colony. There was also Black Star Square (or Independence Square) which commemorates Ghana's independence in 1957, and 'Job 600' an enormous hotel that the Prime Minister Kwame Nkrumah ordered to be built for an international conference. The hotel is now empty and useless and, according to some Ghanaians that I spoke to, a monument to Nkrumah's folly and misuse of funds. In the city, I saw many women dressed in red, apparently the funeral dress for the former Army Chief of Staff, General Emmanuel Kotoko, who was killed earlier in the year. Periodically, there are repeat funerals for him.

As a zoologist, I was particularly interested to see the Cane Rats and Giant Pouched Rats that Dr Griff Ewer, the Professor's wife, was studying. These rats are fascinating animals. Griff had several Cane Rats (*Thryonomys swinderianus*) which were kept in a large enclosure so that she could study their behaviour. Cane Rats are big (adults: 3-5 kg) with large heads and rough textured pelage, and look rather like giant Guinea Pigs. They feed almost exclusively on the thick stems of grasses; a stem is held in one front paw and fed sideways into the mouth while the other paw guides the stem to the correct place. The powerful incisor teeth cut the stem on a diagonal.[4] Cane Rats live in savanna grasslands but they can become pests when they live in sugar cane fields where they delight in eating the sugar cane stems. They are hunted for 'bush meat' – a favourite source of protein for Ghanaians and for many other people in Africa.

On one afternoon, I visited the Botanical Gardens. There is a magnificent collection of palms, many of which were in flower, the huge inflorescences hanging down almost to the ground. Sadly, a heavy afternoon rainstorm, so typical of coastal West Africa, curtailed my visit; but I saw enough to appreciate the marvellous botanical richness of this part of the coast. It is particularly impressive when it is pouring with rain!

After two days in Accra, I set off again. I was not certain how I would travel to Abidjan. The normal route for vehicles is northwards to Kumasi and Sunyani and then, after crossing the Ghana – Côte d'Ivoire border, southwards through Abengourou to Abidjan. However, this route forms two sides of a triangle. It seemed to me that a shorter route along the coast should be possible and more interesting, even though there seemed to be no road through the lagoons on the Ghana-Côte d'Ivoire border. No one whom I talked to in Accra knew whether it was possible to travel to Abidjan this way, but it seemed worth trying; if all failed, I could retrace my steps and go north. Before leaving, I called in at the Customs Office in Accra and asked if there was a Customs Post at Half Assini – the end of the road in Ghana. 'Yes there is,' I was told. 'Can I travel this way to Abidjan?' 'Yes, you can.' So with this heartening news, the Professor took me in his ancient Morris Minor car as far as Cape Coast where he was going to give a talk. It was a dull day, with low cloud drifting in from the sea, and intermittent rain. The normal brilliant tropical colours had faded in a wash of pale grey, and the scenery was very sombre. Rolling low hills of grassland stretched away to the north on our right, quickly to disappear in the mist. Some vultures were sitting beside the road, and in places there were red peppers placed out to dry by the local farmers – an unexpected touch of colour in the drabness! The new road bypassed most of the places on my map – Swedra, Winneba and Saltpond – which was disappointing because I thought my journey would be very close to these places all the time. Near to Saltpond is the village of Abandze where there is the ruin of Fort Amsterdam set on a hill close to the sea.

The coast of Ghana is very different from the other coastlines of West Africa because of the large number of forts, castles and trading posts that were established in the early days of European exploration and trade. At the time of my travels, I did not know enough about this aspect of history, but my interest was stimulated by the brief sightings of some of the forts as I travelled westwards; later I was able to read about their fascinating history.[5] The earliest of the forts in Ghana was Elmina Castle built in 1482 by the Portuguese. It was built, as were all the others, for trade and as a statement of sovereignty. Portugal was not the only European power to build castles; the Netherlands, Denmark, Brandenburg (later part of Prussia), France, Spain, Sweden and Britain also built castles during the fifteenth to eighteenth centuries. There are about twenty castles and forts along the coast, some in excellent condition, others are in various states of decay. Throughout these centuries, castles were attacked, exchanged, and sometimes sold to another European nation. Elmina, for example, remained as a Portuguese possession until 1637 when it was attacked and taken over by the Dutch. It remained as a Dutch possession for nearly 250 years until, in 1872, it became part of the British Gold Coast (1872 – 1960). The situation – of changing ownership and changing allegiances – was rather similar to what was happening on the European continent at the time. At first, the castles and forts were used as trading bases in order to purchase gold and ivory (hence the early names of Gold Coast and Côte d'Ivoire) and West African pepper. These commodities were traded for beads, mirrors, knives, rum, guns, ammunition, and other products from Europe. When the Americas were being colonised, the trade was mostly in slaves who were transported to work in the sugar plantations. The slave trade became the most important and infamous export from the Gold Coast (and other parts of West Africa). It was promoted by the slavers, but with the assistance of some local chiefs and merchants who captured the slaves, often far inland from the coast. The number of slaves transported from the whole of West Africa is estimated to be about six million. But, in addition, many died during capture, or while being held as captives in the forts, and during the sea crossing to America. When slavery was abolished in 1807,[6] the castles and forts lost their purpose. Some are still maintained in good condition as grisly but important reminders of the horrors and cruelty that befell so many West Africans at the hands of Europeans.

The name 'Ghana' is a very ancient name in West African history, but it was not used for the present nation of Ghana until after Independence in 1957. The original Ghana referred to a huge Empire which existed from *c.* 300 AD to 1200 AD. It was located in the far west of West Africa in what is now Mali and the eastern part of Mauritania. The details of its origin and foundation are debatable, but it was a great trading nation with trading routes to the west coast, across the desert to North Africa, and along the Niger river to Timbuktu and other towns further downstream. At the time of its foundation, the Ghana Empire followed some sort of traditional religion but, in about 1000 AD, Islam was introduced by the Almoravids from the north-west of Africa (the region now known as Morocco). However, the invasion by the Almoravids destabilised the Empire and it gradually disintegrated. Most of the original Ghana Empire was incorporated within a new empire – the Mali Empire (not to be confused with the modern nation of Mali). The name 'Ghana' was chosen for the modern nation by Kwame Nkrumah because the old Ghana Empire was a symbol of greatness and wealth in West Africa – even though modern Ghana is geographically a long way from the original Ghana.

In Cape Coast, I said goodbye to Professor Ewer and found my way to the centre of the town to find transport to Takoradi. Beside a petrol station, I found 'Abide With Me', an Austin minibus bound for Takoradi. While waiting for the minibus to depart, I ate my lunch of bread and jam. The forty-five miles to Takoradi passed through more grasslands, a narrow western extension of the Dahomey Gap, with palms growing beside the beaches. At Elmina, I saw the well-preserved old castle in the distance, but sadly I was unable to visit it because the minibus did not stop. Further on, we passed the Komeda Sugar Factory which, according to a notice on the roadside, was managed by 'Technoexport – Czechoslovakia (Prague)'. It seemed strange that Czechoslovakia, at that time a Communist State behind the Iron Curtain, was running a sugar factory in an independent African colony. Beside the road, in several places, the local people were selling red-coloured shrimps. We arrived in Sekondi and then Takoradi. I found both places rather unattractive – probably because they are major ports. Also it was raining, and the lorry park was a sea of mud. I was glad that I had decided that I would not stop here. Thankfully, the last lorry of the day to Half Assini in the far west of Ghana was about to depart. This lorry was very similar to a Nigerian 'mammy-wagon' and the only seat left was on a plank at the back of the lorry. I clambered up, squeezed myself into the remaining space and placed my case under the plank amongst the chickens and the baskets of food and fish. The weather was overcast and it was threatening to rain.

At first, the road followed the coastline, and after a little while we turned off on to the 'New Axim' road further inland. The grasslands of the Dahomey Gap were replaced by scrubby bushland – the sad remnant of what was once wonderful rainforest. The bushland alternated with swamps and extensive patches of reeds. This was wet soggy country and, of necessity, the road was built on ridges well above the waterline. In some places, there were low hills and the road passed though deep cuttings. Everywhere was green and luxuriant, similar to the country close to the Nigeria-Dahomey border. Axim was a small and delightful looking place – rather rural and off the beaten track. A superb old castle, Fort St Antonio, stands near the sea. It was built by the Portuguese in about 1515 and later was taken over by the Dutch and finally by the British in 1872. I was sorry that there was no opportunity to visit the castle, but I could see the turrets, white walls, and gun emplacements.

So far, the road had been good tarmac and it was fairly comfortable sitting in the back of the lorry, but after Axim, the road degenerated into laterite full of potholes and puddles. The distance from Axim to Half Assini was much further than I realised from my map and I feared that we would not arrive until very late. When we arrived at the Ankobra River, we had to wait for an hour before the ferry arrived. There was a sign showing the prices for the ferry (in New Pesewas [NP]; 100 NP = 1 Cedi):

Lorries	40
Car	25
Bicycle and rider	6
Cattle	6
Sheep, goat, pig	3
Passenger	3
Load	1
Timber, per log	20
Lumber [sawn, per piece]	1

While waiting for the ferry, I talked to a Swiss man in a Peugeot car. He worked at the Vegetable Oil Mill at Esiama, further along the road towards Half Assini. The Mill produced coconut oil. Surprisingly, he did not know how long it took to reach Half Assini because he had never been that far. This lack of local knowledge about the country, how long it took to travel from A to B and the state of the roads was something that I encountered frequently during my journeys. By the time the ferry arrived at 6:30p.m., it was almost dark. My fellow passengers chewed dried fish and bread as we bumped along. By now, the road was very bumpy and the lorry was sliding all over the road in the liquid mud. At one place, where we had stopped, we barely started again because the wheels had sunk lower and lower into the mud. There was another problem too – the driver had to stop frequently to fill the leaking radiator using a broken leaky plastic bucket. As time passed – and it became darker and darker – the lorry stopped more frequently to drop off passengers and their loads. At each stop, the passengers quickly disappeared into the darkness as if they had never been. I wondered where they lived and what they did – this part of Ghana seemed so remote and out-of-this-world. Soon there were only a handful of us in the back, and by the time we reached the Police Station at Half Assini, I was the only one left. It was 11:30p.m. and the electricity had been turned off. The driver could not think of any place to take me, but he suggested I might be able to sleep in a cell at the Police Station!

As luck would have it, the (sleepy) policeman on duty told me that some teachers from the secondary school would be coming soon and he thought I could sleep at the school. When the two teachers arrived (to find out why one of their pupils had been arrested), they took me back to their house in the grounds of the school. We walked about a mile through the sleeping town; there was no noise except the crashing of the waves on the beach. One of the teachers, James Ackah, had read Classics at the University of Ghana and had been teaching at Half Assini for about a year. We sat and talked and drank coffee for about an hour and then I went to bed. I certainly had not contemplated that I would spend the night in a comfortable bed with sheets after such a long journey. Unfortunately, I woke at 5:30a.m.; after a wash, I looked at some of James' books before we had a good breakfast of porridge, bread, jam and tea.

149

James showed me around the school and then the school bus took me to the Customs Post adjacent to the Police Station. I had to change all my Ghanaian currency into 'Communauté Financière d'Afrique' francs (CFA francs) because it was illegal to take cedis out of Ghana. I had twenty New Cedis (equivalent to about £20) and these were exchanged for 4,000 CFA francs. I was told that I had to get a bus from Half Assini to Jewi (Gyawue) wharf, but the bus would not leave until later in the morning. The beach was nearby, so I went for a walk along the pale golden sands that sloped gently down to the sea. Large coconut palms swayed in the breeze on the landward side. Further along the beach, to the west, I noticed the blackened rusty form of a ship resting on its side. It was just a mass of dark and rusty metal, with no superstructure and nothing to identify it. Sea and spray lapped at the side of the wreck, and water entered through the holes on the side of her hull. Later, I found out that this was the wreck of S. S. Bakana, a cargo ship of the Elder Dempster Line.[7] She ran aground in bad weather and was wrecked on 27th August 1913 while carrying a cargo of wood from West Africa to Liverpool. Two hundred yards further away there was a huge villa surrounded by a tall concrete wall (shutting out all the view!); apparently this was President Kwame Nkrumah's country retreat. The beach was lovely with hundreds and hundreds of crabs scuttling around on the sand; but the weather was overcast with low grey clouds scudding in from the sea so it was not the sort of day to linger on a 'tropical beach'. On my return to Half Assini, I found a bus about to leave for the wharf. Much to my surprise, the road from Half Assini to the wharf was excellent tarmac, such a contrast to the dreadful road from Axim. I was told that the road was built on the orders of the President so that, if he needed, he could make a quick exit from Ghana to Côte d'Ivoire!

In spite of the remoteness of the wharf, there was a vast sign 'Welcome to Ghana' to greet passengers coming from Côte d'Ivoire (see Chapter 1, Note 3). Since almost everyone who travels this way is a local and familiar with the border country, the notice seemed rather redundant. The ferry from Frambo in Côte d'Ivoire, four miles away on the other side of the lagoon, had not arrived so I spent most of the day sitting on a log, reading and watching the world go by. Almost nothing happened! There were several soldiers and policemen guarding the border (except there was no border to guard), and about twenty other passengers waiting for the ferry.

No one knew when the ferry would come because it belonged to the Côte d'Ivoire and there was no way of contacting the other side of the lagoon. Four of the men waiting for the ferry looked like dark-skinned Sudanese. They wore white *jelebeas* and round flat-topped hats made of orange or white felt which, I was told, are popular in Côte d'Ivoire, Upper Volta and Mali.

The ferry arrived at 4:30p.m., leaving only just enough time to cross the lagoon before dusk. It was small, about 20 ft long with a covered front and seats across the back. Loading the luggage and passengers took forty-five minutes and, by the time we left, the sky was looking very stormy in the west and the light was failing fast. The ferry took thirty minutes to reach Frambo which turned out to be just a simple village, and very different to Half Assini. The Customs Officer looked at everyone's luggage, except mine; he told me there was no resthouse in the village but I could sleep in the Customs shed if I wanted to. There was no bed or light, but I found a rather dirty mattress which I thought would be more comfortable than the concrete floor. With one of my fellow travellers (from Côte d'Ivoire), I walked down the one 'street' in the village. The only food we could find was some bread, a pineapple and a few bananas. The mud and thatch houses were old, dark, and decrepit, and appeared rather sinister in the misty half-light of the forest night; they looked as if they would disintegrate in the next heavy tropical storm and fall to the ground. We found one 'coffee house' with a table and bench and settled ourselves there to eat 'supper' in the light of a kerosene lamp. There was nothing to do or see after supper, so I went to bed in the Customs shed. I was very glad of the old mattress, my sheet sleeping-bag and my inflatable pillow. There were lots of mosquitoes so I had to snuggle down deep in my sleeping bag with my head completely hidden. I did not know where the other passengers had gone to – I assumed they must have been locals who lived in the village.

I was woken at 5:30a.m. and told that a car had arrived and it was going to leave for Abidjan soon. Six of us squeezed into the car and we set off along the muddy track through the rainforest. The trees were some of the largest and tallest I had ever seen in West Africa. It was magnificent; the early morning light filtered through the mist and dew creating a wonderland of soft green and grey. I was in the middle of the back seat, and next to me was a huge African woman who spent the whole time suckling her small child. The track was muddy and slippery. On one part of the track, a big timber lorry was stuck in the mud, and a bus (which had tried to pass the lorry) was also stuck. The bus passengers had got out and were cutting vegetation to place under the wheels so it could gain some traction; liquid mud was flying in all directions! Our car eventually edged its way past the lorry and the bus and we continued on our way. We arrived in Aboisso, on a main road, at 8.15a.m. Here we – the six of us – transferred to another Peugeot car, which sped along a smooth tarmac road towards Abidjan. In the past, all this area was rainforest, but now it was dull secondary bush and plantations. It was a sobering ride after travelling through the lovely rainforests; such changes are (ironically) called 'progress'. We passed several small villages, crossed a toll bridge, and skirted around the coastal city of Grand Bassam. Everywhere seemed rather civilised and clean and there was none of the mess and clutter as there is in many Nigerian villages. The tall white buildings of Abidjan were visible a few miles away – a blinding contrast to the greens, browns, and greys of the 'bush'.

The driver took us to the edge of the city, and I found a taxi to take me to where I could find a bus to ORSTOM (Office de la Recherche Scientifique et Technique Outre-Mer) at Adiopodoumé which also housed the 'Centre Suisse'.[8] The taxi driver charged me 800 CFA francs – very expensive by African standards but as I knew from travelling in some parts of Chad, 'French Africa' is expensive compared with 'British Africa'. Eventually I found a bus going westwards on the correct road; the driver did not know ORSTOM or Adiopodoumé, but he thought he knew a place called 'Centre Suisse'. So I paid my fifty CFA francs and hoped for the best. In fact, the village of Adiopodoumé is only just outside Abidjan, and ORSTOM is south of the village on the edge of a large lagoon and surrounded by a lovely patch of rainforest. My hosts, Pierre Hunkeler and his wife Claudine, lived in a delightful wooden house overlooking some of the forest and the lagoon. After an excellent lunch – it seemed particularly good because I had not eaten since my meagre supper the previous night – we walked through the grounds of ORSTOM and visited some of the well-equipped laboratories. The French have always been particularly good at setting up excellent scientific research stations in their colonies, and maintaining them after each colony attained independence. In the evening, at dusk, we sat on the veranda and watched Mona Monkeys playing in the trees beside the lagoon – a sight I had rarely seen in Nigeria.

I found Abidjan to be a very pleasant city and much nicer than Fort Lamy – the only other French African city that I knew. Some parts were very French, and other parts were very African. We drove into town in Madame Hunkeler's small red Citroen 2CV car (2CV stands for 'deux chevaux-vapeur', i.e. two horse power). The 'deux-chevaux' has a strange 'ladybird' shape, is high off the ground, light in weight, and uses very little fuel. These cars were very common in French African countries at the time, and had the delightful nickname of 'Ugly Duckling'. We stopped at a newspaper stall where French ladies were selling newspapers and postcards, and nearby were local traders selling carvings and leatherwork. There were several delightful park-like gardens full of tropical flowers in the middle of Abidjan, and nearby many French shops sold a huge variety of goods imported from France. The price of these goods was astronomically high by my standards, and I assumed that the salaries of French people in Côte d'Ivoire were equally astronomical. Clearly these shops were for the French and not for the Africans. We also went to buy vegetables at a local market; it was stocked with a greater variety of perishable goods than one ever saw in Nigeria. There were some huge 'supermarket stores'; one of them – 'Monoprix' – sold foods imported mostly from France, and I did not see anything that was imported from Britain. It was surprising to see a French girl working at one of the checkout tills, with five African girls at the others. No doubt in the years to come, the French influence will decrease and the African influence will increase.

IFAN – short for 'Institut Fondamental d'Afrique Noire' – is another excellent French institute in Africa that specialises in the languages, cultures and history of 'French West Africa'. It maintains many museums, cultural centres and scientific research stations in the former French colonies of West Africa, including in Abidjan. We visited the museum where there was a superb collection of carvings and masks. Many of them were symbolic and tokens of fertility. There were also copper weights for weighing gold, each weight marked with symbols to denote the equivalent weight of the gold. Another intriguing exhibit was a balaphon – a sort of xylophone made of calabashes of different sizes to which are attached strips of wood that act as a keyboard. When a padded stick hits one of the wooden keys, the calabash (which acts as a resonator) emits a musical note. The smallest calabash gives the highest note and the largest gives the lowest note. The instrument was several feet in length and had about twenty calabashes. An African musician in the museum gave me a demonstration using two padded sticks; he was able to make the most delightful melodic tunes with great dexterity.

14

CÔTE D'IVOIRE TO MALI

I was sorry to leave Abidjan. It was a delightful place, full of interest, and a pleasant interlude between two long stretches of travelling. I woke to find it was raining hard; the garden and nearby forest were sopping wet – as it often is in this climate. Madame Hunkeler drove me to the Mali Embassy to collect my visa. Much to my surprise, it was ready but it cost CFA 2500 francs (£3. 14. 0). In order to pay, I had to cash some travellers cheques at a local bank (£1 = 650 CFA francs; my £20 cheque = 13,000 CFA francs). One great advantage of travelling in the former French colonies is that most of them (except Mali) retained the CFA currency after independence, rather than fragmenting into a multitude of different national currencies. On the way to the lorry park, we got a puncture so we had to change the tyre in the mud and rain, and consequently I started my journey wet and dirty! At the kiosk at the entrance to the lorry park, I bought my ticket to Bamako and was told that the bus would leave at 3p.m. The price was only CFA 3,000 francs, and an additional CFA 300 francs for my suitcase. The bus was an old-fashioned Renault; it was box-shaped with an almost vertical front, a cab, and a back part with rows of seats where the passengers sat. The sides were open to the elements but there were canvas awnings, tied at the top, which could be rolled down if it rained.[1]

Madame Hunkeler returned to Centre Suisse, and I wandered around the local market where the floors and benches were tiled. There was the usual assortment of goods, all African in origin. Outside there were huge coloured umbrellas and stalls where food and drink could be obtained, as in a typical French café. I found a little restaurant run by a Korean lady; the walls were plastered with posters advertising Korea. I spent a long time there consuming excellent coffee, camembert cheese and long French bread.

Often nothing happens on time in Africa, hence the phrase 'Africa time' which is as important a concept in Africa as 'Greenwich Mean Time' is in the rest of the world. Certainly, this afternoon was a good example of 'Africa Time'. At 5p.m., I wrote in my diary:

Some of the passengers have disappeared and the bus is not full, so the 'chef' and the driver decided that the bus would not leave until tomorrow morning. They took me to the 'Hotel du Nord' just behind the bus park. The hotel overlooks plantations on the edge of town. It is rather decrepit – dirty paint and not that clean – but probably adequate for the night. There is one main room lined by orange, black, and white tiles, wooden tables covered by horrid red-flower design tablecloths, and plastic flowers. Two old refrigerators stand against the wall beside the bar. The bedrooms are on the next floor at the top of a small winding staircase. Mine has a shower and a washbasin, and a double bed with clean pink sheets. I have to pay CFA 800 francs for the night (= sterling 23/-).

There was time before supper to try a local beer. So I bought a bottle of 'Braconi' – fairly potent and without much fizz – and read a scientific paper given to me by Griff Ewer on Ground Squirrels. These squirrels live in grasslands and semi-arid regions in West Africa; they are delightful animals with a complex behaviour and social system. Supper was rather tough Abidjan chicken with peas (250 CFA francs), black coffee (35 CFA francs) and another beer (CFA 75 francs). There was hardly anyone in the hotel restaurant, so I went to bed at 8p.m.

I woke several times during the night because the mattress was squishy and saggy, and it formed a U-shape when I lay on it. It was not conducive to sleep! I got up at 6a.m. and had bread and coffee for breakfast (all that the hotel could offer) and returned to the lorry park. The bus was still there, and numerous people were milling around. The street vendors were selling food, lengths of cloth, torches, sunglasses, finger rings, clothes, washing things and perfume. One vendor was selling iced drinks that he kept cool by having a big block of ice dripping icy water on to the drink bottles below the ice block. In the park, there was a barber, a shoe-cleaner, and even a podiatrist if you wanted your fingernails or toenails trimmed. I could not discover why the bus was not ready to leave or how passengers had booked – nobody seemed to know anything! At 10a.m. four Arabic-looking people arrived in a taxi with an immense amount of luggage – metal trunks, collapsible beds, and mattresses – which were hoisted onto the huge luggage rack on the top of the bus. It was far too much luggage for just four people.

At 12:20 p.m., we left the lorry park at long last... but only to stop 50 metres down the road at a petrol station. By 12:55p.m., we had petrol, oil, air in the tyres, and had completed (yet another) police check. We were ready to go... but the driver had disappeared! Finally we departed, just twenty-five and a half hours late. But, of course, time does not matter in Africa!

The road to the north begins by going westwards along the coast for about twenty miles towards Dabou. It is disappointing country, just secondary forest and plantations. At one place there was a patch of grassland, which looked out-of-place in this environment. We stopped again just before Dabou where there were some roadside stalls. I bought a coconut. Many of the coconuts were germinating (a rather unusual sight) and I could see the 'seedling' emerging through one of the germination pores (round dark brown depressions at one end of the coconut husk). I had lunch (bread and jam, two bananas and part of my coconut) while the driver changed the oil and the Muslims said their prayers. I wondered why the oil change was not done previously – after all, there had been plenty of time!

The first part of the drive northwards was through more (man-made) grasslands and large oil palm plantations. The tarmac road was excellent so we sped along trying to make up for lost time. After two hours or so, the first savanna trees appeared indicating that we had left the rainforest zone and had reached the 'derived savanna'. By the time we arrived in Toumodi, we had entered the Guinea Savanna. Everywhere was green and fresh and very pleasant. The countryside, uncluttered by plantations, was spacious and small hills added greatly to the beauty of the scenery. We stopped for evening prayers, and soon after there was a heavy rainstorm. We had to stop again to roll down the canvas sides of the bus so that we did not get soaked. I was unlucky because the roof leaked just above my seat, and the rain dripped into my lap. I wrapped myself in my plastic raincoat, but still felt rather wet and soggy. At Yamoussoukro, we had to halt by the side of the road because the driver was unable see anything in the blinding rain and mist. As soon as we started again, we had to stop for (yet another) police check; the policeman ordered us to get out so he could look inside the bus. This journey was a succession of stops and starts!

Bouaké was one of the larger towns on the route north. It appeared to be a well-laid out town with trees lining the road, restaurants and two cinemas. It was dark by now and the driver wanted to continue without stopping, probably because he knew there was a good restaurant at Katiola, a few miles further north. At the restaurant, some of the passengers consumed salad and soup, but I thought that salad would not be a good idea while travelling (for obvious reasons – 'tummy plavers' are all too common in this part of the world!). From Bouaké northwards to the border, the road was deeply corrugated laterite, and the bus bumped and rattled and swayed from side to side all the time. Somehow I managed to get some sleep although the lights as we passed a town or village woke me up.

I knew from my map that we would pass through Ferkessedougou. It was such a lovely sounding name and I wondered whether it would be as lovely as its name. When we arrived at 2:30a.m., a thick mist had descended and it was impossible to see anything much except in the headlights of the bus. Huts with thatched roofs lined the deserted streets. It was quiet and there was no one around at this time of night. A few streetlamps cast faint rays of light and I wondered why streetlights were considered necessary in such a remote place. There was the inevitable police check, but in fact nothing was checked. I think I must have slept for about three hours until our bus arrived at the Côte d'Ivoire-Mali border. My first impression on waking in the half-light of dawn was seeing *Acacia* trees – a sure indication that we had left the northern limit of the Guinea Savanna and were now in the Sudan Savanna and in a different climatic regime.

The Côte d'Ivoire Customs Post at Koronami was just a collection of mud huts. We had to wait, together with six other Renault buses, so I took the opportunity to walk along the laterite road. The grasses and trees were wet with dew and rain, and the fresh cool air was lovely to breathe. I did not walk for long, and on my return to the customs hut, I found a lady who was selling a sort of hot porridge made from maize meal. It was good and warming. The Customs Officer appeared eventually looking tired and weary, and he did not know what to do with so many buses and passengers! He looked at my visas for Dahomey and Senegal, but not for Côte d'Ivoire. Unless I had asked, he would not have stamped my passport to show that I had left Côte d'Ivoire legally.

A few kilometers further on, there was a sign 'Bamako 465km' and the road turned from being rough laterite to a smooth wide tarmac – a real treat after bumping about all night – and then we reached the Mali Customs Post. The intervening country between the two Customs Posts is a sort of no-mans-land, neither one country nor the other! We stayed at the Mali Customs Post for about three hours. The place was so disorganised. Lots of people, buses and trucks were waiting under the trees, and no one seemed to know what was happening. When eventually we were attended to, most of our suitcases, except mine, were opened; it was most amusing to see that the inside lids of many suitcases were covered with pictures from French magazines – mostly of white naked women and elegant buildings. I assumed that the cases were purchased like this, and the local people like cases with pictures inside. We had to change our CFA francs because Mali had issued its own currency after a prolonged crisis with France. The Mali currency had been devalued and was now practically worthless except in Mali (1,000 CFA francs = 2,000 Mali francs [MF].) I spent some of the three hours at a little coffee house, and I talked to two missionaries and two French teachers from Bamako who were travelling by bus from Bamako to Abidjan.

The road north from the Customs Post was excellent. The country was relatively unspoilt savanna with grasses 1-2 ft tall, all gloriously green. We passed a few villages of square mud huts with pointed thatched roofs and small round thatched huts for storing maize and other crops. Surrounding each village were fields of maize and groundnuts, and also derelict ground where the trees had been cut for firewood. The bus was stopped at a police checkpoint, and the driver had to pay several hundred francs before we could continue, supposedly because one of the documents was not in order. At the entrance to Sikasso, the only proper town on the road to Bamako, we were stopped at another Customs Post, and had to pay a 200 MF bribe before being allowed to go to the Customs yard (for yet another check); here we had to pay 1,000 MF in order to continue. None of us were pleased about this but if we had not paid we might have been delayed all day. Corruption is very evident in Mali and it seems a necessity of life here!

We stopped for an hour in the Sikasso bus park where several passengers departed and some new passengers got on. I ate some of my bread and jam, and drank some coffee in a 'restaurant' at the park. It was hot and windless, and for once I was feeling hot too. A further delay was a detour to the house of one of the 'bus boys' (for no apparent reason). Then, at long last, we reached the outskirts of the town, and hoped that there were no more customs and police checks.

For the whole afternoon, we sped westwards through the Sudan savanna, over gently rolling hills with long gradual inclines up and down. At the top of one hill, the extensive view was lost in the distance by warm haze. The sky was a brilliant blue, and the vegetation was green and clean – July is the middle of the 'wet season' – and by this time of year the leaves and grasses are at their greenest. The dense growth of grasses hid the earth from where they grew so the scenery looked not unlike an English pasture. The road was almost straight for miles on end; there was hardly any traffic and few villages. Some areas were flooded by the recent rains, and in places there were glimpses of the old laterite road. Mushroom-shaped termite mounds emerged above the grasses near the roadside – and there must have been thousands more that I could not see. I learned later that this new road was financed by an enormous Development Bank loan when Mali severed relations with Senegal; this severance meant that no goods could be transported along the Bamako-Dakar railway or road network. This new road, on which I was travelling, linked Bamako with the coastal ports of Côte d'Ivoire. Now – at the time of my journey – diplomatic relations have been restored between Mali and Senegal, the railway and the roads were functioning again, and the new road is hardly used at all. Near one of the villages, I saw two bullocks pulling a plough… a sure sign that agriculture here had not changed over many centuries.

At 6p.m. there was yet another stop at a Customs Post; every time we were stopped, the procedure became more and more ridiculous and pointless. Every piece of luggage was taken down from the roof rack. I stood around watching, slightly bemused by the proceedings. I wanted to see how thorough the check was going to be… in the end no one looked at my case. What a complete waste of forty-five minutes! Later, we stopped for coffee – thank goodness for all these little coffee stalls and 'restaurants'! By the time we left again, it was already dark. The tarmac had now degenerated into lots of holes, and the bus bumped and rattled a lot more than previously. At

9p.m., we stopped at another Customs Post. Most of the passengers got out and disappeared into the darkness, and it was some time before I realised what had happened. I found a policeman who told me that the driver was asleep and was too tired to go on (not surprisingly), and we would have to wait until the morning before moving on. There was nowhere to sleep and I was very hungry. Luckily I found someone with a huge pot of stewed meat. It smelt excellent, so I paid 100 MF and thoroughly enjoyed a huge lump of meat and lots of gravy which I mopped up with bread. Then I stretched out on one of the seats of the bus and slept moderately well until 5:30a.m. Some of the other passengers reappeared soon after – I had no idea where they spent the night – and we departed at 5:50a.m. just as it was getting light.

I knew that I was entering the country of the three greatest empires of the past in West Africa.[2] Looking at the dry rather desolate scenery around me, with nothing old and substantial by which to remember the glories of the past, it was difficult to believe that great empires had existed here – the same sort of 'difficulty' that I experienced earlier in the journey. The three empires collectively spanned about 1,300 years, from about 300 AD with the founding of the Empire of Ghana to the demise of the Empire of Mali and the subsequent rise and fall of the Empire of Songhai in the early 1600s. The history of these empires is one of internal power struggles, wars, conquest and capitulation. The Ghana Empire predated the other empires and was the smallest in geographical extent but one of the most enduring (see chapter 13). The Empire of Mali arose as a result of the disintegration of the Empire of Ghana; at its height, it was much larger than the Empire of Ghana extending from the Atlantic coast eastwards to the bend in the Niger river. It covered about 1.2 million km^2 and included the modern states of Senegal, southern Mauritania, Mali, northern Burkina Faso, Gambia and western Niger. (Modern Mali includes some of the lands of the old Empire of Mali, and is about the same size although with a different configuration.) The empire was very wealthy because of the gold mines in its territory, and its trading links across the Sahara. There were a series of Mansas (Kings or Emperors in the Mandika language) during the life of the Mali Empire; the best known of these was Musa I (Mansa Musa) who ruled Mali from about 1312–1337 AD. During these years, Mali reached the height of its power and wealth. Mansa Musi is best remembered because of his immense wealth, his pilgrimage to Mecca over the Sahara when it is recorded that he took 60,000 men with him (including 12,000 slaves), and the building of the great mosques in Timbuktu and Gao which still stand today. The Empire of Mali gradually collapsed so that by about 1500 AD it was completely taken over by neighbouring Songhai. The Songhai Empire was the largest of the three great West African Empires; it enjoyed a period of peace and prosperity until about 1600 AD when Berber forces from Morocco invaded the Empire. The Moroccans eventually withdrew and for nearly three centuries there were a series of smaller states, none of which assumed much importance – there seems to be a paucity of records for this period. The French invaded in 1901 – the period of European colonial expansion into Africa – and the old Songai Empire became part of French West Africa. The histories of these three Empires are intricately intertwined; all are characterised by invasions, wars, periods of wealth and greatness, famous leaders, and gradual decline – only to be taken over by a new political entity. All of this is not obvious to the traveller in the 1960s – only the few museums that I was able to visit gave a hint of the rich history of these lands.

My breakfast was just one orange – all that was available – but I knew it would be not too long before we reached Bamako. The country here showed all the signs of environmental degradation due to bad farming, cutting and burning. We stopped only once – to give some petrol to another bus; while this was happening, some of the passengers cut themselves 'tooth sticks' from suitable bushes near the roadside (see also Chapter 6). It was 60km to Bamako, and when we reached the top of a hill, I could see the Niger River in the distance. We had to stop at another Customs Post a few kilometers from Bamako, and while we waited I drank some coffee at a wayside café full of flies. The Customs Officer told me that all these checks were necessary to deter people from buying goods in other countries, and therefore spending their francs outside Mali. An hour and a half later, we set off again accompanied by two policemen on BSA motorcycles. We lost both of them along the way! I was unable to fathom what they were meant to do. We could hardly get lost, and it was highly unlikely that any of us were sufficiently dangerous or undesirable to require an escort. As we got closer to Bamako, I saw many donkeys and donkey-drawn cars taking produce to market. We passed several very ancient French lorries with huge front mudguards and big headlights on each side of the bonnet. Finally we reached the Niger River and crossed over on a wide and spectacular bridge into the tree-lined boulevards of Bamako. The bus finally stopped at the Customs Office beside the railway station. It was 9a.m. The journey from Abidjan had taken forty-four hours!

My first task was to find somewhere to sleep. I did not know my way around, so the Customs Officer took me to the 'Bureau de Tourisme' where I bought a town plan (200 MF). We returned to La Gare (railway station) where I knew that the 'Buffet de la Gare' offered cheap accommodation (800 MF/night), but unfortunately there were no vacancies. So I took a taxi to the 'Hotel Majestic' where I obtained a room for 1730 MF/night. Although more than I wanted to pay, I had a large and airy room, a high ceiling with a ceiling fan, two beds, a shower and a washbasin. My shirt, which I had worn for more than two days, was more dirt than cotton, and it tore in several places when I took it off – I left it in Bamako when I departed! After a much-needed shave and shower, I changed into clean clothes and went in search of breakfast. It was wonderful to have good coffee, French bread and butter (350 MF).

Bamako is lovely. Most of the main streets are lined with trees, usually mango or neem trees. Both species of trees have dense dark green foliage so that, from a distance, the centre of town looks like a forest with only a few buildings jutting above the treetops. The roads are tarmac, but the edges are just sand. Although it is the capital of Mali, Bamako seemed like a French version of a Sudanese provincial town, like Nyala or El Obeid. But there are some good well-designed buildings that add character and substance to the town. I met quite a lot of French people walking about. During my explorations of the town, I found the American Embassy; the embassy was looking after British interests because in 1966 Britain severed diplomatic relations with Mali after the Rhodesian crisis. I talked to the Consul and signed my name in the Visitors Book. From the embassy I walked back to La Gare to enquire about trains to Dakar in Senegal. La Gare is a magnificent colonial-style stone building with 'Chemin de Fer de Dakar au Niger' in large gold capital letters on the front façade. I was told that the next train would depart in three days time, which meant I had almost three days to explore Bamako. Next door to La Gare was the Soviet Showroom – an overt example of the desire of the USSR to have a presence in Africa. It was filled with Soviet-made machinery and Soviet literature; all of it looked very dull and drab.

Back at the hotel I had a 'Salad Nicoise' – olives, sweet peppers, onion, boiled egg, tomatoes, parsley, olive oil and vinegar – for lunch; it tasted so good after the bland bleak meals of the last two days. And then I slept all afternoon!

In the early evening, I visited M. Macher at the 'Departement des Eaux et Forêts' and talked to him about conservation and mammals in Mali. There was hardly any information about the parks and reserves of Mali, and there were no checklists, but he promised to find something for me before I left Bamako. Afterwards, in the cool of the evening, I walked over the Niger River bridge,[3] the same bridge that the bus had crossed earlier in the day. For part of the way I was given a lift by the Director of Radio Mali who kindly stopped and asked if I wanted any assistance. I was looking for a housing estate where one of the teachers I met at the Customs Post had a house – he had said that I could stay in his house if I so wished. The estate was a scruffy region of shacks, more like stewards' quarters in Nigeria. I found the house, knocked on the door, and talked to the steward. The house was very sparsely furnished and unattractive; I decided that I would be better off at the hotel in the centre of town.

The sun was setting as I walked across the bridge again. I was amazed to see lots of African Straw-coloured Fruit-bats flying over the river. Many of them were flying close to the water surface and seemed to be dipping their hindfeet into the water. They were large, dull brown in colour with a wingspan of about two feet. During the day, the fruit-bats rested in the upper branches of the big trees in the centre of Bamako. Sometimes they were quiet; at other times they emitted twittering vocalisations. At dusk, in contrast, when the bats began to fly, the noise was so loud (because there were so many fruit-bats) that it was almost impossible to stand under a tree and hold a conversation with anyone. I learned later that these fruit-bats (scientifically named *Eidolon helvum*) arrive in Bamako at the beginning of the rains in April and stay until the end of July. At maximum, there are probably up to a million of them. They depart in July and are assumed to fly southwards where the trees are fruiting later and for a longer time than in the north. While in this part of Mali, they feed on the fruits of trees in the city, including mangoes.

On my return to the hotel, I found a note from Charles and Joan Bird (whom I did not know) asking me to come to dinner with them. I had forgotten that when I was having breakfast, a young American lady asked if I was David McGill (who I was not!); she told me, he was an American

Peace Corp Volunteer from Gabon and was due in Bamako after travelling from Abidjan. We talked together for a few minutes and I told her what I was doing. So it was a great surprise to be asked out for dinner. The Birds had a lovely house in a pleasant area of Bamako. Charles Bird was based in Bamako for two years while studying the languages of Mali. David McGill (who I discovered had booked the last available room at 'Buffet de la Gare' only a few minutes before I arrived) was also there, and we decided to travel together to Dakar. I went to bed at midnight but the mosquitoes and the heat (even with the ceiling fan on all night) were not conducive to a good night's sleep.

There was heavy rain in the early morning and the streets around the hotel were flooded. After breakfast, I visited the bookshop to buy postcards and a book on Mali, and then I walked to the post office to buy stamps. Later in the morning, Charles and Joan took me to a ceramics factory on the outskirts of town. On the way, we passed the airport where several Russian-made Ilushin aircraft of Air Mali were lined up in front of the air terminal. The laterite road to the ceramics factory looked and felt like tomato soup after so much rain. The ceramics factory was built by North Korea, and started production about one year before. The plates, cups and saucers that I saw were better quality than I expected, and all were for sale locally. The background colour of the ceramics was grey, not white; I was told this is because there was no suitable whitening pigment in Mali. Besides tableware, there were lots of ashtrays with maps of Africa or Mali on them.

On returning to the centre of town, I visited the IFAN museum. There were many lovely pieces of Malian arts and crafts but the museum was dirty and dusty and no one seemed interested in the collections. With care, thought and some work, the museum could be excellent and informative. Finally, for this morning, David and I went to the railway station to buy our train tickets to Dakar, but we were told that no tickets were available so our names were placed on the waiting list. On reflection, we decided it would be better to buy first class tickets because accommodation in second class would be very crowded and very hot. But – as usual – there was a complication; tickets can not be issued without a *'Laissez-Passer'* (i.e. permission to leave the country) which we had to obtain from the police. By this time, the Police station was closed... so we went for lunch at a little Lebanese restaurant full of flies, but at least the Kafta (minced beef with onion, parsley, black pepper and salt) and salad were good. After an afternoon sleep – almost obligatory here at this time of year, we returned to the police station which necessitated walking along the railway lines for 200 yards. We were told to return tomorrow, but I was very insistent, and in the end I persuaded the policeman to give us our *Laissez-Passer* straight away. The rain began to fall as we walked back through the town to the bridge. I watched the fruit-bats again as they emerged from the trees, and took some photos. We had supper in 'The Aquarium' restaurant – good but expensive (900 MF plus 20% tax = 1080 MF).

On my last full day, I wandered around Bamako taking photos; later I was told that photography was not allowed and that I might have been arrested! Evidently, the policemen were not aware of this regulation, because some of the photos were taken while they were watching. A little cobbler in the market mended my sandals for me while I waited.

The Jardin Botanique, close to Bamako Zoo, is delightful and I spent a happy hour there looking at plants before walking to the zoo next door. Much to my surprise, the zoo was well laid out, had lots of trees and vegetation, and many large Whipsnade-style enclosures that provided plenty of room for the animals. In places, huge boulders and rocks emerged from the ground, and some of the enclosures had been landscaped round these natural features. There was an extensive view across the zoo to the Niger River. I made a list of the species of mammals that I saw; there were twenty-two species of African mammals and one yak, as well as many species of birds and reptiles. I wondered how and why a yak from the Himalayas came to be in Bamako.

I had lunch at the Lebanese restaurant again – omelette, salad and bread (300 MF), and then the usual afternoon sleep. Later, I walked to the bridge to watch the fruit-bats again. By 4:30p.m., they were becoming very noisy and the first bats were beginning to fly. I watched them scrambling about among the branches at the tops of the trees. Many of them spent several minutes fanning their wings before flying. I never became tired of watching these bats: the vast numbers, their antics in the trees, and their determined flight with slow wing beats were mesmerising. In the market nearby, I bought some mangoes and tomatoes for the train journey; and then I visited M. Macher again who gave me lots of useful written information about the Parks of Mali that was unobtainable elsewhere.

Finally I collected our tickets and wagon-lit reservations from the station, and enjoyed a drink of Martini and soda with M. Oudot who owns a wireless shop close to the offices of the Departement des Eaux et Forêts. His living room was just like a living room in France; we sat round a table with his wife and some of his friends. They told me that Mali had degenerated since independence, and that many foreigners had departed. Hardly any goods were being imported now, and most of the shops were running out of stock. This was obvious to me because of all the empty shelves in the shops that I visited. M. Oudot was an interesting person because he collected fish from all over Mali for the Natural History Museum in Paris.

The mangoes that I bought in the market in Bamako were the best that I had ever encountered, far better than any mango I had eaten in Sudan and Nigeria. They were huge and about six inches long; the flesh was a rich orange in colour, extremely juicy and without any fibres. One mango was a meal in itself. When I started to eat one in my bedroom, the juice started to run over my shirt; in the end I found that the only way to eat a Mali mango was to sit naked in the bathtub and then to have a shower!

In the evening, David and I and the Birds went to a 'Sikasso Evening'. This was part of a competition for the youth of Mali. The hall where the competition was held was crowded with people, and we only just managed to squeeze in. There was modern dancing and an uninteresting play in French, but the traditional dancing was marvellous, full of colour, vigour and rhythm. As we left. I noticed a huge poster in the Hall which proclaimed "A Bas d'Aggression Imperialiste en Vietman et Tout la Monde". This was the time of the Vietnam War and was clearly a very anti-American statement, expressing the feelings of many people around the world.

It was a short night. I got up at 6a.m. and took a taxi to the railway station. By this time, the station was bustling with people. I was so glad that I had come to Bamako; it was a delightful place, not too big, and rather 'off the beaten track'. Especially I will remember the 'Bamako bats' and the 'Mali mangoes'.

15

BAMAKO TO DAKAR

The Bamako – Dakar railway is one of many fascinating railways in Africa. The first part from Dakar eastwards was built under the French administration in the late 1800s, although the link to Bamako was not completed until the 1920s. In previous years, I had travelled on the Nairobi – Mombasa railway and on the Khartoum – Cairo railway, and I was interested to compare these three railways. My first impression was that the train here was rather run down and needed renovation. The coaches needed a good clean and some new paint. However, the compartment which David and I shared was quite comfortable and clean, but the washing and toilet facilities were not so good.[1]

The train departed fifteen minutes late at 7:45a.m. and travelled slowly away from the Niger River along wooded valleys. The soil was lateritic and looked nutritionally poor. Within about thirty minutes, the track entered typical Southern Guinea savanna, green and pleasant and slightly sandy. The plants in the maize plantations were only 1-2 feet tall, much shorter than in Nigeria at this time of year, probably due to the poor soil and lower rainfall. The track continued in a slightly northerly direction during the course of the day; the vegetation changed to Northern Guinea savanna, and *Acacia* trees and baobab trees became more common. In the valleys, densely leaved green trees clustered together, but on the higher parts of the hills, the ground was bare and arid. Some parts of this country had been burned, and the new growth obscured the blackened soil. In some places, I saw *Ficus* trees, easily identified by their large very dark green leaves, as well as baobab trees resplendent with their new green leaves. The waters of the Senegal river originate in these fragmented rocky hills and flow westwards to empty into the sea north of Dakar.

In the early morning when we left Bamako, the air was cool and refreshing, but as the day wore on, the oven-like heat blasted in through the windows of the train. By midday, the heat was overpowering and soporific, and by afternoon there was nothing much to do except to watch the unchanging scenery pass by. The railway line runs west and south of the Senegal River through mostly uninhabited countryside. Although there is something really fascinating about this unchanging panorama, it does become rather monotonous and dull when the temperature is more than 100°F (c. 38°C). Even when the train reached Kayes in the evening, it was still unbearably hot. David and I walked up and down the railway tracks hoping to cool off – at least this was better than sitting in the boiling carriage.

Several Customs Officers had boarded the train at Kayes, and during the journey to Ambidedi (the last town in Mali – a small scruffy place in the bush) they checked the passports of all the passengers. Most of these Customs Officers were not in uniform and were officious and unhelpful. They wanted to confiscate all Mali currency from passengers, but had no Senegalese currency to offer in exchange. One person looked at my 'Laisser-Passer' and tore away the bottom left corner – presumably so I could not use it again. We reached Ambidedi at 7:50p.m just as the sun was setting and there was a huge lightning storm in the south.

After this unnecessary bureaucracy, we had supper. We had been told that the food was poor or non-existent on the train. Thankfully the Birds had supplied us with an excellent supper (some of it brought into Mali by the American diplomatic service); we enjoyed paté, tomatoes, bread and guavas. Then we walked to the buffet car for lemonade and coffee. By now it was quite dark, hot and steamy. When the train reached the first town in Senegal, Senegalese Customs Officers came on board. At 10p.m., when we were half asleep, a drunk Customs Officer banged on our door; he wanted to see all our documentation and was thoroughly rude and obstructive.

Surprisingly I slept quite well in spite of the heat and the fan that did not work. The bedding was just one sheet and a pillow, but I did not want more than that. The swaying and jolting of the train woke me several times during the night, and I was glad when, at 7:15a.m., we reached Guinguineo where we were able to get out and have a walk. When I looked at my map, I was surprised that we had passed through the big town of Tambacounda during the night and I had not woken when, I assumed, the train must have stopped. It was an overcast morning, and it seemed as if it would rain soon. All around the railway track, the soil was sandy, and horses were ploughing the soil in the groundnut plantations. From here to Dakar, we saw just sand and groundnuts (which are most the important agricultural product grown in Senegal). There were very few trees. It hardly seemed possible that cultivation was possible, but the groundnuts appeared to survive well. There was no grass anywhere.

Breakfast consisted of bread, the last of my Bulgarian red cherry jam (from Ibadan), some coconut (from Abidjan), an orange (local) and water. It was just as well that we had brought our own food – none was available on the train. As the train approached Dakar, the land became more sandy and barren; this was so unexpected because I had envisaged lush maritime vegetation. As I discovered later, Dakar is built on rock and sand dunes. We arrived in Dakar at 11:30a.m., some twenty-seven hours after leaving Bamako. Now that I had travelled on this railway, I concluded that it was not as well organised as either the Nairobi-Mombasa railway or the Khartoum-Cairo railway. Nevertheless, this did not distract from the enjoyment of the countryside, the changing natural and human-made environments which I saw from the window, and the realisation of the vastness of even this small part of the African continent. At Dakar railway station, I said 'au revoir' to David.

Dakar – like Abidjan – is very French. It is a beautiful city full of trees and lovely white buildings. On my first afternoon, after lunch, I bought a 'Guide Bleu' to Dakar; it contained a map so I could find my way around, as well as information about the city. Dakar is built on the Cape Verde peninsula (Cap-Vert in French), the most westerly point on the African mainland. The Cape is a triangular-shaped rocky peninsula covered by sand and with many sandy beaches along its coastline between the rocky outcrops. There are excellent shops – mostly French – in the central area of the city. I walked to Cape Manuel, the southernmost point on the peninsula. It was lovely and refreshing to walk along the pavements with beautiful buildings on one side and the blue sea breaking on the rocky shoreline on the other side. In a way, this seemed so un-African, and far removed from the semi-deserts, savannas and rainforests that I knew well.

Dakar has had a complicated history, as have so many other settlements along the coast of West Africa. This is partly because it is close to Europe and all the early navigators and traders had to sail round the peninsula on their way southwards. Before European colonisation, the peninsula was inhabited by the Lebou people, and was part of the Jolof Empire which extended into modern-day Mauritania and Gambia. The Portuguese were the first to establish settlements on the peninsula and on nearby Gorée Island in the fifteenth century. The peninsula alternated between Portuguese, Dutch and British administrations before being taken over by the French in 1677. Dakar became one of the most important cities in 'La France d'Outre-Mer'. It is hardly surprising that Dakar is so French considering its long association with France which lasted until independence in 1960.

I had accommodation in a little cottage at IFAN, very close to 'L'Assemblée' on 'La Place du Rond-Point de l'Etoile'. Six boulevards meet at Rond-Point, a design very reminiscent of the large roundabouts in Paris. In the evening, I had an excellent evening meal at L'Assemblée for just 400 CFA francs.

On one day, I was given a lift by an electrician along the Cornische Ouest towards the suburb of Fann so I could visit the University and the Zoology Museum at IFAN. The Corniche runs along the coast, with spectacular views of the ocean. The University is modern and well laid out; the buildings are painted white with terracotta roofs, as are so many French and Belgian colonial buildings – lovely to look at and very functional in a hot climate. I discovered that there is a good bus system in Dakar, so I was able to catch a Number ten bus back to the centre of town.

Having travelled so far from Massawa on the coast of the Red Sea, I was determined to reach the most westerly point on the African continent. Here in Dakar (14° 45' N), I was almost at the same latitude as Massawa (15° 36' N). Later in the afternoon, I retraced my steps on another Number ten bus towards Ngor where there is an enormous and ugly tourist hotel, visible from miles around. I got off the bus at the small village of Quenum, and walked along the shore to the tip of Cape Verde. There was no-one else walking along the sands or the rocks. It is a barren landscape – just sand, sea and rock and without any vegetation. I walked as far as I could westwards to the outermost rocks ('Le Pointe des Alamadies') and looked across the

Atlantic Ocean. Nearby there is the wreck of a large ocean-going steamer and, on the furthest outcrop of rock, maybe a mile away, is a lighthouse. Beyond, if I could have seen that far, are the Cape Verde Islands, and further on, thousands of miles across the Atlantic, is the Caribbean with its multitude of tropical islands. At last I had reached my destination!

Walking back to a road, I found a 'plage' full of swimmers and sunbathers – French and Senegalese. The French, of course, wore next to nothing and the Senegalese were more modestly clothed. It was a colourful scene with many brightly coloured sun-umbrellas and other bathing paraphernalia. There were beachside stalls selling drinks and snacks, so I bought myself a cold drink. The road was sandy, with many people and cars, and the usual discarded rubbish of civilisation.

One of the most interesting historical places in Dakar is Gorée Island. The island is about three miles to the south-east of the Cape Verde peninsula. Many boats leave Dakar harbour to take visitors to the island. The boat that I was on was crowded with passengers who were going to spend the day on the island. From a distance, the island looked romantic with its white and colourfully painted houses, terracotta roofs, large green shady trees, rocky coastline, little picturesque sandy streets, and sandy beach. A real holiday island! But Gorée has had a dark and dreadful history because, from here, many slaves were transported in slave ships to the Americas from the mid 1600s to the mid 1800s. Opinions differ as to how many slaves were transported from Gorée, but historical records suggest that it was only a small number compared to the other slave ports on the West African coast. Nevertheless, the island is now an important memorial to all those who were transported from Gorée and other locations in Senegal. I spent the day walking around the island. The houses are built of stone, and often painted in pastel colours. The streets are narrow, often just walkways, and in places bourgainvilleas were flowering, and the fronds of palms and sisal plants rustled in the wind. At the northern end of the island is the huge round stone fort, now the IFAN museum, built in the late 1600s. A lesser known fact about the fort, and its turbulent history, is that the British tried (unsuccessfully) to seize the fort from the French in 1940. Many ships on both sides were sunk or damaged. At that time, Gorée (and Dakar) was controlled by the Vichy government in France which sided with Germany during World War II. Near the fort is the 'Maison des Esclaves' (House of Slaves) with its dungeons and cells where slaves were imprisoned before being transported to the Americas; this is the most heart-wrenching building on the island. The House had been in a state of disrepair for many years, but it had recently been renovated. I was able to walk around – I was the only visitor – and see where the slaves were chained. I could walk on the stairways where slaves once walked, and pass through the doorway onto the rocky shore, as they did before being placed on ships. Now everywhere is clean and painted white – so sanitised where once everything was so brutal.

After three hours of sight-seeing, I went to the beach in search of lunch. The beach was very crowded with French and Sengalese bathers, and far too crowded for my liking. I found only one 'hotel' near the beach – rather expensive but I decided to enjoy it sitting under their huge coloured umbrellas. It was very hot. I had an excellent lunch: Rocquet (probably Red Mullet) with sauce, salad, French bread and butter.

Often one meets interesting people while travelling in out-of-the-way places. On the return boat trip to the harbour, I met two Americans who were conducting a smallpox eradication programme in Bamako, and an Englishman (with a Canadian wife) who was checking civil aviation communications. We decided to have a drink together, followed by tea and magnificent cakes, in a 'Swiss-style' tea-house. It was fascinating hearing about their work and travels, especially about smallpox in Mali. They were amazed that I had travelled overland from Nigeria, and were even more amazed that I had also travelled overland from Khartoum to Nigeria. Their normal mode of transport was by air!

On my last day in Dakar, I took the bus to Hann to find the office of the 'Department d'Eaux et Forêts'. The bus passed through many newish suburbs and along avenues of newly planted trees, and roundabouts with lots of flowers. It was surprising how well everything was growing in the sandy soil. The bus stopped opposite the Department where I spent an informative hour talking to M. Lamine Diop about conservation in Niokolo-Koba National Park – the premier National Park in Senegal. He told me that, as elsewhere in Africa, habitat destruction, hunting, fires, human population pressures, illegal poaching and human poverty are huge problems... and, as a result, the numbers of many species of animals are declining. Next door to the Department is the 'Parc Forestier de Hann' and the Zoological Gardens; the Park is more like a forest with *Eucalyptus, Casuarina* and *Cassia* trees amongst many others. In the zoo, I was particularly delighted to see a herd of Red-fronted Gazelles (a rare species of gazelle of the sub-Sahara), and a Manatee. Manatees are extraordinary mammals; they are totally aquatic and live in freshwater and estuarine habitats along the west coast of Africa (including far inland on the Niger River). Their body shape is similar to that of a whale, and the skin is grey and hairless and often covered by green algae. The eyes are very small and I could hardly make out where they were; more obvious was the large bulbous snout with very long thick vibrissae. This individual was 6-7 feet in length and as it floated motionless just below the surface of the water, it looked just like a piece of rotten wood.

On the Cornische Ouest, there was a fascinating Artisan Village built on a sandy part of the beach. The many little stalls displayed a large selection of Senegalese arts and crafts – especially leatherwork, woodwork, silver jewellery, cloths, and palm weaving. I bought a little wooden statue of a wizened old man carrying a staff, very beautiful and full of character; he is black in colour and presumably made of ebony. Another place for looking at Senegalese art is the IFAN Ethnographic Museum; most of the material here is old and of historical interest. I was intrigued by a series of copper weights used for weighing gold, and the symbols stamped on the copper weights to indicate their weights in gold.

As the sun was setting on my last evening, I sat on the beach looking westwards and ate a mango. This was the end of my long journey across the width of Africa. I had travelled through many environments and many cultures spanning hundreds of years of history. I had come to understand the immense richness of this part of the continent, its turbulent history, its great kingdoms of the past, its amazing resilience in times of stress, and the immenseness and beauty of its landscapes. The journey gave me many challenges and uncertainties; I received kindness from fellow travellers and local people. In retrospect, I was fortunate that I was able to make this journey in the 1960s before the upheavals and the political changes of the post-Independence years that have changed these countries forever.

16

EPILOGUE – FIFTY YEARS ON

I was fortunate that I was able to experience such wonderful journeys in the 1960s. Since then, the ten countries through which I travelled have experienced civic strife, political turmoil and (for some) civil war and military coups. At the time of my travels, all these countries were relatively quiet, and travelling through them was assumed to be quite safe. However, I was never certain whether it was possible to get from one place to another. Questions such as 'Is there any transport?' 'Are the roads passable now?' and 'Where can I stay?' were real concerns for me in many places.

Now, fifty years later (2017), I can look back and reflect on the huge changes that have occurred since the 1960s. These changes mainly concern the political stability (or otherwise) of each country, the increase in the number of people (and the effects of this increase on the environment), and the changes in transport and communications. Some of these have brought progress and happiness; others have brought hardship and unhappiness.

The euphoria of independence and democracy was, sadly, not long-lived in many African countries. It is sobering to relate what has happened in each of the ten countries since I visited; yet it is important to do so for the historical record. A very brief history shows that all of them have suffered from political instability (to a greater or lesser extent) because of tribal animosities and rivalries, corruption, poor economies, high levels of

175

debt, human rights abuse, hardships caused by drought and famine, and the failure of the leaders to accept the Western democratic process.

Eritrea, in 1965, was a Province of Ethiopia but there were already rumblings about Eritrea gaining independence from Ethiopia. 'The Eritrean War of Independence' began in the early 1970s and ended in the 1990s when Eritrea became an independent nation. However, border disputes have continued, even though there has been a UN Peacekeeping Force for many years. Skirmishes on the Eritrean-Ethiopian border still continue, and the dictatorial government has forced many young Eritreans to leave the country and seek refuge elsewhere.

The Sudan has been plagued with ethnic strife for the last fifty years. There have been many changes in government and several military coups, as well as two major civil wars – one in the south and another in the west. In the south, in 1964, the Christian and animist southern Provinces demanded independence from the Arabic Islamic north. Sporadic (and sometimes intense) fighting between the Sudan Peoples Liberation Army (SPLA) and the government of the north occurred for over forty years until the new country of South Sudan was created in 2010. Since 2010, ethnic tensions have resulted in a continuous civil war in South Sudan. In the west, in 2003, war erupted in Darfur between the Sudan Army and the rebel fighters of the Sudan Liberation Movement (the rebel group of the Fur people). The reason for the war was that the Fur (the majority non-Arab ethnic group) accused the government of oppression, and wanted independence from the government in Khartoum. This war has been long and vicious, many thousands of civilians have been killed, and many have been displaced. The situation has been made more complex because different factions and nations have given money and/or weapons to one or the other side of the conflict. Both sides have been accused of genocide and war crimes. Many Fur people have sought refuge in western Chad, causing a major humanitarian crisis for Chad. United Nations and African Union peacekeepers have established many refugee camps in Darfur and in Chad. At the time of writing (2017), the South Sudan is still plagued by civil war, and the conflict in Darfur is ongoing; millions of refugees are living in neighbouring countries.

Chad became independent of its French colonial rule in 1960, although as I travelled through Chad, I realised that the French were still well established in the country. Although there was a democratic government for the first nineteen years, competing factions resulted in three years of civil war, from 1979 to 1982. Nigerian and the African Union intervention re-established a workable government, although tensions between the north and south of the country continued to cause problems. There were conflicts and skirmishes with Libya about the position of the Libya-Chad border. Ethnic tensions, especially between north and south, continued into the early 2000s, and the situation was made worse by the troubles in Darfur which culminated with a declaration of war with Sudan – a war that lasted for five years. Chad now has a democratic government with Presidential elections, but the tensions between the north and south continue and Islamist rebels have tried to destabilise the country.

Nigeria gained independence from Britain in 1960, but in 1967 eastern Nigeria declared itself to be the independent Republic of Biafra. The resulting civil war lasted for three years, until Biafra surrendered. Thereafter, some form of Federal democratic government, either military or civilian, has governed the country, although military coups have always been a part of the political process. Many aspects of life affect the political situation in Nigeria; foremost amongst these are ethnicity, issues related to the production of oil (money, pipelines, and environmental pollution), corruption, economic problems and, more recently, Islamist rebels in the north-east of the country.

Dahomey (now the Republic of Benin) is a former French colony and hence was part of French West Africa. It gained independence from France in 1960. The post-independence years have been marred by many constitutional changes, including a period as a Marxist state ('The People's Republic of Benin'). There have been many coups, counter-coups and periods of economic hardships over the years, but now there is a stable multi-party state with a President as Head of State and Head of government.

Togo became a German Protectorate in 1884 when the European powers divided Africa into colonial "units" at the Treaty of Berlin. The Protectorate lasted until 1914 when Britain and France invaded Togo at the beginning of World War I. The country was divided into 'British Togoland' in the west and 'French Togoland' in the east in 1916, and became a League of Nations mandated territory in 1922. In 1957, after a plebescite, British Togoland merged with Ghana and in 1960 French Togoland became the independent Republic of Togo. Since then, there has been a Presidential parliamentary system and a democratic government, but also periods of military rule and constitutional crises.

Ghana was the first of the West African countries to gain independence in 1956. However, the economy started to decline after independence, and in 1964, the first President, Kwame Nkrumah, suspended the constitution. In 1966, a bloodless military coup overthrew the President and for the next three years, the country was governed by the military. The following years were characterised by alternating civilian and military governments, economic problems (often associated with the variable price of cocoa), excessive debt, and several transitions of power from one government to another. Compared with most other African countries, Ghana has had a relatively peaceful time.

Côte d'Ivoire gained independence in 1960, and remained stable and prosperous under the first President, Félix Houphouët-Boigny, for thirty-three years (1960-1993). Thereafter, the country has been in political turmoil and has suffered two civil wars: the first was in 2002-2004 and ended with the country being split between the rebel-held north and the government-held south. The second civil war was in 2010-2011; it began because the two candidates in the presidential election could not agree who was the winner. Many people were killed and hundreds of thousands were displaced. Peace was restored after intervention by the United Nations, France (the former colonial ruler) and the African Union. Currently, Côte d'Ivoire enjoys a relatively stable political system.

Mali was formerly French Sudan and part of French West Africa. For a short while (1959-1960) it joined with Senegal to form the Mali Federation; this association was short-lived, and the country was granted independence in 1960. It immediately became a one-party State with strong connections to Russia and the eastern communist states. In 1968 (one year after my visit), there was a military coup and the army were in power for about six years until a new constitution was formalised even though the military leaders remained in power. The next few years alternated between a single-party government, anti-government demonstrations and several coups. Unstable government continued for years, made worse by the possibility that the north of the country (where the Tuaregs are the dominant tribe) might secede. In 2012, rebel troops (allied to several fundamental Islamist groups) took over the north of the country; they displaced the Tuareg and destroyed many of the ancient monuments of the Mali and Songai Empires.

Senegal gained independence in 1960, and it maintained a stable democracy under the first President, Léopold Senghor, for twenty years (1960-1980). When Senghor retired, there was a period of uncertainty before the second President, Abdou Diouf, took office; he served four terms (1981-2000). Subsequently there have been only two other Presidents. There was a single period of turmoil in the early 2000s when the southern region of Casamance wanted to secede. Senegal has a democratic presidential system, many political parties, and has adapted to the democratic process very well. It has had one of the best records of peace and democracy of any sub-Saharan nation.

★★★

The fifteenth parallel is a dry region, with low rainfall, high temperatures during most of the year, and low soil fertility. As such, it can only support, on a sustainable basis, a limited number of humans and animals (whether these are wild or domestic animals, or both). This situation was very obvious during my travels – I passed through mile upon mile of seemingly unoccupied country. Here and there, where there was water in permanent and semi-permanent rivers and in wells, there were communities of humans; sometimes there were large towns, in other places just a few huts. I was very aware of the differing numbers of people and livestock, the presence (or absence) of fields for crops, and the extent of natural vegetation (or the lack of it) in different places. South of the fifteenth parallel, where the climate is cooler and wetter and (in general) soils are more fertile, the carrying capacity of the land is higher and there are more people and animals. In the past, there were many 'checks and balances' that kept the human and animal numbers within the carrying capacity of the environment, both in the short-term (e.g. years and decades) or long-term (between generations and centuries). In recent years, and certainly between the time of my travels in 1965-1967 and now (2017), the human population has increased greatly, and this has been a contributory factor to the political upheavals, poverty, desertification and famine suffered by most of the countries across this part of Africa.

A comparison of the number of humans in the ten countries between 1965 and 2015 is shown in Table 1. To take one country – Sudan – as an example: there were 8.73 million people in 1965, and 40.23 million in 2015.

During these fifty years, 31.5 million additional people were added to the population of the Sudan. This means that the population increased 4.61 times, and there are now – on average – about 21.6 people in each square kilometre. Collectively, at the present time (2017), there are just over 253 million more people now in these ten countries than there were in 1965, or to put in another way, there are 3.84 times as many people now as there were in 1965.

Table 1. Area, population numbers, and density in 1965 and 2015 for 10 countries [1]

Country	Area (sq km)	Population 1965 (millions)	Population 2015 (millions)	Actual population increase (millions)	Increase as factor of 1965 population	Current Density (people/ km sq)
Eritrea	117,600	1.58	5.23	3.65	3.31	44.47
Sudan	1,861,484	8.73	40.23	31.50	4.61	21.61
Chad	1,284,000	3.31	14.04	10.73	4.24	10.93
Nigeria	923,768	50.25	182.20	131.95	3.63	197.24
Benin	112,622	2.63	10.88	8.25	4.14	96.61
Togo	56,785	1.71	7.30	5.59	4.27	128.56
Ghana	238,533	7.71	27.41	19.70	3.56	114.91
Côte d'Ivoire	322,463	4.22	22.70	18.48	5.38	70.40
Mali	1,240,000	5.56	17.60	12.04	3.17	14.19
Senegal	196,722	3.65	15.13	11.48	4.15	76.91
(Totals* & Averages #)		89.35 *	342.72 *	253.37 *	3.84 #	77.58 #

I remember that when I first arrived in Nigeria in 1965, the population was about 50 million, and the country seemed to be so densely populated (especially when compared with the Sudan). When I left in 1976 it was about 65 million – and was considered to be far too high to be sustainable. In those years, I saw the destruction of rainforest, the expansion of agriculture in both forest and savanna, the enlargement of towns and villages, and desertification in the northern parts of the country. Now – 2017 – the human population is 2.8 times larger than when I left in 1976.

Each country exhibits a different pattern of population growth. For example, Eritrea and Mali have the slowest rates (increase factor 3.31 and 3.17 respectively) and Côte d'Ivoire has the highest (increase factor 5.38). Any increase in numbers means that there is less space for each person and that there needs to be additional resources (food, water) to support the additional people. Using these criteria, Mali comes out rather well with its comparatively low population numbers and low density; but Mali is a dry country, much of the land is desert and semi-desert, and the carrying capacity of the land is low. Of necessity, it can only sustain fewer people. At the other end of the spectrum is Nigeria – a large country with a large population, high density of people and a comparatively high carrying capacity. All the other countries fit somewhere between these extremes. As expected, the northern, dry countries (Sudan, Chad and Mali) have the lowest population numbers and lowest densities, and the southern wetter countries (Nigeria, Benin, Togo, Ghana, Côte d'Ivoire) have the highest densities. Eritrea is an exception because it has a temperate climate and a high density, and Senegal also has a high density because of its mesic coastal climate. All countries have problems that are due either to large population numbers or high densities, and/ or restraints because of a low carrying capacity and a paucity of natural resources.

Demographers measure the 'fertility rate' (i.e. the average number of young born to a woman during her lifetime), and the 'annual rate of increase' (the percentage increase in the number of people compared to the number in the previous year) in order to understand how populations vary over time, both within and between countries. Both these measures are, in some part, related to cultural and social factors. They help us to understand why populations change in the way they do. Table 2 gives two sets of information ('Fertility Rate' and 'Annual Population Growth Rate') for each of the countries through which I travelled. The average fertility rate in 1965 was 6.51 children for each woman. The average rate dropped by 1.38 children to 5.13 by 2015 but with considerable variation between countries. Only one country (Chad) increased the average fertility rate during these years.

Table 2. Fertility Rates and Annual Population Growth Rate in 1965 and 2015 for 10 countries

Country	Average Fertility Rate (Births per woman) 1965	Average Fertility Rate (Births per woman) 2015	Annual Popln growth rate (%) 1965	Annual Popln growth rate (%) 2015
Eritrea	6.97	4.40	2.51	2.31
Sudan	6.65	4.46	3.10	2.25
Chad	6.10	6.31	1.94	3.32
Nigeria	6.35	5.67	2.17	2.66
Benin	5.86	4.89	1.78	2.65
Togo	6.33	4.69	2.80	2.66
Ghana	6.44	4.25	2.63	2.33
Côte d'Ivoire	6.77	5.10	4.20	2.46
Mali	7.10	6.35	1.25	3.01
Senegal	6.57	5.18	2.86	3.11
Averages	6.51	5.13	2.52	2.68

Although it might be expected that the decrease in fertility rate would result in a decrease in the annual growth rate, this is not necessarily so; in fact, the growth rate increased in six of the ten countries because there is always a lag of many years between a change in fertility and a reduction in growth rate. The African data can be placed in a wider context by comparison with, for example, some European countries. In Denmark, the Fertility Rate fell from 2.55 in 1965 to 1.73 in 2015, and the Annual Growth Rate fell from 0.77% to 0.42%. In Germany, the Fertility Rate fell from 2.13 in 1965 to 1.39 in 2015, and the Annual Population Growth Rate fell from 0.76% to 0.06%. In these two countries, and indeed in all of Europe, Fertility Rates dipped below 0% during 1980-1990, i.e. the number of births fell below replacement level. These comparisons serve to emphasise the very high Fertility Rates and the high Annual Population Growth Rates in Africa. Unless Fertility Rates and Growth Rates decline in coming years, the population numbers of humans in Africa will increase to what most demographers consider to be unsustainable numbers. This will mean even greater changes to the environment, more deforestation in rainforest and savanna woodlands, overuse of water supplies, shortages of food, especially in years when crops fail, and increased desertification in drier regions.

Conflicts between human populations for scarce resources are likely in the future. The challenge for Africa is to balance population numbers with the available resources so all citizens have adequate food, shelter, health support services, education and jobs. The population statistics given here are not consistent with this ideal.

★★★

When I travelled, I had very simple maps and there was no information on what the roads would be like, nor about the size of villages and towns that I would pass through. Now that there are satellite images (such as Google Earth), it is possible to look at detailed photographs of every part of Africa and, as a result, I have been able to retrace my journey across Africa on a computer screen. It has been a fascinating exercise, and I am amazed by the physical changes that have occurred in fifty years, even in countries that have had civil wars and unstable politics. The most obvious change is the increase in size of towns and villages, which now cover much larger areas than they did fifty years ago. This is especially obvious in Khartoum and Ibadan, both places that I knew well. Areas on the periphery of these cities, which formally were countryside, are now covered with houses. There are new roads and bridges, and enormous concrete and glass buildings in the big cities. Little villages have become substantial towns. There is less countryside between neighbouring villages, and there are now villages in places that I remember as being devoid of humans. Forests that I knew are smaller in area and have less dense vegetation. Travelling is much easier now because of huge improvement in the roads – some roads that were just tracks in the sand or constructed of laterite in the 1960s are now tarmac, and there are bridges where previously the dirt road descended into a dry river bed and climbed out on the other side.

★★★

Communications have changed dramatically as well. In both Khartoum and Ibadan, I did not have a telephone at home or in my office, and access to a telephone was limited or non-existent in other places. Telephones –

where they occurred – were land-based using poles and wires that often fell down and were poorly maintained. The most widespread means of personal communication was by letter and telegram. Newspapers and radio were available in many places and were the best way to learn about local and international news. When travelling, I was unable to keep in contact with anyone, and no one could contact me. This was not a worry – in fact it was a rather pleasant feeling being free of the trappings of civilisation for most of the time. Communications in Africa have been revolutionised by the introduction of television and mobile phones. Mobile phones are widespread now and are used in many ways: by businessmen, by farmers for marketing, by banks for transferring money, and by doctors and emergency workers, as well as for communication between families and friends. Television was unknown in Africa in the early 1960s, and I never saw a television set during my travels (and indeed in the period 1963 to 1976). But now television is widespread, and there are even television sets powered by solar panels in villages that have no access to a normal electricity supply. These televisions are used to provide educational material for children (and adults), and to give information about local issues to villagers. All these innovations have made huge beneficial changes to the lifestyles of many people, especially those in rural areas.

★★★

I have often wondered whether other people accomplished the same long journey as mine in previous years. Undoubtedly many Africans from the far west of West Africa travelled much of this route on their way to and from Mecca over the centuries, but written records are very rare or non-existant. I did meet four people in 1967 who had travelled from Bamako to Abidjan (chapter 14), and I met many people who had travelled on the railway from Khartoum to Nyala. The only book in English I have come across that describes a journey similar to mine (but not as extensive) is by Frank Gray, published in 1928.[2] Gray was a retired Liberal Member of Parliament for Oxford, interested in politics, government, administration and development. After leaving parliament, he travelled widely in this part of Africa. Part I of his book describes travels in southern and northern Nigeria, and a long boat trip from the Niger delta to Dahomey, Togoland, the Gold Coast (as these countries were called then), Liberia and Sierra Leone. Part II describes his journey with a companion, Jack Sawyer, in two small Jowett cars – named 'Wait' and 'See' – from Lagos to Kano, and then due east to Khartoum and finally Massawa. The two cars were the 7 hp two-seater economy model; each was modified to have a small platform at the back for luggage, petrol, oil, spare tyres and other necessities. These cars were lightweight, so that they could be pushed, pulled, or lifted out of bogs and sand drifts. In addition, each car pulled a two-wheeled 'Eccles' trailer to carry more petrol and water as required.

Reading Gray's book now, it is amazing that he and Sawyer managed to reach the Red Sea. For most of the way, there were hardly any roads worthy of the name. Their route was mostly the same as mine, but in the opposite direction. They took two local men with them: one was 'Bismark', a Nigerian mechanic who could also turn his hand to anything else that needed doing, and the second was Peter, a cook and steward. Later, other cooks and guides replaced Peter because it was necessary to have someone who spoke the local language. Many comments in the book give an idea of the immense problems of the journey. Even in southern Nigeria, where some of the roads just north of Ibadan were newly constructed, Gray recorded that the road was no more than a track; in many places it descended down a steep bank to a narrow bridge (without any protective railings), over a dry stream-bed and then up the other side. At night, they often lost their way and had to ask local villagers to find the road again. Sometimes, one of the cars slid off the road into a ditch and had to be pulled and pushed onto the road again.

Gray had a great capacity to seek out government officials who invariably offered hospitality. After crossing the Niger River and passing through Zungeru, the party reached Kagara. Here they had their first night in the open. They unloaded the platform on the back of one of the cars, and spread a mosquito net over the top covering their beds. They obtained water and firewood from the locals, and Peter cooked some food. They went to bed at 9p.m., got up at 3a.m., and were ready to set off at dawn. All went well until 11a.m. when 'Wait' developed a smell of burning rubber. They had to stop and make repairs. It was exceedingly hot. There were many amusing incidents throughout their travels, such as when they passed through the village of Bernin Gwari: Gray saw two motorcycles at the foot of a cliff-like hill. Thinking that there must be Europeans around, he and Sawyer found a path that led them to the top of the hill. At the top was 'Government House', where there were two young Political Officers. When one of them asked: "Where are you going to?" Gray replied, "To the Red Sea." "Good God," he said, "come and have some lunch."

On the way to Kano, Gray made a detour to visit *"the Lieutenant-Governor, Mr Palmer"* in Kaduna who, in previous years, had travelled by foot and by horse from Nigeria to Khartoum.[3] Gray recorded that Mr Palmer gave him advice and information and was full of enthusiasm. He did not record anything about the advice he was given, but undoubtedly it must have been about the necessity to carry adequate water, remain hydrated, and reduce exposure to the sun – all essential survival skills in hot arid countries.

When Gray arrived in Kano, he recorded that *'there was some excitement at the arrival of 'See', the first car in the world to reach Kano from Lagos on its own wheels... My host told me that the locals, when told the car had been driven all the way from Lagos to Kano were slow to believe it, and at first said of the cars 'Him no fit come Lagos'!'* At Kano, the cars and trailers were loaded up with a huge supply of petrol (184 gallons for each car, enough to travel from Maiduguri to El Obeid in the Sudan), enough food for the whole journey, water, and oil. Because all these essential supplies weighed so much, they abandoned spare clothing, firearms, ammunition, and camp beds. The road east of Kano was dreadful; it was no more than a dry weather track and the 'bridges' were simply logs of trees covered by sand. On one occasion, the wheels of the cars became lodged in the gaps between the logs; the only way to proceed was to carry the cars over the bridge. Thereafter, they avoided bridges and made detours along the edge of the river or stream bed until they found a place where there was a natural descent into the dry river bed. (If it had been the wet season, the river beds would have been full of water, and the roads would have been impassable.) It was always scorching hot. During the 100 mile journey from Dikwa to the Chari River, they averaged just seven miles an hour, mostly in second gear, rarely in top gear, and frequently in bottom gear. This slow progress was typical of most days on the way to Khartoum.

After two days trying to cross the Chari River, and becoming hopelessly stuck on the sand banks of the river, the two cars set off for Mongo. There were many adventures; Joseph the cook fell off the car with all the 'chop boxes', one of the cars drove into a concealed hole which broke the universal joint and bent several rods of the steering mechanism, and they had to drive through miles of *'an impossible confusion of sand dunes, dry grass, rock, stream beds and scrub'*. Gray recorded that on one day and the following half-day: *"we fought loose dry sand over a dreary waste; for seventy miles we saw but two living souls. There was sand everywhere, in our eyes and in our mouths. Sitting under the burning sun, and over our engines, we drove on with a thirst more powerful than any that had parched our throats since we left Lagos.'*

In Mongo, there was a rare surprise. Gray found a local blacksmith who had just an anvil, a hammer and a pair of pliers. With simple bellows made of goat skin, the blacksmith created a furnace and was able to straighten the twisted metal of the steering mechanism and the gear box – *'an achievement of which any English blacksmith might be proud'*. Simple repairs like this allowed the two cars to continue their journey. On the following day, Gray recorded his frustrations at the hardships and slow progress as they travelled eastwards across Chad: '... *we were impeded by bush and sand, engulfed by a broken bridge, and there were many riverbeds of sand to be crossed. For eleven hours we have driven, for the most part under blinding sun so hot that the hands could not be placed upon the exposed metal of the cars. All day we drove through sand, pallid grass and withered bush... and we covered only sixty miles. Twenty miles we passed without seeing [another human]....'* It was such slow going; on the following days, the cars covered only fifty-three, seventy-eight, twenty-eight, forty-five and thirty-six miles each day.

Eventually, they reached Abecher (Abeché) where there was a European depot and they could replenish some of their stores. There were a considerable number of French officials, including a Captain Commandant, who administered this lonely isolated part of Africa. The road from Abecher to Adré, the border post with the Sudan, was sometimes good (*'we managed as much as fourteen miles per hour'*) and sometimes bad (*'just a quarter of a mile in an hour'*). At Adré, surprisingly, there was plenty of water, and fresh fish were available in the market (*'We had fresh fish for dinner. How we enjoyed it!'*). They met two French officers *'who in the kindest and most genial way, entertained us far into the night and provided us with an escort to take us two miles to the British Sudan border.'* No doubt, European visitors were much appreciated in such a lonely outpost – and were few and far between.

It took Gray and his party four days to reach El Fasher, via Kebkebia (Kabkabiya). Their route was north of Jebel Marra (whereas my route was south of Jebel Marra). Gray described the scenery as just bush and scrub, and lots of sand. By this stage of the journey, he was able to use the position of the sun for navigation, and he was learning to notice subtle changes in the landscape and vegetation to ascertain where the next water source might be. He noted that the Sudan was well organised. In places there were white-painted stones to indicate where roads were claimed to be; these were very welcome for without them there was nothing to distinguish the road from the sand plain they traversed. Dwellings and offices were well-kept and orderly. Before reaching El Fasher, the road passed over Jebel Gerda, a rocky area of boulders, splinters of rock and steep gradients. Although it was hot during the day, the nights were cool and it was pleasant to sit around a camp fire. El Fasher was an outpost of the British Empire with an English Governor and a thriving British community. Gray and his party stayed in El Fasher for two nights, and thoroughly enjoyed the kindness and welcome given to them.

The journey from El Fasher to Um Kedada and El Obeid was full of adventure and problems. Often, Gray and his party became hopelessly lost. When this happened, they had to cast around until they found some sort of track going in approximately the correct direction. A typical day started by getting up at 4a.m., having a cup of tea, and moving off at dawn. This had the advantage, both for the cars and for themselves, of travelling in comparative coolness. But as they struggled on, for about twelve hours, the temperature increased. Often at nightfall, they did not know exactly where they were. It was often easier to move away from the 'road' (where the sand was soft) to harder ground at the side where the tyres could gain some traction and it was possible to travel faster. However, this often resulted in mishaps and accidents. Running repairs to the front axles and the steering rods were frequent. Gray commented that these amazing cars seemed to run as well with crooked parts as with straight parts! At Nahud, they were greeted by two Englishmen – the government representative and a police officer – and they found a supply of petrol and tyres awaiting their arrival (neither of which they needed for the final drive to El Obeid and Khartoum). They learned that they had now passed over the huge area of 'bottomless sand' and that the rest of the journey would be on more or less hard ground. It took two more days to reach El Obeid; it was a comparatively easy journey because the 'road' followed the line of the telegraph posts, water was available, and firewood, eggs and chickens could be purchased at villages. At the time, El Obeid was the railhead, and the railway line from El Obeid to Nyala (on which I travelled) had not been built.

From El Obeid, they travelled on sandy 'roads' close to the railway line and could follow the telegraph posts, but after El Rahad, they took a more north-easterly direction towards the White Nile. Their local guide took them in the wrong direction, they became lost again, and the clutch on one of the cars had to be replaced (a repair that took six hours in the blistering sun). By this time, Gray was becoming even more frustrated with the attitudes of the local people with respect to time, distance and direction. When the guide was questioned about where they were, and where was the village that he said they would find, the guide replied, "It no be far, it no be near." It transpired that the village, said to be one day's walk away, was in fact six day's walk away! After a few more days of heat, exhaustion, extricating the cars from holes, and mechanical failures, they reached the White Nile at El Duem, crossed the river on a barge, and man-handled the cars up the sandy bank on the other side. Finally they reached Khartoum and drove into the courtyard of The Grand Hotel. One of the cars, after the engine had been turned off, refused to start again and would not move!

After a few days of rest and repairs to the cars, Gray and Sawyer set off on the last leg of the journey, from Khartoum to Kassala and Massawa. The Acting Governor of the Sudan, General Huddleston, arranged that Captain Haywood (a military officer) should escort them to where the Kassala road began – evidently it was very difficult to find. (An interesting comment; the road was also difficult to find in 1965!) The officer insisted that Gray should send a wire (i.e. a telegram) on arrival in Kassala, and told Gray that, 'If we do not hear from you in four days, all of us will turn out to search (for you).' The 'road' across the Butana Plain – once found – was relatively easy to follow at first, and they passed several wells where bulls were pulling buckets of water from the well. Then they became completely lost in rough flat country amongst huge tussocks of grass. They managed to travel just ten miles in five hours! Ironically, that night, they were short of water (having assumed that wells would be found easily on the journey). That night, they could not have any soup because the water they carried had to be reserved for the car radiators. They were unable to see any fires during the night that would indicate the presence of humans. On the following morning, they set off in roughly the correct direction and found a cluster of nomadic mat-dwellings where they were welcomed by some helpful Arab nomads who guided them to Jebel Qeili. Gray now realised what Captain Haywood meant when he said he would send a search party to look for them… it was easy to get lost on these vast semi-desert plains. They reached Jebel Qeili and found numerous wells where they obtained water. These were the same wells near where I camped at Jebel Qeili (chapter 4) some forty years later.

The winding tracks through high grass continued eastwards towards Kassala. They were told that they had to reach a ford where they could cross the Atbara river. To their surprise, the Atbara river at this time of year was just a huge dry sandy riverbed. Nearby, there was a lake, or rather part of the river where the water had not flowed downstream and had not soaked into the substrate. It was extremely difficult to find a way through the confusion of sand dunes, paths, bushes and former rushing watercourses. After pulling and pushing the cars up the sandy bank on the other side, there were no tracks leading towards Kassala. They became lost again but continued on until they saw the black easily-recognisable profile of Jebel Kassala in the distance. They came to the Marub river where they found a causeway, so it was relatively easy to cross. On arrival in Kassala, Gray located the 'European colony' and drove to the home of the Chief of Police where he and Sawyer stayed for the night. After settling in, Gray had dinner with the Governor of the Province. His last comment about Kassala was, *'All was well – the last outpost of the British Empire has been reached.'*

Finally – and in great contrast to the flat sands and plains – the cars wended their way up through the mountains of Ethiopia. Gray and Sawyer enjoyed the change although they were well aware that any mistakes in driving could result in falling over the steep edge of the narrow mountain track. The temperature became cooler as they ascended on to the Ethiopian plateau. They camped for the night within the fold of the hills and were joined by some local travellers who enjoyed the warmth of the fire, and who also acted as sentries. Surprisingly (to me), they did not stop in Keren even though they were impressed by the picturesqueness of the town and its European buildings, and the number of Italians who were engaged in business there. They continued up through the mountains towards Asmara; the track was built for camels, not for cars, and Gray was fearful of falling headlong downwards over the cliff into the valley 1,000 feet below. They did not stop in Asmara but hurried onto the eastern edge of the plateau where they looked out over the vast valley that led down to the Red Sea. They were able to see two shelves cut into the steep rocky sides of the valley: one was for the railway and one was for camels. The shelves zig-zagged across the side of the valley, gradually descending towards the sea; sometimes the shelves were visible, sometimes they were hidden by the folds of the hills; sometimes the railway was above the camel track, and sometimes it was below it. (These comments were very similar to mine in 1965!) They started to drive down the camel track; but soon it became extremely cold, and heavy wet cloud enveloped them. Driving in these conditions was rather treacherous so they stopped for the night beside a cluster of huts, where the locals lent them a hut so they could escape the biting cold. They shivered all night, even though they lit a fire with goat manure because there was no firewood.

On the final day of their journey, they woke at 2:30a.m. so they could be off by dawn. As Gray recorded — it was far too cold to lie still. They continued along the camel track. On the sharp corners, the cars could not get round on their own lock, so they had to be manually assisted! There were delays when strings of camels wanted to pass by. Eventually, they arrived on the sandy coastal plain where they had to drive for nearly a mile along a dry river-bed to find a place where the cars could drive up the sandy bank. It was extremely hot in Massawa — even hotter (and much more humid) than any other place that Gray and Sawyer had encountered since leaving Lagos two months previously. The locals were amazed at 'Wait' and 'See', and naturally were not able to comprehend where these cars had come from. Although there were a few cars in Massawa, they were used only in the town and for driving a few miles up the coast. The authorities at the time did not promote the use of cars and roads because they wanted people and goods to travel on the newly completed railway to Asmara. After just three days, Gray and Sawyer boarded a ship to return to England. Gray did not record what happened to 'Wait' and 'See'. I hope they also went to England; surely the makers — Jowett — would have been very proud to see their cars again after such an amazing journey.

★★★

Reading Gray's book made me realise the enormous changes that had occurred during the forty years between his journey in 1924 and mine in 1965-1967. Similarly, the changes from 1965 to the present time have altered the landscapes, ecology and lifestyles of the whole region. During the next forty to fifty years, there are likely to be changes that are difficult to imagine. The pressures resulting from even larger human populations, fewer natural habitats, climate change, better communications, quicker means of transport, inter-tribal conflict, political instability, and religious-based terrorism will have far-reaching consequences. The beneficial effects of better economic management, universal education, improved road and rail transport, and ecological changes (to limit the effects of desertification) may be outweighed by the increasing number of humans, and shortages of food and water. What is certain is that the Africa of the 1920s and the 1960s can never return, and that journeys such as described in this book will become distant memories of how it was in the olden days.

NOTES

Chapter 1. Prologue

1. Stevenson-Hamilton 1940. My original copy was lost many years ago, but I was able to find a second-hand copy on an internet bookshop in 2016.
2. Holbach, Maud. *Dalmatia* (1908), *Bosnia and Herzegovena* (1910), *In the Steps of Richard Coeur de Lion* (1912), and *Bible Ways in Bible Lands* (1912).
3. Côte d'Ivoire is sometimes referred to as the Ivory Coast in the English language. I prefer to use 'Côte d'Ivoire' as has been used by the French in colonial times, and by the residents of the country now. The postage stamps use the term 'Republique de Côte d'Ivoire'.
4. The dates of each of these travels were: Eritrea (2nd December 1965 – 7th December 1965) – this journey also included travels to southern Ethiopia (7th December – 24th December 1965) that are not included here; Butana (17th November 1965 – 21st November 1965); Jebel Marra (6th November – 24th November 1964); Khartoum to Ibadan (29th March – 20th April 1965); Ibadan to Dakar (22nd June – 11th July 1967). The costs of travel in £ Sterling (not counting food, and accommodation where necessary) was £21/4/6d (Khartoum to Ibadan) and £19/16/6d (Ibadan to Dakar).

Chapter 2. A Brief Introduction to the 15th North Parallel

1. Bovill 1968b.
2. Moorehead 1960.

3. Oliver 1965.
4. Smith 1984. See also *www.britannica.com/science/intertropical-convergence-zone*
5. There has been a lot of research into the morphological and physiological responses of animals and plants to semi-arid and arid environments. Many chapters in e.g. Cloudsley-Thompson (1984) are devoted to these topics.
6. Ullendorf 1965.
7. Trimingham 1962.
8. Fage 1978.
9. e.g. Trimingham 1962, Palmer 1936.
10. Bovill 1968a.

Chapter 3. Eritrea and Ethiopia

1. At the time of my travel, Eritrea was a Province of Ethiopia. It became an independent country in 1991 after many years of civil war. The present southern border is c. 90 km south of Asmara. Adua and Axum are in Ethiopia, just south of the Eritrean border.
2. Ullendorf 1965.

Chapter 4. The Butana Plains

1. Most of the information in this chapter is based on my travel diary.
2. I have not been able to find any reference to these giraffe engravings in any books on African rock art. Maybe this is the first time that these engravings have been recorded and photographed.

Chapter 5. Khartoum in the 1960s

1. Moorehead 1960.
2. Moorehead 1962.
3. Rzóska 1976. Also website *www.fao.org/nr/water/faonile* gives numerical details for water flow at different parts of the Nile.
4. Oliver 1965.
5. Eltahir 1988.
6. Arkell 1947, 1949.

7. Rilly (no date), Arkell 1955.
8. Author's notes and photographs.
9. The southern Provinces gained independence from the Sudan in 2011, and are now the independent nation of 'South Sudan'.
10. Halfayat el Muluk. I recorded the name of the village, as given to me by the local people, in my field notebook in the early 1960s. At the time, it seemed a rather primitive poor village of no special significance, in a very degraded and rather barren landscape. Many years later, when reading Arkell (1955), I was surprised to see that the village was identified on his Map 11 labelled 'The Sudan, AD 1700-1821'. On p. 225, Arkell recorded that in 1821, Ismail Pasha (a son of Muhammad Ali, the Viceroy or Khedive of Egypt) led a large army southwards along the Nile Valley in order to crush the Fung Kingdom (Fung Dynasty). The Kingdom stretched from near Dongola to south of Sennar and had ruled for nearly 300 years. Ismail Pasha first captured Dongola and then continued south towards Sennar, the capital city of the Kingdom. On the way, he rested his army at Halfayat el Muluk before continuing to Sennar. This military expedition of 1821 ended the Fung Kingdom, and its lands became part of Egypt and hence part of the Ottoman Empire. So the village was of some significance in the changing fortunes in this part of the Sudan! Moorehead (1962) gives a wonderful and detailed description of the military expedition and also mentions "Halfaya" – a shortened name for Halfayat el Muluk.
11. Happold 1967b.
12. Rzóska 1984.
13. Carlisle 1968.
14. The total number of species of birds recorded in Khartoum Province is 351 – an incredibly high number for such a small area. There are 128 'resident' species, 38 'local migrant' species, 13 'African migrant' species, and 172 'Palearctic migrant' species. For many of the smaller Palearctic species, there are so many individuals of certain species that the numbers seen (and caught in mist-nets) is mind-boggling! Details of numbers of species of birds are taken from maps and details given by Nikolaus 1987, with a few additional species recorded since 1987 by Tom Jenner (*pers. comm.* 2015).
15. Cave and MacDonald 1955.
16. Happold 1967a.

17. My studies of small mammals of Khartoum were published in several scientific journals. See, e.g., Happold 1967a, b, 1969, 1970 for a few examples.
18. Happold 1968.

Chapter 6. Khartoum to Western Sudan

1. Most of the information in this chapter is based on my travel diary.
2. Churchill 1899 refers briefly to the Battle of Shaykan. See also: *https:// en.wikipedia.org/wiki/Battle_of_El_Obeid*

Chapter 7. Jebel Marra

1. Jebel Marra was previously the second highest mountain after Mount Kinyeti (10, 456 ft; 3,187m) in the Imatong Mountains of Equatoria Province; but Mount Kinyeti is now in the new nation of South Sudan.
2. Harrison and Jackson 1958.
3. Bailey-Watts and Rogers 1964/65.
4. Lévêque 1990.
5. Green *et al.* 1979.
6. Thomas and Hinton 1923.
7. Happold 1966.

Chapter 8. Western Sudan

1. Most of the information in this chapter is based on my travel diary.
2. Arkell 1955.

Chapter 9. Chad

1. Most of the information in this chapter is based on my travel diary.
2. Nachtigal 1879/1881. This enormous work consists of four volumes: v.1 Tripoli and Fezzan; v.2. Kawar, Bornu, Kanem, Borku, Ennedi; v.3. The Chad Basin and Bagirmi; v.4. Wadai and Darfur. Nachtigal's impressions of Kukawa are recorded in v.4.
3. There are many books about the rock art of the Sahara. See, e.g. Lhote

1959, Willcox 1984. The term rock engraving (or petroglyph) refers to an image cut into the rock; rock painting refers to an image made of paint applied to the surface of the rock (usually in a cave or a very shady place).

4. See chapter 7, and Lévêque 1990.
5. Brunet *et al*. 2002.
6. See Glossary for details.

Chapter 10. Fort Lamy and Westwards to Nigeria

1. Most of the information in this chapter is based on my travel diary.
2. Lemoalle *et al*. 2012.
3. Fry 1971. Other interesting information (including satellite photographs of the shrinking lake) can be found by typing 'Lake Chad' into an internet browser.
4. In Nigeria and Sudan, vehicles now drive on the right hand side of the road (as in all the countries of the former 'French West Africa' and 'French Central Africa').

Chapter 11. Nigeria

1. Most of the information in this chapter is based on my travel diary.
2. Bovill 1968a.
3. Barth 1857-1858. See also Kemper 2012 – a good easy-to-read and informative volume about Barth's travels.
4. The identity of the trees in Barth's house is uncertain. The name 'korna-tree' is probably a local name for a species of *Ziziphus*. Plants of this genus are widespread in arid habitats, and some species are trees, others are shrubs. The meaning of 'caoutchouc tree' is less certain. Caoutchouc means 'rubber ' or 'latex', a (usually) white sticky substance produced by special cells in many species of plants. Barth's 'caoutchouc tree' cannot be the well known commercial rubber tree because this species grows only in the wet tropics, and was introduced into southern Nigeria only in the early 1900s. There are several species of latex-producing trees and vines in arid areas of northern Africa. It is unlikely that we will ever know the identity of Barth's 'caoutchouc tree'. (J. R. Timberlake, *pers. comm.* 2017.)

5. My first impression of Kano (in 1965) was rather unfavourable; however subsequent visits revealed that it was a fascinating place with a rich history and many wonderful old buildings.

6. At the time, Ahmadu Bello University was a new foundation. It was founded in 1962 and named to commemorate Sir Ahmadu Bello (1910–1986). He was a descendant of Usman dan Fodio, and was the Sardauna of Sokoto. He was Leader of the Northern People's Congress and the first and the only Premier of Northern Nigeria; he played a leading role during the negotiations for Nigeria's Independence. Sir Ahmadu Bello was assassinated in January 1966 in the coup that toppled Nigeria's first post-independence government.

Chapter 12. Ibadan in the 1960s

1. Most of the information in this chapter is based on my notes, letters, collections and photographs.

2. Two other leading politicians were also assassinated during the coup: Sir Abubakar Tafawa Balewa (Prime Minister), and Samuel Akintola (Premier of Western Nigeria).

3. I lived in Ibadan from 1966 to 1976 (except for short periods when I was on leave).

4. Elgood 1960.

5. Hopkins 1965.

Chapter 13. Ghana and Westwards to the Côte d'Ivoire

1. Most of the information in this chapter is based on my notes, letters, collections and photographs.

2. Elephantiasis is a parasitic infection caused by very small filarial nematode worms that are transmitted from human to human by female mosquitoes. The larvae of the worms are taken up by a mosquito when it bites an infected human, and the larvae are injected by the mosquito when, later on, it feeds on another human. The larvae grow to adults in the lymphatic system of humans, causing blockages and hence swellings, of arms, legs, scrotum, etc. There are several species of these filarial worms. Elephantiasis is widespread in the tropics.

3. The Kingdom of Dahomey existed from c. 1600 until c. 1894 when it became part of the French West Africa. It gained independence in 1960 and changed its name to the Republic of Benin. This is the same name as the city of Benin in Nigeria (well known for its famous Benin brasses) and the State of Benin (which has the city of Benin as its state capital). The name change caused annoyance and confusion at first.

4. Ewer 1969. Further information may be obtained by searching the internet, using the scientific name or vernacular name.

5. There are many publications about the European forts and castles in Ghana. For details and references see: *http://www.colonialvoyage.com/ european-forts-ghana/* ; *https://en.wikipedia.org/wiki/List_of_castles_in_ Ghana*

6. 1807 is the date when the 'Abolition of Slave Trade' Act passed through the British Parliament. However, different European countries banned the trade at different dates. Even so, illegal slavery continued for many years after the various Acts were passed, and it was not until about 1848 that slavery was finally and completely abolished on the West African coast.

7. The Elder Dempster Line was the major British shipping line that carried passengers and freight between Liverpool and the ports of West Africa. The line was named after its founders (Alexander Elder and John Dempster). It began service in 1868 (as Elder Dempsey and Company, changing its name and ownership over the years) and continued until 1974. Before air travel, the Elder Dempster ships were the most important means of transport for expatriates travelling between England and West Africa.

8. 'Centre Suisse' is an abbreviation for 'Centre Suisse de Recherches Scientifique en Côte d'Ivoire', a Swiss scientific agency (CSRS). The Centre, in 1967, was housed in the grounds of ORSTOM at Adiopodoumé, near Abidjan.

Chapter 14. Côte d'Ivoire to Mali

1. Most of the information in this chapter is based on my notes, letters, collections and photographs.

2. There are many publications about the great empires of this part of Africa; see e.g. Oliver and Fage 1962, Reader 1997, Packenham

1991. Especially informative is Davidson 1965. There are also many informative websites such as: *https://en.wikipedia.org/wiki/African_empires*

3. Bamako is situated on the Upper Niger river. The waters flow downstream eventually entering the sea at the Niger delta in southern Nigeria. Prior to this journey, I had seen the Niger river several times at Jebba in Nigeria. The waters which I saw flowing under the bridge at Bamako had to travel 2,500 miles (4,000km) to reach Jebba, and then a further 400 miles (650km) to the sea at the Niger Delta.

Chapter 15. Bamako to Dakar

1. Most of the information in this chapter is based on my notes, letters, collections and photographs.

Chapter 16. Epilogue – Fifty years On

1. United Nations, Department of Economic and Social Affairs, Population Division. World Population Prospects: The 2015 Revision. See also: www.un.org/en/development/desa/… /pdf/fertility/world-fertility-patterns-2015.pdf and www.worldometers.info

2. Gray 1928.

3. Herbert Richmond Palmer (1877–1958), later Sir Herbert Palmer, was educated at Oundle and at Cambridge where he read law. He joined the Colonial Service in 1904 and served for twenty-six years in Nigeria (successively) as Resident in Katsina, Resident in Kano Province, Resident in Bornu Province, and finally as Lieutenant-General of Northern Nigeria. Not only was he a first-class administrator, he was an historian, Arabic scholar and author. After leaving Nigeria, he was Governor and Commander-in-Chief of The Gambia (1930-1933) and Governor and Commander-in-Chief of Cyprus (1933-1939). In later life, he practiced law in Keswick and wrote about his African experiences.

GLOSSARY

adire cloth. An indigo-dyed cloth made by the Yoruba women of south-western Nigeria. Often a hand-painted design is drawn with cassava starch paste before the cloth is immersed in the dye; this results in white or pale blue designs on a dark blue background.

African Humid Period. A period 15,000 – 5,000 years BP *(q.v.)* when the area now called the Sahara Desert had more rainfall, was more humid, and was covered by savanna vegetation. There were large lakes and flowing rivers. At this time, many of the larger mammals now associated with the savannas further south, were abundant. Many of these mammals (and some birds and humans with their cattle) are depicted in the rock art found on the rocks and in the caves of Sahara mountains.

agbada. Nigerian name for the long coat-like apparel worn by Nigerian men.

angareeb. A Sudanese bed made of wood and rope netting.

annual rate of increase. The percentage increase in the number of people compared to the number in the previous year (e.g. 2%/year).

a.s.l. *(abbrev.)* 'Above Sea Level'.

bamia. Sudanese name for ochra – a nutritious vegetable. The edible parts are the green seed pods which are harvested when about 10cm in length. Often served with stewed meat – the cooked dish of meat and ochra is sometimes also called 'bamia'.

Bight of Benin. Geographical term for the ocean adjacent to the West African coast from the southernmost point of Ghana (west of Takoradi) to the easternmost part of the Niger delta in Nigeria.

201

buba. Nigerian name for the blouse worn by Nigerian women.

BP. (*abbrev.*) 'before present' (geological term). Some authorities prefer the term 'm.y.a.' (millions of years ago).

bushmeat. Meat derived from wild animals.

caldera. Large circular hollow, resulting from the collapse of the central part of a volcano after an eruption, often shaped like a pudding bowl. Some caldera contain a lake at the bottom of the hollow (as at Jebel Marra).

carrying capacity. A biological term referring to the maximum of individuals (of one species, or a community of species) that can be supported in a stated area of land on a continuous basis without adverse ecological effects.

CFA. (*abbrev.*) 'Communauté Financière Africaine' – group of African countries with a common economic framework and a common currency (the CFA franc).

chop box. A box, usually made of wood, for storing food when on safari. An old British colonial term.

copra. The dried flesh, or dried kernel, of the fruit of the coconut palm (*Cocos nucifera*). Coconut oil is extracted from copra. The outside fibrous part of the coconut fruit is called coir and is used for making mats and ropes and for stuffing mattresses.

damureah. A cheap form of cotton cloth – usually coarse in texture without any dye or embroidery.

density. The number of individuals of animals and/or plants in a stated area of land (e.g. 100/ha, 15/sq. km).

derived savanna. A habitat which was formerly rainforest but is now savanna. Derived savanna is maintained by agriculture and forestry activities, overgrazing by domestic animals, and fire.

dura. A species of domesticated grass (*Sorgum bicolor*) grown for its grain. It is used to make bread and porridge, and as food for domestic animals. Dura is cultivated in semi-arid climates in Sudan and further west to Senegal (and in similar climates throughout the world). Also called millet or sorghum.

fertility rate. The average number of young born to a woman during her reproductive lifetime.

ful musri. Lightly mashed broad beans garnished with olive oil and cheese.

Fulani. A large ethnic group spread across the Sudan and Sahel savanna zones. In Nigeria, the Fulani are mostly nomadic herdsmen who walk their cattle from the north to the markets in the south of the country.

gari. Nigerian name for flour made from the roots of the cassava plant.

gela. A long piece of cloth used as a head tie by women in Nigeria. The cloth is wound around the top and sides of the head, usually in an elaborate and complicated manner.

Guinea Savanna Zone. This wide biotic zone may be divided into the Northern Guinea Savanna and the Southern Guinea Savanna. It is characterised by tall trees such as *Daniellia*, *Lophira* and *Afzelia*. Grasses are tall and dense especially in low-lying ground. The environment is much less harsh than in the Sudan and Sahel savannas to the north, the wet season is seven to eight months/year, usually with a period of lesser rainfall in July and August. Mean annual rainfall is fairly high (800-1500 mm/year), and relatively predictable (more so than further north). Mean maximum temperatures are high for most of the year, but lower during the 'winter season' (see also chapter 5 for details).

Gulf of Guinea. The area of sea bordering the West African coast from Ghana (Cape Three Points) to Cape Lopez in Gabon. The Gulf opens out into the Atlantic Ocean. Many rivers flow into the gulf from the African mainland. It contains several islands which follow the line of volcanoes on mainland Cameroun; these include Bioko (formerly Fernanado Poo), Principe, São Tomé, and Annobón. The meridian 0° 00' latitude and 0° 00 longitude is in the Gulf of Guinea, south of Cape Three Points and west of São Tomé.

haboob. Sudanese name for the dust-laden winds which blow from the desert in December to March (cf. harmattan, *q.v.*).

haffir. (*Arabic*) Man-made dam containing water for domestic animals.

harmattan. Nigerian name for the dust-laden winds which blow from the desert in December to March (cf. haboob, *q.v.*).

Holocene. The geological epoch that began about 11,700 years BP, after the Pleistocene and after the last Ice Age. Both the Holocene and the Pleistocene are part of the Quaternary Period (2.5 million years BP).

Ice Ages. The periods during the Pleistocene when ice covered the northern parts of the Northern Hemisphere; as a consequence, the Rainforest Zone in West Africa (and further east) moved southwards, was fragmented, and occupied a much smaller area than previously.

There were about eight Ice Ages during the Pleistocene. The times in between the Ice Ages ('interglacials') allowed the rainforest zone to move northwards and most of the present-day Sahara was savanna. See also Inter-glacials (*q.v.*).

IFAN. (*abbrev.*) 'Institut Français d'Afrique Noire' – a French cultural and scientific organisation which established many research centers and museums in French West Africa during the colonial years. The Institut (now 'Institut Fondamental d'Afrique Noire') continues its work in the (now) independent nations of francophone West Africa.

inselberg. Large isolated rocky hill surrounded by flat land. Inselbergs (or groups of neighbouring inselbergs) vary in size from a few hectares to hundreds of hectares in area, and are of varying height. A word used mainly in West Africa. (German: *insel* = island; *berg* = hill). cf. jebel (*q.v.*)

Inter-tropical Convergence Zone (ITCZ). The zone, or band, of cloud and rain that moves north and south across the Equator, within the tropics. The zone makes one traverse each year from its most northerly latitude (during the Northern Hemisphere summer), to its most southerly latitude (during the Northern Hemisphere winter), and then returns to the most northerly latitude again. It is associated with low atmospheric pressure, and widespread heavy rains and thunderstorms. It is responsible for the wet and dry seasons in the tropics.

inter-glacials. The periods between the glacials during the Ice Ages (*q.v.*)

iro. Nigerian word for a cloth worn by women which is wrapped around the waist and legs; maybe simple in design or highly coloured and decorated.

jebel. Large isolated rocky hill surrounded by flat land. Arabic word, similar in meaning to inselberg (*q.v.*).

jelabiya. A long white robe, extending from neck to feet, with sleeves, worn by men in the hot semi-arid regions of the northern half of Africa.

ju-ju. Traditional 'black magic'. Ju-ju markets in West Africa sell many animal and plant parts believed to have magical properties; ju-ju is considered to provide cures from illness and safety against evil spirits.

kafta. A culinary dish, originally from Lebanon, made with ground beef, onions, parsley, black pepper and salt.

khor. A stream bed which now never flows with water.

kisra. A thin pancake-like bread made from fermented sorghum flour.

lamoon. A Sudanese cold drink made from limes and/or lemons, with water and ice.

laterite. A soil and rock type rich in iron and aluminium, and reddish-cinnamon in colour. Widespread in West Africa where heavy rain has eroded the topsoil. Laterite is very low in organic nutrients and unsuitable for agriculture. When compacted (as when roads are made), it forms a hard surface that can be graded to produce a surface suitable for motor vehicles. Laterite roads develop a corrugated surface in the dry season with constant use. Most non-tarmac roads in the non-sandy regions of Africa are made of laterite.

lb. *(abbrev. for one pound in weight)* 1lb (imperial system) = 16 ounzes (imperial system) = 453 grams (metric system).

mammy-wagon. A Nigerian word for a 1-ton lorry converted into a 'bus'. The back part is fitted with wooden benches and has a covered roof. Used for transporting people, farm products and livestock. Many mammy-wagons are painted in bright colours, highly decorated, and often emblazoned with mottos such as 'Trust in God', 'Jesus saves us' and 'Blessed are the pure in heart'.

Maria Theresa dollar. An important currency, named after Empress Maria Theresa, ruler of the Austria-Hungarian Empire, 1740–1780. The Maria Theresa thaler or dollar (MTT) was, and still is, a large silver coin. It was used as an official trade coinage in the Middle East, India and parts of Africa (especially Ethiopia). Thalers were introduced into Ethiopia in the 1750s and 1760s, and were a prized and valuable possession among the local people. Since 1780, any new thaler is dated as 1780 – even though minted many years later. Thalers have spread westwards from Ethiopia, and can still be seen as part of a necklace in many parts of Africa. MTTs are still minted in Austria.

millefiore. A type of bead made of glass at the Murano factory in Venice. The name 'millefiori' is a combination of the Italian words "mille" (thousand) and "fiori" (flowers) and refers to the beautiful designs and patterns on each bead. A typical millefiore bead is circular in cross section (10-15mm diameter), with a hole (3-5mm dia.) through the centre, and 10-40mm in length. European traders used Millefiore beads in previous centuries to purchase goods and slaves in West Africa, hence the term 'African trade beads'. (There were many other types of beads that were used as currency in West Africa).

mist-net. A special very fine-meshed net for catching live bats, similar to the net used by ornithologists for catching birds. The bats are unharmed and can be released after identification and taking measurements, etc.

neem. A large tree (*Azadirachta indica*) in the mahogany family, indigenous to the Indian subcontinent. Widely planted in Africa as a shade tree. Resistant to drought. Crushed dried neem leaves can be used as an insecticide.

ORSTOM (*abbrev.*) Office de la Recherche Scientifique et Technique Outre-Mer. French scientific institute now called 'Institut français de recherche scientifique pour le développement en coopération'.

Palearctic. Biogeographical term for the temperate regions of the Eurasian landmass. It includes the terrestrial environments of Europe, Siberia, the Mahgreb (in North Africa), the Arabian Deserts, Western and Central Asia (north of the Himalaya Mountains), and Japan.

piastre. Unit of currency in the Sudan (100 piastres = One Sudanese pound).

Population Growth Rate. The rate, expressed as a percentage, of the increase in numbers of individuals compared with the previous rate (usually the previous year). For example, if a population of 1000 in Year 1 increases to 1050 in Year 2, the population growth rate is 5%. Growth rates may be for all individuals, or males, or females, or specified age groups.

qoz. (*Arabic*) Deposits of fine silty sand, usually blown from desert habitats.

Quaternary Period. Geological Period (from *c.* 2.6 millions BP; may be divided into the Holocene (present to 100,000 years BP) and the Pleistocene (100,000 years BP to 2.6 million years BP).

racouba. (*Arabic*) A simple shelter or grass hut made from branches of trees and covered with grass thatch.

rainforest. The Rainforest Biotic Zone is the most southerly of the vegetation zones in West Africa. It is bordered by the Guinea Savanna (*q.v.*) to the north and by the sea to the south. In some locations, tongues of rainforest extend northwards into the Guinea savanna, especially along rivers. There is a rich diversity of trees, shrubs and climbers in the rainforest, and there are layers of vegetation at different heights above the forest floor, culminating in the canopy and emergent strata (up to 100m above ground level). The climate is warm and moist.

Annual rainfall is 1600-2000mm/year (or higher in some places), and the rainy season lasts for eight to ten months (with a short period of lesser rainfall in the middle). The dry cooler season lasts for only about two months. Annual mean maximum temperature is *c.* 30°C and annual minimum is *c.* 20°C. Seasonal variation in climate is much less obvious than in the savannas.

Ramadan. The annual religious observance by Muslims to commemorate the revelation of the Koran to Mohammad. Ramadan is the ninth month of the Islamic year. The beginning of Ramadan begins with the first sighting of the new moon in the ninth month and lasts for twenty-eight days. Hence the actual date (in the Gregorian calendar) varies from year to year. During Ramadan, Muslims fast from dawn to dusk.

Sahel Savanna Zone. The Sahel Savanna Zone is immediately south of the Sahara Desert and north of the Sudan Savanna Zone (*q.v.*). This zone is characterised by *Acacia* and *Commiphora*, and a perennial grass *Andropogon gayanus.* The environment is harsh, the wet season is limited to three to four months/year, rainfall is limited (*c.* 100mm /year in the north, 350-400mm/year in the south), and is spasmodic and unpredictable. Mean maximum temperatures are high for most of the year (34°C), but lower during the 'winter season' (see also chapter 5 for details).

shadoof (shaduf). A structure made of wooden poles, ropes, and a bucket. The bucket, attached to a rope, is lowered into a river (or other water source) and, when full, is raised up to ground level. The water is poured into an irrigation channel where it flows to the fields where crops are growing. Shadoofs are very common along the Nile river where rich Nile silt (deposited during the floods) enables crops to be grown when the river is not in flood (see chapter 5).

shama (shamma). A dress with a full skirt falling to below knees (or to the ankles), made of cotton and often bordered by decorative patterns, worn by men and women in Ethiopia. The shama is either white (for men) or more colourful and decorated (for women).

shifta. An Ethiopian bandit.

Sudan/Soudan. The name has – confusingly – been used to refer to two different geographical areas in the past. [1] Anglo-Egyptian Sudan, now the Republic of Sudan. [2] French Soudan – the large area of West Africa (Afrique Occidentale Française) under French control during the colonial era (*c.* 1880 – 1960). Afrique Occidentale Française included the

207

countries now known as Senegal, Mauritania, Guinea, Côte d'Ivoire, Dahomey, Mali, Upper Volta (Burkina Faso), and Niger. The French language is still the main language spoken throughout these ex-French territories, and also in 'French Equatorial Africa' (Afrique Equatoriale Française), now known as Gabon, Congo (Brazzaville), Central African Republic, Chad, and Cameroun (British/French Trusteeship since 1920).

Sudan Savanna Zone. A biotic zone south of the Sahel Savanna Zone (*q.v.*) and north of the Guinea Savanna Zone (*q.v*). This zone is characterised by *Parkia, Combretum Anogeissus* and *Adansonia (*baobab*)* trees, and low growing grasses. The environment is quite harsh; the wet season is limited to two to six months/year, rainfall is limited (500-800mm/year) and is spasmodic and unpredictable. Mean maximum temperatures are high for most of the year, but lower during the 'winter season' (see also chapter 5 for details).

Sudd. The vast area of swamps and water in Sudan/South Sudan where the White Nile spreads out over the flat landscape. Its size varies during the year according to the inflow of water from Lake Victoria and the East African highlands; the average size is 30,000km^2 but it may enlarge to *c*. 130,000km^2 after severe flooding. The Sudd contains waterways, lagoons, and extensive impenetrable areas of reeds and papyrus. The water is shallow, and navigation through the Sudd is possible only with small shallow boats.

suq. (*Arabic*). A local market; also *suq lorry* – lorry taking people and goods to market.

tabag. A beautifully coloured food cover made of raffia, palm fronds or dried reeds, shaped like a wide flattened conical hat.

tamia. A favourite snack in the Sudan made of chickpeas, onions, bread and spices rolled into a ball and then deep-fried.

tarbush. A small flat-topped conical hat, similar to a fez, worn by men in Muslim countries.

tasali. Melon seeds which can be chewed to pass the time; frequently sold in small paper packets at railway stations in the Sudan.

tobe (thoub, toob tiab, tyab). Long piece of wide cloth wrapped around the head and body; the commonest form of clothing worn by women in the Sudan (see also chapter 6).

travellers cheques. Voucher cheques issued by banks that may be cashed at any bank in the world. Travellers cheques were a convenient way of taking money overseas in addition to cash. Travellers cheques were available in denominations of US$ 10, 20, 50 and 100. In Africa (in the 1960s), banks were present only in big towns and cities; obtaining adequate cash during my travels was difficult and it was essential to plan my monetary requirements before each part of the journey. Cashing travellers cheques was possible only if the receipt of purchase (with purchaser's name) and identity documents (e.g. passport, with photo and signature) were presented to the bank. (Internet banking, credit cards and debit cards did not exist in the 1960s!)

wadi. (*Arabic*) A dry river bed or stream bed which may flow at certain times of the year during and after the wet season. Some large wadis have pools of water during the dry season if the underlying soil, clay or rock prevents water seepage into underlying strata.

zanzameer. A thick canvas bag with a short glass spout with a screw top; water evaporates through the canvas keeping the water inside cool and pleasant to drink.

REFERENCES

Arkell, A. J. 1947. Early Khartoum. *Antiquity* 84:172-181.

Arkell, A. J. 1949. *Early Khartoum*, Oxford University Press

Arkell, A. J. 1955. *A history of the Sudan. From the Earliest times to 1821*. The Athlone Press, University of London. 249 pp + 24 Plates.

Bailey-Watts, A. E. and Rogers, J. F. 1964/65. Scientific Results of the Jebel Marra Expedition: (2) The Fish Collection. *Twelve Annual Report, Hydrobiological Research Unit, University of Khartoum, Sudan*: 7-9.

Barth, H. 1857-1858. *Reisen und Entdeckungen in Nord- und Central-Afrika in den Jahren 1849 bis 1855*. 4 vols (trans: Travels and Discoveries of North and Central Africa). Ward Lock & Co., London. [Minerva Library of Famous Books 1890].

Bovill, E. W. 1968a. *The Golden Trade of the Moors*. (2nd Edn.) Oxford University Press, London. 293 pp. + maps.

Boville, E. W. 1968b. *The Niger Explored*. Oxford University Press, London. 263 pp + photos + maps.

Brunet, M., Guy, F., Pilbeam, D. *et al.* 2002. A new hominid from the Upper Miocene of Chad, central Africa. *Nature* 418(6894): 145-151.

Carlisle, D. B. 1968. *Triops* (Entomostraca) eggs killed only by boiling. *Science* 161: 279-280.

Cave, F. O. and Macdonald, J. D. 1955. *Birds of the Sudan. Their Identification and Distribution*. Oliver and Boyd, Edinburgh. 444 pp + maps + photos + 12 coloured plates.

Churchill, Winston S. 1899. *The River War* (2nd Edn 1902, First Four Square Edition 1964). 351 pp.

Cloudsley-Thompson, J. L. 1984. *Sahara Desert* (Key Environment Series). Pergamon Press, Oxford. 348 pp.

Davidson, B, 1965. *The growth of African Civilisation. A History of West Africa 1000 – 1800*. Longmans, London. 320 pp.

Elgood, J. H. 1960. *Birds of the West African Town and Garden*. Longmans (West African Nature Handbooks). 65 pp.

Eltahir, E. A. B. 1988. Tests for the suspected trend in annual rainfall series in central and western Sudan. *Sudan Engineering Journal* 30: 37-50.

Ewer, R. F. 1969. Form and function in the Grass Cutter, *Thryonomys swinderianus* Temm. (Rodentia, Thryonomidae). *Ghana Journal of Science* 9: 131-141.

Fage, J. D. 1978. *An Atlas of African History*. (2d Edn.). Edward Arnold, London. 71 maps + Appendix + Index. No pagination.

Fry, C. H. 1971. Lake Chad: Retrospect and Prospect. *The Nigerian Field* 36(3):100-114.

Gray, F. 1928. *My Two African Journeys*. Methuen, London. 271 pp. + photos + maps.

Green, J., el Moghraby, A. I. and Ali, O. M. M. 1979. Biological observations on the crater lakes of Jebel Marra. *Journal of Zoology (London)* 189: 493-502.

Happold D. C. D. 1966. The mammals of Jebel Marra, Sudan. *Journal of Zoology (London)* 149: 126-136.

Happold D. C. D. 1967a. Biology of the jerboa, *Jaculus jaculus butleri* (Rodentia, Dipodidae) in the Sudan. *Journal of Zoology (London)* 151: 257-275.

Happold D. C. D. 1967b. *Gerbillus (Dipodillus) campestris* (Gerbillinae, Rodentia) from the Sudan. *Journal of Natural History* 1: 315-317.

Happold D. C. D. 1968. Seasonal distribution of adult dragonflies at Khartoum, Sudan. *Revue de zoologie et botanique Africaine* 77: 50-61.

Happold D. C. D. 1969. Observations on *Gerbillus pyramidum* (Gerbillinae, Rodentia) at Khartoum, Sudan. *Mammalia* 32: 43-53.

Happold D. C. D. 1970. Reproduction and development of the Sudanese jerboa, *Jaculus jaculus butleri* (Rodentia, Dipodidae). *Journal of Zoology (London)* 162: 505-515.

Harrison, M. N. and Jackson, J. K. 1958. Ecological Classification of the vegetation of the Sudan. *Forests Department, Ministry of Agriculture, Forests Bulletin* 2 (n.s.). 35 pp + maps.

Hopkins, B. 1965. *Forest and Savanna. An Introduction to Tropical Plant Evology with special reference to West Africa.* Heinemann. 100 pp.

Kemper, S. 2012. *A Labyrinth of Kingdoms. 10,000 miles through Islamic Africa.* W. W. Norton, New York. 415 pp.

Lemoalle, J., Bader, J-C., Leblanc, M. and Sedick, A. 2012. Recent changes in Lake Chad: Observations, simulations and management options (1973 – 2011). *Global and Planetary Change* 80-81: 247-254.

Lévêque, C. 1990. Relict tropical fish fauna in Central Sahara. *Ichthyological Exploration of Freshwaters* 1: 39-48.

Lhote, H. 1959. *The Search for the Tassili Frescoes. The Story of the Prehistoric Rock-paintings of the Sahara.* (English Translation). Hutchinson, London. 236 pp. + photos + maps.

Moorehead, A. 1960. *The White Nile.* Hamish Hamilton, London. 385 pp.

Moorehead, A. 1962. *The Blue Nile.* Hamish Hamilton, London. 308 pp.

Nachtigal, G. 1879 / 1881. *Sahara and the Sudan.* 4 vols. (Translated from original German by Fisher, G. B. & Fisher, H. J. 1974-1987). C. Hurst, London.

Nikolaus, G. 1987. Distribution Atlas of Sudan's birds with notes on habitat and status. *Bonner Zoologisches Monographien* 25. 322 pp + 938 maps.

Oliver J. 1965. Guide to the Natural History of Khartoum Province. Part II. The Climate of Khartoum Province. *Sudan Notes and Records* 54. 40 pp.

Oliver, R. and Fage, J. D, 1963. *A Short History of Africa.* Penguin Books, London. 280 pp.

Packenham, T. 1991. *The Scramble for Africa 1876 – 1912.* Weidenfeld and Nicolson. 738 pp. (Abacus paperback 1992).

Palmer, Sir Richmond, 1936. *The Bornu Sahara and Sudan.* John Murray, London. 296 pp + photos.

Reader, J. 1997. *Africa. A Biography of the Continent.* Penguin. London. 803 pp.

Rilly, C. [No date]. *The Sudan National Museum in Khartoum. An Illustrated Guide for Visitors.* Section Française de la Direction des Antiquités du Soudan. http://sfdas.com/IMG/pdf/livretmuse_etenglight.pdf 87 pp.

Rzóska, J. 1976. Nile Waters – Hydrology Past and Present. In: *The Nile, Biology of an Ancient River.* ed. Julian Rzóska) Dr W. Junk, The Hague. (Monographiae Biologicae 29). pp 145-153.

Rzóska, J. 1984. Temporary and Other Waters. In: *Sahara Desert* (Ed. J. L. Cloudsley-Thompson). Pergamon Press, Oxford. 105-114 pp.

Smith, G. 1984. Climate. In: *Sahara Desert* (ed. J. L. Cloudsley-Thompson). Pergamon Press, Oxford. pp 17-30.

Stevenson-Hamilton, J. 1940. *Our South African National Parks*. (In English and Afrikaans) Cape Times Limited, Cape Town. 102 pp + photos + cigarette cards.

Thomas, O. and Hinton, M. A. C. 1923. On the mammals obtained in Darfur by the Lynes-Lowe Expedition. *Proceedings of the Zoological Society of London* 1923: 247-271.

Trimingham, J. S. 1962. *A History of Islam in West Africa*. Oxford University Press, London. 262 pp.

Ullendorf, E. 1965. *The Ethiopians. An Introduction to the Country and People*. (2nd Edn.). Oxford University Press, London. 235 pp. + 16 plates + 1 map.

Willcox, A. R. 1984. *The Rock Art of Africa*. Holmes & Meier, New York. 287 pp.+ maps + illust.

INDEX